*How a
Woman
Ages*

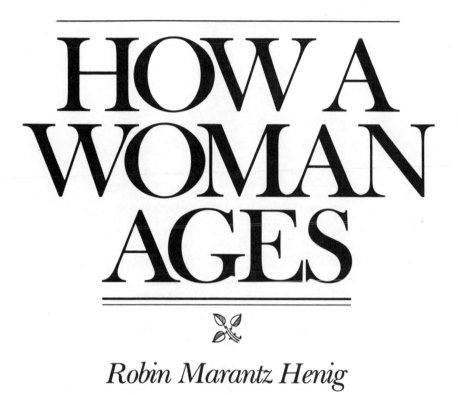

HOW A WOMAN AGES

Robin Marantz Henig

AND THE EDITORS OF
ESQUIRE

A Ballantine/Esquire Press Book
Ballantine Books · New York

*Robin Marantz Henig
dedicates this book to
her mother, Clare Marantz,
and her daughters, Jessica and Samantha.*

Library of Congress Catalog Card Number:
84-91667
ISBN 0-345-31780-7

Manufactured in the United States of America
First edition: June 1985
10 9 8 7 6 5 4 3 2 1

We advise the reader to consult with a physician before
beginning any program of diet and exercise. The authors
disclaim any liability, personal or otherwise, resulting
from the procedures in this book.

ACKNOWLEDGMENTS

Robin Marantz Henig and the editors of Esquire would like to thank the dozens of medical professionals, researchers in the field of gerontology, and others who have given generously of their time and knowledge in the preparation of this book. In particular, we would like to thank: T. Franklin Williams, M.D., Jane Shure, and Marian Emr of the National Institute on Aging, Bethesda, Md.; Reubin Andres, M.D., Jordan Tobin, M.D., Jerome Fleg, M.D., David Arenberg, Ph.D., Chris Plato, M.D., and Jan Ehrman of the Gerontology Research Center, Baltimore, Md.; Morris Notelovitz, M.D., University of Florida, Gainesville, Fla.; William Kannel, M.D., Boston University, Boston, Mass.; Elaine Eaker, M.D., the National Heart, Lung, and Blood Institute, Bethesda, Md.; Robert N. Butler, M.D., and Diane Meier, M.D., Mount Sinai Medical Center, New York, N.Y.; Stanton Cohn, M.D., Brookhaven National Laboratory, Brookhaven, N.Y.; Vincent Cristofalo, Ph.D., Arthur Kligman, M.D., Ingrid Waldron, M.D., and Mary Ann Forceia, M.D., University of Pennsylvania, Philadelphia, Pa.; Barbara Gilchrest, M.D., Harvard University, Boston, Mass.; Frederick McDuffie, M.D., The Arthritis Foundation, Atlanta, Ga.; Ron White, The American Lung Association, New York, N.Y.; Frances Purifoy, M.D., University of Louisville, Louisville, Ky.; Edwin Dale, M.D., Emory University, Atlanta, Ga.; Robert McGandy, M.D., Tufts University, Boston, Mass.; Jean Emory, Ph.D., Washington, D.C.; Bruce Baum, D.D.S., and Martha Somerman, D.D.S., National Institute of Dental Research, Bethesda, Md.; Jane Porcino, Ph.D., State University of New York at Stony Brook, Stony Brook, N.Y.; JoAnn Cannon, Ph.D., and Laura Altschul, Inward Bound, Inc., Chicago, Ill.; Linda Campanelli, Ph.D., University of Maryland, College Park, Md.; and Tish Sommers and Alice Quinlan, the Older Woman's League, Washington, D.C.

CONTENTS

PREFACE

In May 1982, when *Esquire* published a cover story called "The Aging Male Body," the issue was a near sellout at the newsstand. Everyone, it seemed, wanted to know exactly what happened to a man as he grew older. Men who had just begun to feel intimations of their mortality—men in their 30s and 40s—were particularly eager for information. As a result, in 1984, Esquire Press published *How a Man Ages,* which offered a complete head-to-toe examination of what a man could expect—mentally, physically, sexually—as the years marched on. Now, with *How a Woman Ages,* we are here to tell the equally fascinating story of the maturing woman.

The signals of approaching middle age can cause a man or a woman a good bit of anxiety. Luckily, however, there is much that we can learn and much that we can do to adjust to these changes. We have many options. Especially nowadays. Today, this country is in the midst of a fitness boom. We have discovered the value of exercise and good nutrition, and we are learning more each day about the ways that our bodies respond to training. The health-conscious individual today can thus benefit from the wealth of new information coming out of scientific and medical circles. Biological research, the new field of sports medicine, and new studies of the aging are all contributing to our understanding of the changes the body undergoes over time.

We take the position that none of the marks of age that occur in a healthy person are cause for alarm—only thinking or neglect can make them so. Because the whole person is body *and* psyche, a commitment to fitness can make an enormous difference to one's mental health, just as a positive attitude toward physical change can have an effect on how the body works. In these pages, we focus on the physical aspects of aging, because we believe that the habits of fitness established early in life will greatly enhance one's total sense of well-being as time goes on.

For too many years Americans have worshipped youth. Today, as our demographic makeup is changing, and as the baby boom moves into middle age, we are looking anew at the aging process, trying to see it with clear eyes, without prejudice.

All over this country, there are vital men and women who are helping to revise our expectations of growing older. Many of these people might once have been considered "past their prime," but they are proving in large numbers that vitality is not synonymous with youth. Valuing their health and strength, they work to keep fit—not so they can compete with 20-year-olds, but because they believe that a strong body feels good and looks good at any age. They finish marathons. They go on Outward Bound trips. They demonstrate with their lives how a sense of well-being is fostered by reaching out to new people, new interests, new physical experiences. They are our pioneers in the aging game. Those in the next generation, men and women in their 20s and 30s, will reap the benefits of their shining examples.

In *How a Woman Ages,* you will find much scientific and medical evidence for a more hopeful view of aging. You will also learn about the predictable changes that accompany a woman down the road from the age of 30, and what can be done to stave off or ameliorate age-related disorders. You will learn to recognize the "symptoms" of aging for what they are, and you will find, we hope, reassurance in the fact that much of what once seemed inevitable about aging is no longer considered so.

We believe that when we commit ourselves to pursuing our physical potential, we can find all sorts of benefits. Our concentration improves. We are more productive. We have a greater desire, it seems, to develop the interests and relationships that really matter to us. We discover that age-related changes do not mean the end of our prowess or our attractiveness. And, as we stretch ourselves toward new goals, discover new insights, and open up to new experiences, each passing year can be better than the one before.

—the Editors of Esquire

INTRODUCTION

What they don't tell you often enough is that each half of life has its youth and its old age. As Victor Hugo wrote, 40 is the old age of youth; 50 is the youth of old age. It is during the ten or 12 years in between, beginning in the late 30s, that most of us feel out on a limb; suspicious of the future, our knees gone weak, we dread to fall but fear to jump. As the first furrows in our faces suggest the mystifying seasons to come, we imagine the worst—the drought-stricken ruin of our skin, a sudden barrenness in the pit of creation, a winter of sensuality—and the seat of all our imaginings is ignorance.

"Openness to change" is one of those totems to which we pay lip service. Isn't it supposed to be the secret of an exciting and productive middle age? In practice, most of my efforts and probably yours, as we slouch toward middle age, go into gaining control, trying to know it all, reducing the necessity to change and the inclination to take risks.

Our efforts are spurred by the illusion that if we simply pop enough vitamins, slather on enough cream, scallopine enough flesh off our thighs, and lube and tune the hydraulic system of our sex lives to dredge up the desperate juices indefinitely, we will be armed against the invasions of age. Many people slip into an approach that might be called life prevention. And in this grasping for control, something very precious we had as children is lost—the exposure to surprise.

How, if we don't march ourselves out to the end of a limb and jump in a new direction now and then, shall we continue to learn? And if we do not continue to learn, how shall we continue to develop? Because children are repeatedly faced with novel and challenging experiences, they are constantly developing the plasticity to deal with them. The quickest way to learn, in my experience, is to interrupt your everyday, predictable existence. Put yourself on the line. Introduce a new test or adventure of the heart and, in that one domain, give up some control.

Coming upon the promontory of true middle age myself, I refused to surrender to the urge for more control. I was scared, very scared, suspended in my dreams over a gulf of unfathomable proportions. But now, after two years, I look back, having attempted a first play, adopted a second child, and entered a new state of marriage. And they said there were no more surprises.

The mutual shock of physical ruin I had expected to register when my classmates and I came together for a twenty-fifth college reunion did not occur. My first impression was, what healthy and handsome people are these! They looked ten years younger than the generation ahead of us had looked on entering their middle 40s. We have at least two advantages: We passed through childhood before meat became a pharmaceutical product, and the fitness movement caught us before we turned 40. But the baby-boom generation right behind us is even more fortunate. They have the facts to formulate a healthy life-style and the time to use them in preparing for an energetic old age.

Challenges need to be introduced, but one needn't be successful at each new endeavor. My first play, for instance, is still sitting, unfinished, on an old floppy disc; I shall try another one day, I know I shall. One intrinsic reward for putting oneself back into the wobbly-kneed state of a learner is the return of a sense of playfulness and delight. What joy it was for me to put on jeans and leg warmers and plod through snow to acting class, to be sweaty-palmed before a Shakespeare exam again, to feel as if a great sloughing-off of old cells was being expedited by the sharp edge of uncertainty. In that amateur state, one is simply forced to stop taking oneself so seriously.

But even if we are relatively satisfied with the stage we are now in, we cannot help wondering, "What will it be like to be sixty, or seventy? Do I really want to be eighty-five?" Most women, lacking any pleasant or exact images of such ages, put such questions quickly out of mind: "Too depressing." There has not been a book to paint the picture in straightforward detail, until this one.

At every fork in the journey of my life I have met my mother, the shadow of my age, and silently asked, "What's next?"

At 40, she seemed old. But at 50, divorced, she bounced back, started a new business, trimmed down, and took to painting her toenails again. She was courted and married, and, at the age of 53, she confided later, she celebrated what was surely her sexual peak.

Then, at 64, abruptly, a reckless energy overtook her. She had always smoked, but now she chain-smoked—leaving the butts, livid with bright lipstick, in defiant little heaps. Her drinking became careless and coarse. She ate meats drowned in sauces in death-house portions. No one could talk to her. It was as if she had entered a tunnel beyond the great gray parking lot of middle age and, convinced there was no road beyond, had begun to spin and slam off the walls, determined to inflict as many little deaths as she could before the controls were taken away from her.

"Don't tell me how to live my life," she sandbagged against my imprecations. "I don't tell you how to live yours." Her statements were punctuated by a shudder of the lungs. "I only have a few years left. What I do with them is none of your affair."

But it was, of course. We do not alone endure the verdict of our later years. We may sentence a mate or children to unnecessary internment. Not having yet broken into my own 40s, I found it terrifying to meet myself, in my mother, beyond middle age. "Is this what's next?" Why, I agonized, when she was enjoying freedom from serious illness and a happy marriage, would this lovely woman of 64 drive herself perversely toward an untimely end? She must have settled arbitrarily on a check-out time, I thought.

(From this book I later gained an insight. A woman's genes and health habits largely determine how she will age, but only until she reaches 60 or 65. After that, her psychological attitude—whether she marshals her energies, or resigns herself to join the walking dead—becomes far more important.)

All at once, a few blocks from the graveyard, at the age of 69, my mother swerved in the opposite direction. She started exercising three times a week: lifting dumbbells, hanging from parallel bars. After being a smoker for 50 years, she awoke one morning and reached for the pack of old friends and crushed them. No tapering off, no therapeutic programs. She has not smoked since.

Inexplicably, my mother had entered her third spring.

Visiting her recently, in her seventy-fourth year, I puzzled over what had revived the old sunniness of her nature. What indefinite treaty had she made with the armies of old age?

She said, "I guess I thought it would be almost over at seventy. Instead, I found I was still feeling good. Well," she admitted, "the emphysema focused for me what I had to do to live longer and still feel good. But I was enjoying the trip. I got excited about it all over again. I wanted an extended itinerary!"

My mother confirmed an attitude that is dangerously common in so many of us. Even though the stage we are in may feel far richer than we had ever anticipated, we look ahead to the *next* stage and know—with an absolute, aggressively uninformed, let's-don't-talk-about-it conviction—that it will be straight downhill from there. Yet if we fail to conspire in our own irreversible deterioration, we will probably arrive at the new stage, rummage around, surprised, and say, "Why, this isn't so bad at all. If only I had known, I would have taken better care of myself."

My mother is wily now in guarding her health. She is different from some of the widows at her garden club whose conversations are assaults of memory, set in the stopped time prior to their husbands' deaths: "Henry will love this," or "Al never loses at Bingo." My mother's life is in the here and now. She keeps learning and hungering to learn.

"Now, sex," she said during my last visit, this tiny white-haired woman who knits stocking caps. "As a woman ages, she initiates the sex with her partner more often." I asked how that made her partner feel. "Oh, a man feels flattered," she said definitively, then chuckled, "and he *never* has a 'headache.' "

It is one of the great surprises of aging, this unanticipated sexual abandon, and you will hear older women talk freely about it in this book. It seems an internal wildness grows in some women like a fantastic tropical vegetation—even, or perhaps most easily—within the neat borders of marriage.

At the end of my last visit home, I said, "Do you know, Mom, at the age of seventy-four you can expect to live until you are eighty-seven." I thought she might groan.

"Why not?" she said. "My mother lived to be eighty-nine."

The women who survive and triumph in advancing age are those who can adapt to change. At every stage, they will surprise themselves by pulling off some cartwheel of thought or action they never attempted before. Rather than fuss over each slight physical decrement, why not focus on the natural territory for self-improvement that opens up in later years—our psychological capacities? At least two significant changes of personality commonly occur with age, and these are changes for the better. Older people are not as likely to blame others for their problems, and they don't indulge in escapist behavior as readily as when they were younger. They know it does no good. Experience, one presumes, has triumphed over illusion. And the closer one comes to confronting one's own mortality, the more dramatically one's personality may be spurred to change—for as Samuel Johnson said about waiting to be hanged, it concentrates the mind wonderfully.

You will find in perusing the following pages that there is less to fear and more to look forward to as a woman ages than most of us thought. So, don't be afraid of your own second and third flowerings. A woman can scarcely hope to fulfill the goals of her youth until she is over forty. And then, for as long as she continues to surprise herself, she may do whatever she dreams she can.

Here's wishing you never run out of surprises.

Gail Sheehy
New York City

1
How a Woman Ages

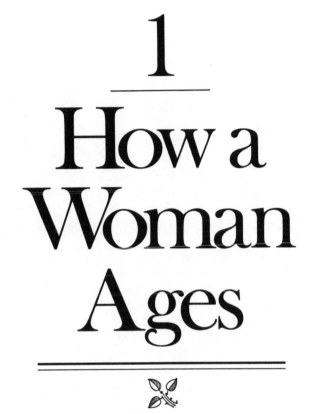

When feminist Gloria Steinem turned 50 in 1984, the whole world watched. Her thoughts about her landmark birthday appeared in dozens of major newspapers and in *Ms.*, the magazine she had helped create. She threw herself a big birthday bash at the Waldorf Astoria in New York, and 800 celebrities came. "Fifty is what forty used to be," said Steinem, attributing the good looks and good health of her peers to their improved lives after feminism. "Self-esteem and a measure of success keep us going: not just in our heads but in our bodies."[1]

Aging is usually perceived as a gloomy subject. But in truth, as Steinem's remark affirms, there's much cause for optimism. What we know about aging is based on the current generation of over-65s. Tomorrow's elderly—the current generation of young adults—will be different from today's elderly because of the personal, cultural, and scientific environment in which they are aging. And the changes will almost uniformly be changes for the better.

The woman who grows old in the twenty-first century will have benefited from a lifetime of better medical care, more conscientious eating and exercising habits, improved living conditions, and better education. She will be part of a large mass of aging Americans—the baby-boomers gone gray—and will no doubt benefit from the sheer quantity of women who are aging along with her. And she will be among the first to benefit from the latest scientific information to emerge from the relatively new field of longevity research. As a result, her "golden years" will probably be more comfortable, more healthful, and more fulfilling than were those of her mother or grandmother.

How a woman ages depends on a combination of several factors, most importantly her family history and her life-style. The relative importance of each factor is just beginning to be understood. Heredity certainly plays a significant—most say a major—role in sealing a woman's future. But even heredity can be overcome. According to Linda Campanelli, associate director of the Adult Health and Development Program at the University of Maryland, a woman's genes determine how she will age *until she reaches the age of 60 or 65.* After that, says Campanelli, she's on her own. Then the influence of her life-style, especially the life-style she adopted in youth, becomes far more important.[2]

This is heartening news indeed, because life-styles are remediable. And indications are that the life-style of today's typical 30-year-old is far

3

healthier than that of any previous crop. Because of their more prudent youth, the men and women from the baby-boom generation—who will reach their "golden years" in the twenty-first century—are likely to look, act, and feel at the age of 60 much the way a 40-year-old does today.

The health habits that can stave off old age are the health habits that mothers have been pushing for as long as we can remember. The difference is that now scientific evidence supports their admonitions—and now hundreds of thousands of young people are taking the advice to heart. The habits are simple: exercising, eating a balanced diet, eating enough fiber, drinking plenty of milk and water, dental flossing daily, cutting out smoking, and protecting oneself from the sun. By following these rules, a woman can minimize her chances of encountering some of the most common ills of old age—heart disease, digestive problems, osteoporosis, some forms of cancer, periodontal disease, even wrinkles.

Some scientists now are exploring ways in which old age itself might actually be avoided (see Chapter 12). This extension of longevity would involve a qualitative leap beyond prudence. It would require a truly disciplined life-style. Researchers such as Dr. Roy Walford of UCLA are trying to see whether extreme measures—lifelong undernutrition, lowering of body temperature, megadoses of certain vitamins or minerals—can push the average human life-span beyond the currently accepted limit of about 100 years.[3]

Life Changes

As a woman ages, no matter how healthy she remains, she will no doubt undergo certain changes. She will have less muscle strength, less lung power, less bone mass, less flexibility with each passing decade. But most of these changes have little, if any, effect on a woman's overall functioning. And many of these changes are changes for the better. In terms of intelligence and sexual responsiveness, for example, most women actually improve in the course of a lifetime.

Even for the systems that do show some decline, there is good news. In almost every instance, a woman in her 30s or 40s can begin taking steps now to minimize the effects of aging. Brittle bones can be avoided by getting enough exercise, and enough dietary calcium, beginning early in life. Wrinkles can be avoided by protecting the skin from the sun, beginning early in life. Heart disease can be avoided by eating a low-fat diet and engaging in lots of heart-thumping exercise, beginning early in life. If a theme seems to be emerging here, it is this: A healthy

Life Expectancy:
The Gender Gap Widens

In the years since 1930, the "gender gap" in life expectancy—the number of years by which an average woman can expect to outlive an average man—has grown from 3.5 years to nearly eight. And at any particular age, a woman can look forward to more years of remaining life than a man can. One fact should be noted, though: The female advantage in "remaining life expectancy" shrinks with age. A one-year-old girl can expect to live 7.6 years longer than a one-year-old boy, but a woman of 60 can expect to live only five years more than a man of the same age.

LIFE EXPECTANCY AT BIRTH

Year Born	Male	Female	Female Advantage
1930	58.1	61.6	3.5
1940	60.8	65.2	4.4
1950	65.6	71.1	5.5
1960	66.6	73.1	6.5
1970	67.1	74.8	7.7
1980 (est.)	69.9	77.8	7.9

REMAINING LIFE EXPECTANCY

For a person who in 1978 was age	Male	Female	Female Advantage
1	70.2	77.8	7.6
10	61.5	68.9	7.4
20	52.0	59.1	7.1
30	42.8	49.5	6.7
40	33.6	39.9	6.3
50	24.8	30.7	5.9
60	17.2	22.3	5.1
70	11.1	14.8	3.7

Source: Bureau of the Census, *Statistical Abstract of the United States 1981* (Washington, D.C.: U.S. Department of Commerce, 1981), pp. 69, 70.

life-style, *beginning early in life,* can mean the difference between a vigorous old age and a decrepit one—or no old age at all.

Gerontologists, specialists in the study of aging, are leading the way toward a new understanding of how a woman ages. In the process, they are dashing all myths of the inevitability of certain changes. Their most dramatic findings reiterate the same theme: Changes that were once thought to be inevitable with age are not inevitable. Many conditions are preventable, or they occur—when they occur at all—at a far more advanced age than commonly thought. Among the supposedly unavoidable declines of old age that we now know may indeed be avoided are:

Heart disease. A high-risk woman can protect herself with diet, exercise, and control of high blood pressure.

Digestive disease. Fiber in the diet seems to prevent almost every digestive complaint associated with old age.

Pain. Physical conditions that often produce pain, such as menstrual cramps or arthritis, will not interfere with functioning in a woman with a well-toned body and a cheerful mental attitude.

Tooth and gum disease. A woman can keep her teeth for life if she takes care of them, with such habits as daily flossing and regular professional removal of plaque.

A stressful menopause. While hot flashes and vaginal dryness often accompany the "change of life," many women go through menopause with no symptoms and emerge from it feeling more energetic, livelier, and sexier than ever before.

Senility. The vast majority of older women, like older men, retain their intellectual functioning until they die.

Obesity. Although it becomes harder to lose weight after menopause, a woman of any age, if she eats less and exercises more, can maintain the weight she achieved in her 20s or 30s.

Flabbiness. Once again, it takes more discipline the older a woman gets, but a conscientious exercise regimen can keep her body limber, supple, and relatively taut.

Wrinkles. Even these can be forestalled if a woman avoids sunbathing and scrupulously uses sunscreens when outdoors.

In the chapters that follow, we will take a look at the female body and the changes it undergoes over time. The tour is organized according to organ systems. Some systems will show the effects of age more clearly than others. But in almost every instance, the most debilitating declines associated with aging are also, fortuitously, among the most preventable.

Our examination of the aging woman's body proceeds from the outside in. We begin, in Chapter 2, with a look at body shape and muscle tone. One of the most universal changes observed in the aging female body is the replacement of a substantial portion of lean body mass (muscle) with fat. Today's statistics show that a woman in her 30s has about 33 percent body fat; in a woman of 60, the proportion of body fat has risen to 42 percent.[4] But just because increased fattiness is common with age is no reason to think it must happen to everyone. For women who are in their 60s and 70s today, sweaty exercise during young adulthood was *verboten*. Even the sportiest among them did little more than accompany their husbands in some golf or, at most, a bit of social tennis.

In contrast, many women in their 20s and 30s today—women who will be 60 in the twenty-first century—will have spent their entire adult lives exercising vigorously; devoting hours each week to jogging, swimming, biking; going to aerobic dance classes and working out on Nautilus machines. The payoff is sure to be a firmer, trimmer body that won't wear out as quickly. If they keep working at it, these women will probably avoid the increased flabbiness that seemed to their mothers' generation to be a natural part of aging.

A recent study of 59 women runners over the age of 40 confirms this optimistic prediction. These women, who have been running for just four years on the average, run a good deal (an average of 31 miles per week) and maintain remarkably low proportions of body fat as they age. The proportion increases with age, but only slightly: 22 percent for women runners in their 40s, 24 percent for women runners in their 50s, and 26 percent for women runners over 60.[5] Even the oldest of these women is far leaner than is the typical sedentary woman 30 years her junior.

Based again on observations of currently old women, a woman's overall shape seems to change subtly over the years. Her breasts droop, her waistline thickens, and her hips, thighs, and buttocks grow broader. Many of these changes can be attributed to the lifelong effects of gravity. But many are a function of a sedentary life-style. Once again, observers believe that the current group of exercise-conscious 30-year-olds will maintain a youthful silhouette far longer than their mothers did.

In Chapter 3 we move on to the skin and hair, which tend to show their age emphatically—especially in women. Gloria Steinem says that the most-repeated quote of her career was the statement she made on her fortieth birthday, when a reporter, probably meaning to be kind, said to her, "But you don't look forty." Shot back Steinem: "This is what forty looks like!"[6] When women can accept their aging faces, wrinkles and all, as looking good, as carrying the signs of a life well lived, then all mid-life and older women will benefit. This is the true "beauty"—complete with a history and character that glow from within—that baby-boom women can hope to achieve in the next century.

A woman's skin ages about ten years earlier than a man's; because it is less oily, it is more susceptible to the drying effects of time. A woman also misses out on the best friend of an aging man's skin—the daily shave.[7] A woman can, however, invest in special skin-sloughing soaps, sponges, and facials to achieve the same effect of removing dead skin cells. And she can follow the advice of many dermatologists, who urge women—and men—to wear a sunscreen every single day. Sun damage accounts for many of the changes seen in aging skin, particularly wrinkles and "liver spots," and is the cause of skin cancer, the third most common cancer in women over 50.[8] And since about 80 percent of sun damage occurs before the age of 20, sunscreens should be slathered on infants and children as well.

Chapter 4, a look at teeth, bones, and joints, is full of good news for women in their 30s or 40s: Most of the common problems of the musculoskeletal system can be avoided in late life by a few simple life-style changes now. Periodontal gum disease, which is the single biggest cause of tooth loss in persons over 45, is by no means a "normal" part of aging; it is a bacterial infection that can be prevented by regular plaque removal by a dentist or hygienist, frequent tooth-brushing, and daily dental flossing.[9] Osteoporosis, the thinning of bones that accounts for 200,000 hip and wrist fractures in the United States every year, also is not inevitable, even though it is quite common (it affects one out of every four white women over 65).[10] It can be prevented by a lifelong regimen of regular weight-bearing exercise and sufficient intake (1,000 to 1,500 grams a day) of dietary calcium. And osteoarthritis, the swelling and stiffening of major joints that affects everyone over 55 to some degree, can be made less debilitating in women who maintain their normal weight and keep their supporting muscles limber.

Age-related changes in the reproductive system, the subject of Chapter 5, are the most obvious a woman undergoes. And they have become the symbol for all other changes. A woman is defined by the state of her ovaries; gerontologists, gynecologists, and women themselves routinely refer to women as either pre- or post-menopausal.

In this chapter we describe, decade by decade, the physiological events of menstruation and pregnancy. A woman of 38 will have a different experience getting and being pregnant than will a woman of 24. As a woman ages, the changes in her reproductive system usually can be reliably predicted. On average, at about the age of 35 her fertility declines; by 45 her menstrual periods become irregular; by 55 her periods cease altogether; and by 65 her vagina becomes drier and smaller. But while the changes might be predictable, a woman's experience of them is not. A woman who has all the children she wants by age 30 will never notice her declining fertility. A woman who suffered from premenstrual tension during her 30s will welcome the cessation of periods. A woman who maintains an active sex life will keep her vagina supple and well-lubricated, avoiding what physicians call the "senile vagina syndrome."

As a woman's reproductive life draws to a close, menopause may be welcomed as a kind of liberation—from menstruation, from contraception, from fear of pregnancy. Every woman experiences this time of life in an individual way, just as every woman experiences menstruation, pregnancy, and childbirth idiosyncratically. Indeed, some researchers are beginning to investigate the question of whether a woman's experiences of earlier reproductive stages can give a clue as to how she will experience menopause.[11] Until the results are in, a woman can take comfort in the knowledge that she will probably discover, to her surprise, that menopause is far from the end of life; it is simply an introduction to life's final, and potentially most rewarding, stage.

Traditionally, women have been thought to be protected from coronary heart disease, the topic of Chapter 6. During the years before menopause, when her male peers are experiencing heart attacks and atherosclerosis at an alarming rate, a woman's attention is focused on other matters. A heart attack in a woman in her 40s or 50s is rare indeed. But after menopause, when the protective effects of natural estrogen are removed, the rate of heart disease increases significantly. Women, especially those whose parents or siblings had heart attacks before the age of 60, should stop smoking, stop eating fatty, salty, cholesterol-laden foods, and begin controlling hypertension by the time they are 30. They should avoid the birth control pill after the age of 35, measure their blood levels of cholesterol and triglycerides after the age of 40, and maintain a blood pressure no higher than 140/90 no matter what their age. And, perhaps most important, they should perform vigorous, aerobic exercise for at least half an hour three times a week.

Chapter 7 describes age-related changes in the respiratory system, probably the most resilient system in the body. Although changes in lung function can be expected with age, they generally are changes that do not interfere with day-to-day activity. In terms of her ability to breathe, and to keep the ratio of oxygen to carbon dioxide at an appropriate level, a woman is likely to maintain healthy functioning throughout her life.

One significant change that does occur, however, is a change in a woman's—or a man's—forced vital capacity (FVC). The FVC is the amount of air that can be forcibly expelled after a big inhalation. Gerontologists have come to use FVC as a measure of a person's functional, as opposed to chronological, age. Research is now under way to see whether a specific decline in FVC can somehow help compute an individual's remaining life expectancy.[12] The measurement has been called a "measure of vigor" as well as "an indicator of biologic aging."

A new consensus about the healthful way to eat has emerged in the last ten years. As described in Chapter 8, nutritionists now believe that too much food can hasten the aging process; that fats, sugar, and cholesterol are to be avoided, that antioxidants, such as vitamins E and C, can actually retard aging at the cellular level; and that certain foods, primarily natural grains and vegetables, can be considered active promoters of good health.

There is no proven diet for long life, but experts have found that long-lived people do tend to share certain eating habits. They tend to eat breakfast every day; to eat a variety of foods in moderation; to maintain their ideal weight; and to avoid fats, salt, sugar, and cholesterol. They eat lots of complex carbohydrates and fiber, drink lots of water, and drink alcohol only in moderation. These habits can help prevent some of the most common digestive complaints of those who live in the West. Fiber and water are useful in avoiding such age-related conditions as diverticulosis, constipation, stomach cramps, gallstones, and spastic colon; a low-fat diet is often helpful as well.

In this chapter, we also describe the changes in nutritional needs that occur as a woman ages. With each passing decade, a woman needs fewer and fewer calories to keep her body functioning; therefore, she must be sure that the food she does eat is "nutritionally dense." Most older women need more calcium, chromium, vitamin B_{12}, and dietary fiber than they did in youth. A woman who is aware of her changing needs can keep herself healthy with each meal she plans.

The five senses—seeing, hearing, touching, smelling, and tasting—are explored in Chapter 9. Each sense undergoes a change with age, some more than others, and once again it is a woman's mental attitude that helps determine whether the change will be a minor inconvenience or a handicap.

A woman of 65 has one chance in four of losing some degree of hearing in the conversational range of sound.[13] Hearing loss is not inevitable with age, but the major preventable cause of hearing loss—excessive noise exposure—is so ubiquitous that it is virtually impossible to avoid. Excessive noise is everywhere, on a street corner, a crowded beach, a subway train, even inside a house when the dishwasher, the air conditioner, and the television set are turned on. Young women and men today are engaged in a living experiment with noise-induced hearing loss; never before have persons been exposed to so much noise for so long a time. In a particularly noisy work environment, ear protection most certainly helps reduce the damage done to the delicate cilia of the inner ear. And avoidance of self-induced noise—particularly the blaring kind heard at rock concerts and from the headphones of portable radios—is crucial.

One of the few inevitable changes that comes about with age occurs in vision. Presbyopia, the gradual inability of the lens to focus on nearby objects, usually occurs in the early 40s.[14] It is easily treated with reading glasses or, if an individual already wears glasses, a new bifocal prescription in which the reading lens is inserted into the bottom half of the spectacle lens. As a woman ages, she is more likely to encounter more serious vision problems as well—including cataracts, senile macular degeneration, and glaucoma—but there is good news here, too. New methods of treatment, particularly using laser beams, offer hope of normal vision to those with these conditions.

A woman's sense of taste also changes with age, as the number of taste buds on the tongue declines. Some of this decline can be prevented with good oral hygiene, with an adequate intake of iron and riboflavin, and by not smoking. The sense of smell changes, too, which indirectly impairs an individual's appetite and makes it even more imperative to maintain a "nutritionally dense" diet. Finally, skin sensitivity becomes impaired with age, becoming less responsive to real stimuli, such as changes in temperature, and more responsive to imaginary stimuli, such as itchiness. But awareness is all. A woman who expects such small changes can make adjustments in her health and body care routines, and will feel less helpless as she becomes less sensuous.

Furthermore, if a woman loses some of her senses with age, she can expect to lose none of her sensualness. Yes, Virginia, there *is* sex after 60. As we find in Chapter 10, a 60-year-old woman—or even a woman of 70 or 80—is just as capable of having an orgasm as she was at 20. In fact, some women find that their sexual drive actually increases with age, peaking after menopause when the fear of pregnancy has finally passed. Physiologically, a woman is most sexually responsive in her mid- to late 30s, and she remains at that same high plateau for decades.[15]

What sex researchers have learned in recent years is that the best way to keep the vagina and pelvic muscles in good working order is to use them. Vaginal atrophy can be avoided in women who achieve orgasm at least once a week, either by masturbation or sexual intercourse.[16] In addition, "pelvic floor" exercises, described in Chapter 10, can also help keep the vaginal muscles well-toned.

One of the biggest barriers to expression of heterosexuality among women past 65 is demographic. There simply are not enough men their age to go around. For every 100 women between 45 and 64 there are 91 men; for every 100 women over 65 there are only 68 men.[17] That is why some outspoken advocates are urging older women to look to younger male partners. In one recent survey of mature sexuality, 83 percent of respondents (aged 60 to 91) endorsed the notion of older women/younger men couplings.[18] In addition, demographics may also lead more and more women into sexual relationships with other women. And for women who practice masturbation, this sexual outlet can continue for as long as they live.

In Chapter 11 we look at one of the most pervasive, and insidious, misconceptions about aging: the belief that everyone will "go senile" if he or she lives long enough. The truth about the aging brain is far more encouraging. The vast majority of persons—about 95 percent, by most estimates—will never develop senile dementia (the medical term for "senility") no matter how long they live.[19]

A few changes in mental functioning can be expected, particularly in memory and in speed, but a woman or man can expect to stay as intelligent as ever far into old age. Most individuals as they age will find themselves becoming more forgetful, and they will find that learning, recalling, and thinking occur more slowly than before. If a person knows to expect these changes, he or she can allow more time for mental activities, and can use memory aids like lists and reminders to accomplish a day's tasks.

As with so many other organs of the body, the brain is one for which the maxim "Use it or lose it" applies perfectly. A woman can best retain intellectual functioning by remaining mentally active for as long as she lives. This includes reading, thinking, interacting with others (including persons from all generations), working, writing, learning new skills. The better-educated woman of the future will no doubt be better prepared to retain her intellectual abilities because she will be more likely to have developed habits, professions, and social circles for which mental liveliness is required.

Future Stock

"The best is yet to be," said the poet Robert Browning about old age. He was talking about an individual's life-span, but he might just as well have been talking about the aging of entire generations. For each new group of cohorts, the last years of life get better and better, and "old age" arrives at a later and later date. We explore the reasons for this trend in Chapter 12.

Women born around the turn of the century were old by the time they were 50. Women born in the 1920s and 1930s, who today are in their 50s and 60s, can generally look forward to at least ten more years of good health before they join the ranks of the aged. And women born in the 1950s and 1960s, the baby-boom generation, probably will retain

The Rectangular Curve

One way of plotting survival data is to show what percentage of a population survives from birth to a fixed maximum life-span of 100. The survival curves for 1910 and 1970 below are calculated from age-specific mortality rates (number of deaths per year per 1,000 individuals entering each age), starting with 100,000 live births. The curve for 1970 takes its distinctive shape from the lower infant mortality rates and increased survival at older ages. This phenomenon is known among statisticians and gerontologists as "rectangularization of the survival curve," and it promises to be the shape of the future in longevity.

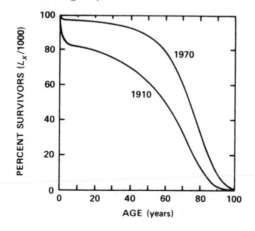

their health, their abilities, and even their looks until they are far into their 70s or 80s.

We can ascribe the good fortune of tomorrow's older woman to a number of factors. Her life expectancy is at an all-time high (a woman who is 30 today can expect to live to 76), in large part because of the conquest of the infectious diseases that once killed girls during infancy and women during childbirth.[20] Her health habits are at an all-time high, too; she is exercising more, eating better, and has access to more effective means of birth control. She is better educated than her predecessors, and with her education come privileges—good jobs, good income, enough leisure, enough mental stimulation—that make life easier and longer.

Today's woman in her 30s also has the strength of numbers on her side. As part of the baby boom, she has always benefited from being a member of an age cohort that vocally defined the "best" age to be. As her generation, an enormous blip on the population curve, moves slowly toward the older end of the scale, the balance of power in the population continually shifts in her favor. This is the generation that has grown accustomed to demanding, and occasionally receiving, enlightened social policies designed for its particular age bracket. There is every reason to think this trend will continue into the next century, when the baby-boomers go gray.

Longevity researchers are furiously working to unlock the secrets of what makes us age and die, and today's young woman might be among the first to benefit from these early findings. Researchers are finding that the body seems programmed to die by a certain age—about 100 to 120 years—because of the work of such agents as "free radicals" and the mysterious "death hormone." Laboratory experiments have successfully extended the life-span of certain animals by mitigating the action of these age agents. The next step is to apply these findings to human beings.

The woman who is in her 30s today has everything going for her. As she ages, her privileges and expanded opportunities will no doubt translate into better health, better attitudes, and overall better aging. But we must be careful not to be too smug in our optimistic predictions. The well-being of tomorrow's older woman depends largely on political and social strides that can be made today.

The very opportunities that have liberated women and allow them access to fuller lives may have an unexpected effect: They may prove to be stressful in terms of health and life expectancy. It is too early to tell what the health impact is on a woman who tries to be superwoman—who holds down a good job, keeps a stable home, raises a child or two, without the support of government-provided child care or other subsidies. As women gain more power in the political realm, perhaps they can wield their influence to find ways to reduce the stresses unique to women in the 1980s and 1990s.

Almost every healthy older woman suggests a formula for successful aging that contains four basic components: good genes, good luck, good habits, and good attitude. There's not much a woman can do about the first two, but habits and attitude are something she *can* influence, and change, her whole life long.

It may seem like hocus-pocus to imply that a woman can "think" herself into a longer and more healthy life-span. But it's not. At the University of California at Berkeley, for example, researchers Paul Mussen, Marjorie Honzik, and Dorothy Eichorn found that people who were happy at 30 tended to be happy at 70. And they tended to be relatively healthy, too. "Health problems in old age," they concluded, "were clearly foreshadowed in early years."[21] The most significant predictor of a healthy, happy old age was a healthy, happy youth. That means that it's never too early to start setting in motion the life-style that will lead to an old age that really is the best that is yet to be.

2

The Shape of Things to Come

The female body is infinitely variable. For a glimpse of its true variety, forget *Playboy* magazine or prime-time television or even the museum of art. Head instead for the woman's locker room at the community pool. Lap swimmers, especially those who exercise mid-morning, come in all ages and all states of fitness. The range is evident as they peel off their bathing suits and head for the showers.

A 50-year-old body looks 50 years old, even if the woman, once she's dressed, looks as svelte and stylish as someone 20 years younger. This is not all bad. Although older bodies might jiggle a little more, they tend to be carried with greater confidence and grace than the bodies of the 20-year-old speed swimmers with the rippleless thighs. Younger women might have bodies that look most like those in the fashion magazines, but many of them haven't yet developed the self-assurance to carry them off.

For a woman in her 30s, that mid-morning locker-room scene might seem like a glimpse into the future. She might imagine that the rolling midriffs and sagging breasts so common among today's 50- and 60-year-olds will await her, too, when she passes menopause. But it need not be. In 20 or 25 years, when today's 30-ish woman can no longer escape the fact that she is "mid-life," the locker-room scene she is part of will be inhabited by an extraordinary group of other "mid-life" women—women who have spent their entire adult lives exercising.

Today's young woman will most likely enter her 60s looking quite different—leaner, trimmer, younger—than her mother does today. Most of the improvement will be attributable to her new, healthier lifestyle. If she has kept her weight low and her exercise level high, she might escape the flabbiness that had seemed, to her sedentary elders, an inevitable hazard of growing old.

The body shape of a 60-year-old woman in the year 2010 will also be *perceived* differently. The ideal "beautiful body," as defined by the ad agencies and fashion magazines on Madison Avenue, is usually responsive to the physical condition of the majority of the population. Ten years ago, when the population "blip" of the baby boom was in its 20s, the ideal was the hipless, chestless gamine look. Today, as the baby-boom generation gets older, our definition of chic has been revised a bit to make room for a little extra flesh. Magazines geared to "big beautiful women" are developing devoted followings; large-size fashions are moving away from dowdy housedresses toward more stylish clothes that actually reveal the body underneath; and some of our most sultry woman performers—Bette Midler, Jennifer Holliday, Bernadette Peters—are, in the Yiddish phrase for well-rounded and sexy, "zaftig," and they plan to stay that way.

And in the year 2010, when an estimated 36 percent of the female population is over the age of 50 (compared to just 28 percent in 1984),[1] the style-setters will simply have to accept a few additional bulges, curves, and valleys in the terrain of the beautiful body.

What Was Up Must Come Down

Many forces are at work to determine a woman's body shape. When a woman is in her 20s or 30s, her shape usually can be traced to a few specific influences: her family heritage, her exercise habits, her tendency to eat too much or too little. But by her 40s and 50s, many other factors have come into play: childbearing history, past surgery, posture, and, most relentlessly, gravity.

Gravity plays a nasty trick on the aging body. Eventually, despite her best efforts, a woman will notice the inexorable movement of body fat downward—straight to the hips, thighs, and buttocks. Gravity is what makes a woman's breasts sag. Gravity is what makes her abdomen droop. Gravity is what makes her buttocks drag.

"Ask anyone over 35, when did you first begin to feel old?" writes Gail Sheehy in her 1976 best-seller, *Passages*. "Was it when you looked at yourself in the buff and realized that everything was half an inch lower?"[2] There's nothing like a change in body shape to bring home the truth of aging. And changed shape is something few people can escape.

Breast sag, for example, happens to everyone. Because breasts are composed of nothing more than skin and fat, there are no muscles to keep toned in order to prevent sagging, although surrounding muscle tissue can be strengthened and firmed. All older breasts sag at least a little. Smaller breasts sag less, because there's less to sag, but all women's breasts eventually show the effect of skin inflexibility—and gravity.

Breast-feeding advocates insist that nursing doesn't change the shape or elevation of the breasts—pregnancy itself does that, they say—but mothers who have nursed say otherwise. And experts still disagree about whether going braless accelerates the inevitable. "If you spend your life without a bra," says Dr. Christine Haycock, a surgeon at the New Jersey Medical College, "you end up with your breasts hanging down to your navel."[3] Most physicians are less convinced. As with so many things, they say, the amount of breast sag a woman will have depends largely on heredity—how do her aunts and mother look?—and partly on her keeping fit all over. Many doctors even contradict the assertion that jogging braless will lead to breast sag. The only reason to wear a running bra, they say, is for comfort today, not breast tone tomorrow.

For a woman facing a major breast disease, particularly breast cancer, concerns about a little sagging seem trivial indeed. A woman undergoing a mastectomy has a good deal more psychological and emotional work to do to accustom herself to a new, radically altered body shape than does a woman whose breasts hang lower than they used to. We will describe breast cancer, and its causes and treatments, later in this chapter; for now, suffice it to say that less extreme changes in breast tone can usually be hidden from most of the world with a well-fitting brassiere.

Fat Redistribution: From Hourglass to Carafe

On the average, an older body is fattier. An average 20-year-old woman's body is 16.5 percent muscle, 47 percent nonmuscle lean tissue (organs and connective tissue), 10 percent bone, and 26.5 percent fat. A male in his 20s, by comparison, has 30 percent muscle and just 18 percent fat.[4] The difference between women and men increases with age: Both sexes become fattier, but women become more so.

Dr. Stanton Cohn of the Brookhaven National Laboratory on Long Island recently used sophisticated nuclear scanning devices on 62 women, aged 20 to 79, to chart the steady increase in the proportion of body fat from one decade to the next. In their 30s and 40s, the women had an average of 33 percent fat; in their 50s, 42 percent. Then began a slight decline: In their 60s, these women had an average of 37 percent body fat; in their 70s, 36 percent.[5]

These statistics, of course, are based on women who are elderly now, women who thought it unseemly to engage in sweaty exercise and who assumed it was inevitable to gain ten or 20 pounds after the birth of each child. With this in mind, we can look at what has happened to the "average" aged body, and be hopeful that, if the current fitness trend continues, it need not happen to the aged body of the future.

Excess fat settles in different places at different stages of life. The female hormone estrogen is mostly responsible for this shifting pattern.

Building Muscle

Some forms of exercise are better than others for building muscular endurance, muscular strength, and overall stamina and flexibility. According to the President's Council on Physical Fitness and Sports, the following activities, engaged in at least four times a week for at least one-half hour each time, can be rated as follows (on a scale of 1 to 21):

	Muscular Endurance	Muscular Strength	Stamina	Flexibility
Jogging	20	17	21	9
Swimming	20	14	21	15
Skiing (Nordic)	19	15	19	14
Biking	18	16	19	9
Handball, Squash	18	15	19	16
Skiing (Alpine)	18	15	16	14
Skating	17	15	18	13
Tennis	16	14	16	14
Walking	14	11	13	7
Calisthenics	13	16	10	19
Golf	8	9	8	8
Softball	7	8	9	7

According to Dr. Doreen Gluckin, author of *The Body at Thirty*, the excess weight that a woman gains during adolescence and young adulthood is distributed evenly around her body. In contrast, weight gain in her 30s and 40s goes straight to her hips and thighs; in her 50s and 60s to her waistline.[6] By the age of 60, then, a woman who has been steadily gaining about a pound a year will have a figure that is decidedly pear-shaped.

Not only that, but the shape will be puckery, not smooth, because of "cellulite." Some women are bothered, as they grow older, by these bumpy fat pockets on thighs and buttocks that seem somehow more sinister than other fat. But cellulite is just regular fat that is arranged differently. Women, unlike men, collect their thigh and buttocks fat in little subcutaneous pouches formed by a grid of tough connective tissue. Excess fat pours out of the top of these separate pouches, creating bumps and lumps. The process begins in puberty, but age makes it more noticeable, as the connective tissue becomes stiffer and the skin holding the fat in place becomes looser. Weight loss and exercise will minimize cellulite by decreasing the fat deposits in the problem areas. But even with exercise, thigh and buttock fat will still be arranged in little bundles.

Cellulite, because it is so prevalent, has been big business for youth hawkers. Every woman's magazine includes a few classified ads for products that promise to roll away, wash away, or pound away that lumpy fat. In her book *The Over-30 6-Week All-Natural Health and Beauty Plan,* former model Elizabeth Martin takes on cellulite with a vengeance. It will disappear, she says, with the right exercises (such as "thigh slaps," in which a woman rolls vigorously on her hips and smashes her legs to the floor after each roll), the right equipment (a loofah sponge, used daily for a brisk rubdown of the problem areas), and the right foods (no muscle meats).[7] But doctors tend to be nonbelievers. They say cellulite is a hereditary condition, and the only thing a woman can do is minimize it.

Some gerontologists have made a living out of measuring the various skinfold thicknesses, arm or leg circumferences, and other bodily proportions of individuals at various ages. Based on these "anthropometric" measurements, they then chart the typical changes over time of an "average" female body. Once again, a reminder is in order: These findings are true only for today's elderly woman. Tomorrow's fitness-conscious adult might be quite another matter.

In general, the shoulders tend to narrow, the chest size to grow, and the pelvis to widen over the years.[8] These changes are comparable to the changes in a man's body, but they tend to occur ten to 20 years *later* in women than in men. Chest size in women, for example, reaches its maximum between age 55 and 64; in men, the maximum is between 45 and 54. An expanded chest could be something to look forward to—the average measurement is 36.2 inches in the late 50s, up more than three inches from the early 20s—except that those numbers are really measuring the broadness of the rib cage, not the size of the breasts. In addition, as we have pointed out, the broader chest is often accompanied by flatter, less rounded breasts.

After age 65, a woman's chest gradually shrinks, to an average of about 34.8 inches in her late 70s. The pelvis, in contrast, keeps widening throughout life, from an average distance between pelvic bones of 26.52 centimeters at age 25 to 29.83 centimeters at age 85.

Muscle Changes over Time

Like brain cells, muscle cells do not regenerate. Once a muscle has been subjected to the stress of misuse or overuse, it cannot repair itself. But like brain cells, muscle cells occasionally are capable of changing function in order to take over the work of nearby damaged cells. In this way, a person is able to continue walking, running, dancing, and moving even though some muscle cells might have been damaged over time.

Muscles do not perform as well at 60 as they did at 20. But gerontologists are not sure how much of this change is the result of normal aging, and how much is a reflection of the sedentary life-style of most 60-year-olds. Many of the changes typically observed in muscle performance over a lifetime are now thought to be the result not of aging but of deconditioning. The good news is that an individual can become *re*conditioned, too. Studies have shown, for instance, a twofold increase in oxygen metabolism to the muscles during exercise after a brief training session.[9] But while anyone, at any age, can develop stronger and more efficient muscles as a result of exercise training, such conditioning is best begun early in life. The younger you are, the more "trainable" your muscles.[10]

According to exercise physiologists Laurence Morehouse and Augustus Miller, Jr., researchers are not surprised when they see a 70-year-old woman with greater muscle strength than another woman of 30. The reason is simple: The older woman might simply be in better shape. "When activity is taken into account," they say, "age and sex differences in strength and endurance are nearly obliterated."[11]

Under a microscope, an aged muscle reveals a loss of cells, atrophy of cells, accumulation of fat and collagen, and loss of contractility. Aging muscles are less flexible than young muscles, and are more susceptible to strains, pulls, and cramping. This makes exercising relatively more hazardous as a woman ages. But the correct response to this new susceptibility is not retirement to the rocking chair; the correct response is greater care in exercising, particularly in warming up and cooling down.

To prevent injuries to the muscle caused by the very exercise designed to strengthen it, good warm-up is essential. Also useful are the following reminders:

· During a workout, don't forget to breathe. When muscles fail to get enough oxygen during exercise, cramping can result.
· Take enough calcium in your diet. Leg cramps have been associated with calcium deficiency.
· Maintain good posture. Keeping the body properly aligned helps ensure that each muscle is carrying the proportion of weight it was meant to carry.

Tucks and Sucks: Plastic Surgery for the Body

After the age of 35, a woman's excess fat becomes harder and harder to exercise or diet away. This is partly because weight gain in mid-life usually occurs below the belt, where it is most tenacious. So some women opt for the quick fix of plastic surgery.

Almost overnight, it seems, cosmetic plastic surgeons have gotten into body sculpting. If the abdominal muscles are too slack, the surgeon can tighten them; if the breasts are too droopy, the surgeon can make them smaller and somewhat firmer; if the thighs are too big, the surgeon can actually suck out the excess fat with a special hose.

It is important to note that these procedures are riskier and less successful than plastic surgery on the face and neck. Body skin is thicker than facial skin, and it tends to heal irregularly, with large visible scars that might even pucker or remain permanently depigmented. Some observers, including the authors of plastic surgery textbooks, are astonished that so many women are willing to trade unsightly scars for an improved silhouette.[12] But body surgery is big business for plastic surgeons, and the rate of increase in these major procedures is even more rapid than is the rate of increase for cosmetic surgery above the neck.

Dr. Elissa Melamed, author of *Mirror, Mirror: The Terror of Not Being Young,* has a theory about why women are oblivious to the risks of the surgery. It is partly out of wishful thinking, she writes, and partly because the procedures are often made to sound so harmless. Women's magazines tend to obscure the fact "that a normal, healthy body is being cut into," says Melamed. "*Cosmo* trills: 'Aren't you curious about what's new in nose, bosom, and derriere bobs?' . . . All the talk about 'tummy tucks' and 'nose bobs' is calculated to make us feel as if we are not living tissue, but dress fabric." [13]

In each "body tuck" procedure, the operation itself is relatively straightforward. The surgeon makes an incision near the unwanted fat, draws out a predetermined amount of excess fat and skin, tightens up the underlying muscle if that is necessary, and closes everything back up with a suture line.

The goal is to make the incision in a spot where the suture scar will be least noticeable—in a natural fold, such as the fold between buttocks and upper thigh, or in a hidden spot, such as along the pubic hairline. But often good camouflaging is impossible. There is no good place, for instance, to put the incision line for a thigh reduction operation. "You may not choose to expose your body in a swim suit if the scars do not

Keeping in Shape

The shape and firmness of your body is directly related to muscle strength, which can only be developed through exercise. Maintaining muscle tone is important not only for reducing flab and creating a supple, athletic look, but for improving posture and reinforcing the body's skeletal structure. Studies show that exercise prevents much of the bone loss that accompanies aging. Without muscle strength, the simplest movements become labored: Climbing several flights of stairs or hoisting bags of heavy groceries may leave you feeling sore the next day. Even active women run the risk of neglecting key muscle groups. With the possible exception of swimming and dancing, few physical activities work all those areas that are likely to weaken over time: the abdomen, buttocks, hips, thighs, and upper arms.

What's needed to round out a sports regimen, or to start you off on a fitness program, is a series of light calisthenics. Those described here are not "spot reducers" intended to trim off inches and pounds, but exercises that link one muscle group to another for near-total toning. The sequence should take about 15 minutes to complete, and should be done from three to five times per week.

First some general tips and precautions:

- Wear clothes that allow you to move freely, i.e., a sweat suit, leotard and tights, gym shorts and T-shirt.
- Exercise to music. It will lift your spirits and keep you moving rhythmically and energetically.
- Exercise on a thick rug or well-cushioned mat.
- Maintain correct posture and alignment. Keep abdomen pulled in, chest lifted, shoulders down, buttocks tucked, chin level with the floor. Think of creating a straight line from your ear to your ankle.
- Protect your lower back. For standing exercises, keep your pelvis rotated slightly forward so that your back is flat and elongated. Knees should be slightly bent. For floor exercises, keep your lower back pressed firmly to the floor. It helps to think of your navel pushing through to your spine. If your stomach or back muscles are weak, work with a towel or your hands underneath the small of the back.
- Pulse, don't bounce. For any stretch movements, avoid sudden, jerky motions. Move gently, as though the stretch were an extension of your breathing.
- Keep breathing. It will help you regulate your movements and sustain holding positions. The general rule is to exhale during the strenuous part of the exercise, inhale on the easy stretch.

Remember that a total conditioning program should exercise joints and cardiovascular organs as well as muscles. See Keeping Limber (pages 78–79) and Keeping Aerobically Fit (pages 158–159).

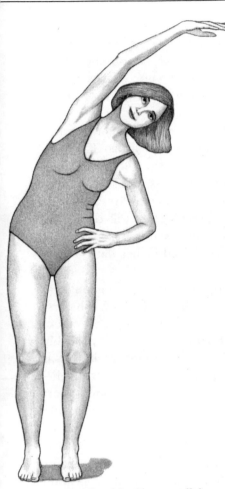

Don't let the elbows thrust forward as you lift; the motion should come from your stomach muscles. Repeat 16 times.

Hips. Lie on your left side, knees bent, with your lower legs behind you at a 45-degree angle. Rest the weight of your upper body on your left elbow and forearm. Keeping your knee level with your ankle and your foot flexed, raise and then lower your right leg. Be careful not to arch your back. Keep your abdomen pulled in and your buttock muscles taut. Use your right hand in front of you for balance and support. Lift leg 16 times, and repeat on your right side.

Waist. Stand with feet in parallel position, one hand on your hip and one arm curved overhead. With your hips facing front and your shoulders relaxed, bend sideways at the waist and pulse gently for 8 counts. Repeat on other side. Alternate left and right, 4 sets, 8 counts each set.

Buttocks. Start on bent knees, your weight supported by your forearms. Your arms should be parallel and directly under your shoulders. Your back should be flat, your pelvis rotated slightly forward, and your abdomen pulled in. Extend your right leg behind you and off the floor. With your foot flexed and slightly turned out, alternately lift and lower the leg. Tighten your buttocks as you lift. Do 8 times on each side, then repeat.

Thighs. Lie on your left side with the weight of your upper body resting on your elbow and forearm. Your left leg should be straight, in line with your hips. Your right leg should be bent at a right angle in front of the hip, the knee resting on the floor. Keeping your left leg straight and toes pointed, lift it a few inches off the floor and lower to starting position. Do 2 sets of 8 counts each, resting in between, then repeat on the other side.

Arms. Stand with feet parallel and hip-width apart, arms extended to either side at shoulder level. Your palms should face the floor. Keeping your arms and hands taut, make small circles forward for 8 counts, then backward for 8 counts. Repeat, making large circles forward for 8 counts, then backward for 8 counts. Complete entire sequence 4 times.

Abdomen. Lie flat on the floor, knees bent, hands behind the head. Keeping your lower back pressed to the floor and your elbows extended directly to the side, curl up one vertebra at a time, lifting your upper back until your shoulder blades clear the floor.

please you," write Drs. Ralph Dicker and Victor Syracuse in *Consultation with a Plastic Surgeon*. But they don't consider this reason enough to steer clear of the operation. "The improved way your clothes will fit may be the satisfaction you are seeking, making scars tolerable under the circumstances."[14]

Dicker and Syracuse also minimize the impact of scars after removal of what they call "bat wing deformity"—flabby upper arms. This "deformity," they write, can make a woman self-conscious in a sleeveless dress, and an operation will correct that awkwardness with ease. On the other hand, the operation will create unsightly long scars along the upper arms. Not to worry: "Wearing a sleeved dress will cover any evidence of this surgery." The irony of this "solution"—forcing a woman back under cover to hide her scars instead of her flab—seems to escape the two surgeons.

All of these lipectomy ("fat removal") operations require about two weeks of hospitalization and another two or three weeks of convalescence. After abdominal surgery, the patient must wear support stockings and an abdominal girdle for several months, and she will probably experience some discomfort when coughing or sneezing and, at least at first, considerable discomfort when sitting or walking. The same discomfort may be experienced after thigh or buttocks reduction operations. Arm surgery is usually done on one arm at a time, because the patient cannot use her arm for at least one or two weeks afterward.

It should go without saying that none of these cosmetic "body tucks" should be entered into lightly. The risks are many; after all, this is major surgery. Cosmetically, the results aren't always satisfactory; the location and extent of scarring are difficult to predict, and occasionally a belly button can be lost or put awry. Medically, the risks are far more serious. In addition to the risk of general anesthesia, the operation can lead to postoperative infection, hemorrhage, or fat embolism in the lung or brain. These complications can severely impair and, rarely, even kill the patient—all for the surgical sculpting of a perfectly healthy body.

Breast Restructuring

In our bosom-oriented culture, a woman sometimes focuses on her breast size or shape as the determinant of her sexuality, her attractiveness, even her value as a woman. She might find that during mid-life it becomes terribly important for her finally to have the breasts she's always wanted. Distressed, perhaps, by changes already occurring in her breast contours, and the contours of most other parts of her body, a woman might turn to "mammoplasty" (breast reconstruction) as the one improvement that will make her look her best.

Three things can be done to breasts to make them conform to society's image of how a breast should look. First, large breasts can be reduced. Second, small breasts can be augmented. And third, breasts removed for treatment of breast cancer can be reconstructed.

Breast reduction is similar to the lipectomy techniques used in other regions of the body. An incision is made in the fold just under the breasts, through which excess fat and skin are removed. Then the skin is stitched back together, and the scar eventually lightens and is all but hidden by the folded skin. For older women whose large breasts have sagged, this operation can provide a lift for the breasts as well; they become not only smaller (women can be reduced from a DD cup to a C), but firmer and more elevated.

Breast augmentation is more complicated. The surgeon makes an incision, again in the fold just under the breast, and forms a small pocket between the breast's glandular tissue and the chest wall. Into this pocket he slips a breast-shaped implant filled with silicone gel. The implant is barely smaller than the pocket, so it should not move, but just to be sure, some implants have an adhesive backing that attaches to the tendons of the chest and holds the implant in place. Because all of the breast tissue remains near the surface—merely elevated by the pillow-like implant—a woman usually retains sensation in the breast, the ability to nurse, and the ability to continue breast self-examinations. (Liquid silicone injections, which are no longer used for breast reconstruction, have been linked in the past with some cases of breast cancer. To date, no such problems have been associated with the use of silicone-filled implants; unlike liquid silicone, the silicone in the implants does not migrate.)

For augmentation or reduction procedures, hospitalization is required for three to five days. Complete recovery usually takes about three weeks, during which time the patient cannot lift things, move her arms, or otherwise strain herself. Because they are done under general anesthesia, these operations carry the same major risks as does other body-contouring surgery.

Breast reconstruction after cancer surgery is a somewhat different matter. The risk-benefit equation is computed differently, because the woman involved, who has had a malignant tumor removed, has both more to gain and more to lose (see the following section). As a breast cancer patient, she is at higher risk for developing cancer again, and might be concerned by the chance she will miss a tumor developing in some of the tissue underneath the implant. But because her alternative is to have no breast at all, she might be a little more willing than another woman to take a few risks.

However, for women faced with normal changes in body shapes, body-contouring surgery, which is not only risky but expensive (costing upwards of $3,000 for each procedure), is often an unsatisfactory alternative. Most women would be better off adjusting their self-image to their new shape. This can be done; a woman of 60 who dresses in becoming styles, maintains her normal weight, and continues to exercise vigorously three times a week might not come out shaped like a 30-year-old, but she will certainly look fit, attractive, and even sexy. In light of the media image of the ideal shape, a woman needs a lot of self-confidence to be happy in this approach. But as more and more women maintain their physical fitness as they age, there will be a generally more positive image of the sexually attractive older woman. And this should reduce the pressure on women in their 50s and 60s to correct nature's "flaws" with the surgeon's tools.

Breast Cancer

As breast cancer reaches almost epidemic proportions among middle-aged American women, the fear of breast cancer has become epidemic among their daughters. To a young, cancer-free woman, the mastectomy itself seems the worst part of a diagnosis of breast cancer. How could a woman go through life without a breast? But to a woman who has gone through the testing, the diagnosis, and the operation, the amputation usually is the least of her worries. She is terrified not by the loss of a breast, to which most women eventually learn to adjust, but by death from cancer.

Rosalie Stahl, 55, is one woman who has been there. In the eight years since her own mastectomy, Stahl has counseled scores of other mastectomy patients as part of the Reach for Recovery program of the American Cancer Society. And she believes they say one thing while meaning quite another. "How [mastectomy patients look and how] they dress is a superficial thing," she tells author Curtis Bill Pepper in *We the Victors*. "I think the main concern is, 'Will this recur? Am I going to die?' "[15]

One in 11 American women will eventually develop breast cancer, most often between the ages of 45 and 55. Usually, the diagnosis means treatment that is disfiguring. The profoundly mutilating Halsted radical mastectomy (removal of the breast, lymph nodes under the arms, and a layer of chest muscle, fat, and skin), once the routine treatment for all breast cancers, is almost never used today. It was condemned by the American Cancer Society and the National Cancer Institute in 1979, after studies found the radical mastectomy was no more effective at preventing recurrence than were the less disfiguring methods available: the modified radical mastectomy, which removes the breast and lymph nodes but keeps the chest wall intact, and the simple mastectomy, which removes the breast only. But even these more conservative treatments completely alter a woman's shape and her view of her own body.

Breast Cancer Risk— A Personal Profile

Many factors have been associated with an increased risk for breast cancer. Some of these are beyond a woman's control, such as her menstrual and family histories. But some, particularly diet and smoking habits, are risk factors that a woman can change at any age.

Women with breast-cancer-risk factors over which they have no control are women who

- are over the age of 40;
- have close female relatives (mother, grandmother, sisters, aunts) who had breast cancer or other cancer before menopause;
- began menstruating early (before age 12) and went through menopause late (after age 50);
- have fibrocystic breasts (that is, breasts with many small, benign lumps that tend to become tender premenstrually); or
- are members of certain ethnic groups—European Jews, northern Europeans, or affluent American blacks.

Women with breast-cancer-risk factors over which they have some degree of control are women who

- are overweight;
- smoke;
- eat high-fat diets;
- began sexual activity late in life;
- used estrogen or birth control pills for more than 10 years;
- had a first child after the age of 35, or are childless;
- did not nurse their babies; or
- live in the northeastern United States, especially in urban or industrialized areas.

"For a long time, I would bathe, and find I had a washcloth on my chest. I didn't do it on purpose, but there it was," recalls Rosalie Stahl. "Subconsciously, I was protecting myself from seeing it. I cried an awful lot. Every time I passed a mirror, I wondered why did this happen to me. What did I do that was wrong for my body?"[16]

Occasionally, mastectomy can be avoided altogether in the treatment of breast cancer, and most or all of the breast can be saved. When a lump is detected early enough, the surgeon might treat it with a lumpectomy (removal of the tumor only) or quadrantectomy (removal of the tumor plus a wedge of normal breast tissue). These less extensive procedures are usually followed by removal of the lymph nodes under the arms, radiation therapy of the affected breast, and sometimes chemotherapy.

Women for whom the loss of a breast is psychologically devastating often choose to have breast reconstruction after the mastectomy. This procedure is much like breast augmentation for small-breasted women. During the mastectomy, the surgeon saves a flap of skin and, if possible, the nipple. When the chest skin heals, usually after six months or so, an

---

Reducing the Risk

Even though the risk of breast cancer is relatively high, a woman can take steps to minimize the chance of developing the disease—and to catch it in its early, most treatable stages should the cancer occur. Among the most prudent steps any woman can take to reduce her risk of breast cancer:

- Lose weight.
- Reduce fat intake.
- Avoid pills containing estrogen.
- Stop smoking.

And to detect breast cancer as early as possible, the American Cancer Society recommends the following:

- Perform a complete breast self-examination once a month for the rest of your life.
- Have a mammogram (a breast X ray) taken once between the ages of 35 and 40 to serve as a base-line picture against which to compare future mammograms.
- Have a mammogram every year after the age of 50 (for high-risk women over 35 and for women between 40 and 50, mammography every other year is recommended).
- Have an annual physical examination that includes a thorough breast examination by a physician.

implant filled with silicone gel can then be surgically inserted. Most major insurance carriers now cover breast reconstruction as a noncosmetic procedure. Women who decide against breast reconstruction can use a prosthesis—a soft, natural-feeling artificial breast that slips easily into a pocketed brassiere.

Who is at risk? Breast cancer is the most common cancer among women. According to the National Cancer Institute, 85 out of every 100,000 women have breast cancer; it is the leading cause of female cancer deaths. But not every woman is equally at risk of developing the disease. Some of the risk factors are beyond a woman's control; others can be minimized by a change in her eating habits or other behaviors.

One of the major determinants of a woman's risk of breast cancer is her personal family history. According to medical journalist Jane Brody, author of *Jane Brody's Guide to Personal Health,* "If a female relative had cancer in only one breast, the risk to a woman was only slightly greater than that faced by the average woman in the population [about 9 percent]. However, if the relative had cancer in both breasts, the risk to other females in the family was 5½ times higher. If the cancer was bilateral (in both breasts) and also occurred before menopause, the risk to her relatives was 9 times higher than expected, giving them a nearly 50 percent chance of developing breast cancer." [17]

The Weight/Age Controversy

The average American woman will put on about 15 pounds between age 30 and age 70—without even trying. (Remember, though, that this "average" woman is from the generation that rarely exercised and that expected increased girth as the inevitable consequence of aging.) Cosmetically, some of that extra weight may actually be an improvement, plumping out facial wrinkles, softening the body's contours. And, remarkably, some gerontologists now actually believe that chubbiness is protective, in terms of longevity, for people who are over age 50 or so.

"We're not sure whether the average individual's gain in fat has the same metabolic meaning in an older person as in a younger person," says Dr. Jordan Tobin, director of the Baltimore Longitudinal Study of the National Institutes on Aging (NIA). In Tobin's study of extraordinarily healthy people as they change over time, anthropometric measurements have been one central component. And scientists are now trying to decipher whether the changes they've detected over a 25-year span are simply the changes that *do* happen with age or whether they're the changes that *should* happen.

A 35-year-old woman with 45 percent body fat carries around a lot more fat than her peers, whose body fat makes up an average of 33 percent of their weight. This means she may run the risk of developing a host of other problems—diabetes, high blood pressure, cardiovascular disease, breast cancer, even arthritis—associated with obesity. But a 55-year-old woman with the same 45 percent body fat is just a few percentage points above the average of 42 percent, and she is far more likely than a younger woman to be perfectly healthy, perfectly normal, and in no special danger of developing any fat-associated disease.

A lively debate has gone on recently about whether a little bit of fat is really bad for women in middle and old age. The leading "pro-chubby" proponent is Dr. Reubin Andres, clinical director of the Gerontology Research Center of the NIA. Andres has recalculated mortality statistics of life insurance actuarial tables and has found that individuals in the lower weight groups seem to have *higher* death rates than those whose weight is a little above what is considered normal.

"The weight charts we now use give a single number for adults without differentiating by age," Andres says. "The weight they give isn't bad if you're forty years old. But it's too high if you're younger, and too low if you're older."

Andres has devised his own scale of "desirable" weight—desirable in terms of *longevity,* not looks—that gives far more slack to older people. His formula, as reported in the May 1984 issue of *American Health,* is as follows: Divide your height, in inches, by 66; multiply the result by itself; multiply that result by your age plus 100. This is the weight that is in the middle of your "safe" range, which generally means that 15 pounds more or less than that is considered acceptable.

Say a woman is 5 feet 8 inches. According to Andres's formula, at the age of 30 she can safely weigh about 138—give or take 15 pounds. But at the age of 50, her "ideal weight" shoots up to 159. Andres has computed that this fictitious woman probably would not suffer any obesity-related illnesses until her weight was at least 15 pounds higher than these upper limits. And, he adds, if she turns 50 weighing much *less* than about 141, she might be putting herself in a group at somewhat higher risk of dying.

Andres and his "pro-chubby" views are in a distinct minority. The most serious criticism of Andres's findings, and one that he himself admits to, is that he has not accounted for other factors, particularly smoking, in determining death rates of persons in different weight categories. As he himself points out, any group of individuals who weigh less than normal is likely to include a higher than normal proportion of smokers—which is itself a major contributor to early death. So until such issues are researched further, the conventional wisdom remains that thin is in. "It's always better, in terms of life expectancy, to be on the thin side," says Stanton Cohn of Brookhaven. "We always recommend exercise and weight loss for our older patients with a good deal of fat."

Some researchers, especially those who study the ravages of atherosclerosis (plaque accumulation on the blood vessel walls), go so far as to say that the typical life insurance table weight charts are too *high* for everyone, even the middle-aged and elderly. Dr. Ernest Aegerter, a cardiologist formerly with Temple University, has devised his own ideal weight chart, computed as the weights at which an individual of any age is least likely to encounter *cardiovascular* disease. In his chart, our 5-foot-8 woman would be permitted to weigh just 128 pounds.[18] "Most of us are too fat for our own good," Aegerter writes. "If you are 30 years old and your weight is normal, your life expectancy is around 72 years. For each 4 pounds you are overweight, you lose about one year of life."[19]

Another objection to Andres's theory is that it flagrantly contradicts a leading theory of life prolongation—the theory of calorie deprivation. In 40 years of studies using rats and mice, longevity researchers have been able to double and sometimes triple and quadruple their animals' life-spans by underfeeding them from the time of weaning. This work has not yet been duplicated in human beings, for several reasons. First, it would take 100 years or more to know whether food restriction has had any effect. Second, it would be ethically objectionable to restrict food intake in one- or two-year-old children—children who, scientists know, are doing the bulk of their growing, especially in terms of brain development and organization. Undernutrition at this time, and at puberty as well, would probably have adverse consequences that could last a lifetime, even an artificially prolonged lifetime.

But if we wait until adulthood to begin calorie restriction, wouldn't that—given the animal evidence—already be too late? Not necessarily, says Dr. Roy Walford, a gerontologist at the University of California, Los Angeles. Underfeeding beginning in adulthood might be time enough to have a significant effect on life expectancy. Walford was one of the first to report, in 1979, that underfeeding rats *beginning in middle age* has almost as dramatic a life-prolonging effect as underfeeding

How Much Should You Weigh?

The quest for the "ideal weight" consumes researchers almost as fiercely as it does the American woman. A particular weight can be ideal for any number of reasons: because it makes a woman look her best, because it guarantees her the longest life, because it minimizes her risk of cardiovascular disease. Scientists have yet to agree on one number that satisfies all these standards. Here are two "ideal weight" charts to illustrate the wide range of what is considered a desirable goal.

METROPOLITAN LIFE INSURANCE CHART (1959 edition)

Height measured with 2-inch heels; weight taken with street clothes. For light frames subtract 7 pounds, for heavy frames add 10 pounds.

Height	Weight
5′0″	113
5′1″	116
5′2″	120
5′3″	124
5′4″	128
5′5″	132
5′6″	136
5′7″	140
5′8″	144
5′9″	148
5′10″	152
5′11″	157

ERNEST AEGERTER'S MODIFIED ADULT WEIGHT TABLE

Height measured without shoes; weight taken without clothes. For light frames subtract 5 pounds, for heavy frames add 9 pounds.

Height	Weight
5′0″	101
5′1″	104
5′2″	107
5′3″	1·10
5′4″	113
5′5″	116
5′6″	120
5′7″	124
5′8″	128
5′9″	132
5′10″	136
5′11″	140

beginning at the time of weaning. And he has taken his findings from the laboratory to his own dining room. Beginning in his own middle age, Walford has followed a regime of "undernutrition without malnutrition" in an effort to prolong his life-span. Walford fasts for two consecutive days every week, and on the other five days he eats about 2,140 calories daily.[20] He tries to keep weight loss to no more than one pound per month. His goal: to lose 20 to 25 percent of his body weight over four to six years.

So what is an aging woman to do? Allow her weight to creep upward, as Andres suggests? Or severely restrict her food intake, beginning in her 30s or 40s, in the expectation that she might, like Moses, live to be 120? Is the goal the zaftig glow of well-being, or the lean and hungry look?

As expected, prudent nutritionists and physicians tend to recommend a pathway somewhere in between. Most will say that women, as well as men, should have as their lifetime weight goal the amount they weighed at age 25. But it's not so easy to keep weight on an even keel. Caloric needs decline dramatically with age, because fat proportionally increases. It takes fewer calories to fuel up fat cells than it takes to fuel up muscle and bone.

For each decade past the age of 20, researchers estimate, caloric requirements decline by 2 percent to 8 percent. "This is why so many people gain unwanted weight in middle age," writes Jane Brody of *The New York Times* in *Jane Brody's Nutrition Book*. "They may eat no more at 50 than they did at 25, but they're less active now and their bodies contain more fat, so they burn fewer calories."[21] A woman who maintained her weight in college on 2,500 calories a day will need just 2,250 calories a day at age 40 to maintain the same weight, and just 2,140 calories by age 50. By the age of 60, her calorie needs could drop to as little as 1,970 a day—crash-diet levels to a young woman in her teens.

For a woman who stays fit and active into her middle and late years, the decrease in calorie needs will be less extreme. A woman who exercises like a 30-year-old will probably continue, with slight modifications, to be able to eat like a 30-year-old. There is one difference, however: *Some* decline in caloric needs will be inevitable over time, because *some* increase in the proportion of body fat always occurs no matter how well a woman exercises. And body fat cells burn up calories more slowly than muscle cells.

It's hard to adjust to these lower energy needs in later life, especially since many women are tempted to turn to food as solace for disappointments suffered in middle age. But the battle to keep weight down goes beyond fashion. It is probably a central component of good health. Dr. Andres notwithstanding, most physicians believe that excess weight causes certain diseases and exacerbates others. Obesity has been blamed

Healthful Weight Loss

In his book *Maximum Life Span,* Dr. Roy Walford of the University of Southern California promotes "undernutrition without malnutrition." By eating few calories and by supplementing the diet with various vitamins and antioxidants (see page 181), Walford says, a person can increase his or her chances of living to be over 100. Whether or not this is true, that person's weight will inevitably decline.

Medical journalist Jane Brody advocates a diet plan that is sensible, well-balanced, and low in calories. In *Jane Brody's Nutrition Book,* she outlines a diet developed by the Columbia University Institute of Human Nutrition. But to Brody, weight loss is a goal to achieve not for the sake of a longer life, but for the sake of a healthier one.

THE WALFORD DIET—A TYPICAL 1,500-CALORIE DAY

Breakfast
1 Tbsp. brewers' yeast in
    low-sodium tomato juice
⅔ cup rye cereal
3 Tbsp. wheat germ
1 Tbsp. wheat bran
½ cup strawberries
1¼ cup skim milk

Lunch
*2 sweet potatoes and
    2 pears
2 cups spinach
½ cup buttermilk

Dinner
*Computer chicken
*Lima bean salad
Any remaining sweet potatoes and
    pears
1 cup green beans
1 cup grapefruit

* Special recipe
Adapted from *Maximum Life Span* by Roy L. Walford, M.D., by permission of
    W. W. Norton & Co., Inc. Copyright © 1983 by Roy L. Walford.

THE BRODY DIET—A TYPICAL 1,500-CALORIE DAY

Breakfast
½ grapefruit
1 slice whole-wheat bread
1½ cups puffed cereal
1 tsp. margarine
1 cup skim milk
Coffee

Lunch
½ cup tuna
2 slices bread
2 tsp. mayonnaise
1 tsp. oil
3 slices tomato
½ cup diced pineapple
Lettuce, pickles, lemon juice,
    vinegar

Dinner
½ cup string beans
4 ounces chicken (no skin)
½ cup mashed potatoes
2 tsp. margarine
½ cup sherbet
2 dates
Lettuce, radishes, soy sauce,
    parsley

Snack
1 cup skim milk
1½ inch square angel food cake
Coffee

Adapted from *Jane Brody's Nutrition Book* by Jane Brody, by permission of W. W.
    Norton & Co., Inc. Copyright © 1981 by Jane Brody.

for heart disease, high blood pressure, diabetes, gallbladder disease, and certain forms of cancer (such as breast cancer); it worsens the problems of arthritis, backache, and osteoporosis; and it increases the risk of any major surgery. All other things being equal, staying trim *is* better.

A sensible diet has also been shown not only to keep one's weight down, but also to reduce the risk of heart disease and some forms of cancer. Such a diet is low in fat, low in cholesterol, and high in complex carbohydrates. Although it differs in terms of food types from the typical American diet, it can be easily achieved with some simple substitutions: margarine instead of butter, skim milk instead of whole milk, yogurt instead of sour cream, chicken or fish instead of red meat, whole grains (such as bulgar wheat or whole wheat pasta) instead of starchy rice or noodles, fresh fruit instead of sugary sweets. In a sensible low-fat diet, meals are built around grains and vegetables instead of around meat dishes, and healthful snacks—raw vegetables, skim milk and fruit, whole-grain muffins—are as important as the meals themselves in keeping energy levels high and keeping impulse eating low.

Two meal plans—one from Roy Walford's *Maximum Life Span,* the other from *Jane Brody's Nutrition Book*—are suggested on the opposite page. They are offered here not as strict guidelines, but as sources of inspiration. Good eating, in the proper quantities, is one of the few steps we can take—alone, every day, without a doctor's prescription—in health maintenance and promotion.

Looking Good Anyway

When it comes to looks, attitude is everything. Carriage, posture, a spring in the step, a seductive twist to the hips can go a long way toward making a woman look younger and more alive.

The key to feeling good, and looking good, is activity. A woman of any age can get out of her easy chair, and away from the temptations of the kitchen, just by walking a few brisk miles a day. Once she feels the high of exercise, she may want to try more elaborate forms—jogging, swimming, biking. Millie Brown, a previously sedentary woman, began in this way and ended up training for, and completing, at age 43 the 1983 "Iron Man" triathlon in which she swam two miles, biked 50 miles, and ran 26 miles in one incredible 17-hour stretch. (She finished last, but she finished.)

However aggressively she wants to pursue her goal, be it a walk around the park or a triathlon of her own, a woman must remember that muscle tone, flexibility, and a fit body are within her reach at any age. The work is harder and the improvements less striking as she ages, but a woman can always make herself look and feel better by getting moving.

Maintenance:
Muscles and Body Shape

A woman's body assumes a different shape over time: Muscles lose their elasticity, weight shifts, shoulders narrow, and the pelvis widens. Considering all the changes that take place, it's comforting to know that exercise, healthy eating habits, and good posture—even surgery, where warranted—can help a body retain much of its original grace and vigor.

- In addition to eating healthy foods (see Chapter 8), you should remember that a woman needs fewer calories as she gets older. If you were able to maintain your weight in your 20s on 2,500 calories a day, you will need just 2,250 calories a day at age 40 to maintain the same weight, and just 2,140 calories at age 50.

- Exercise is the only way to maintain muscle tone and develop firmness. Once muscle tissue has been damaged, it cannot replace itself, but slack muscles can be reconditioned. Concentrate on movements that work all the major muscle groups, with particular emphasis on the abdomen and the buttocks, and engage in exercises or sports that build aerobic capacity. And get plenty of calcium in your diet, since leg cramps have also been associated with calcium deficiency.

- The inevitable sagging of the bust line can be somewhat forestalled by regular exercise that tones the muscles supporting the breasts. A new bra that gives greater support for bigger breasts or some extra padding for smaller breasts can do a lot for maintaining a woman's good feelings about her figure.

- After age 35, excess fat that accumulates around the waist and the hips leads some women to opt for "body tucks" to have the fat removed. Breast surgery can also be performed for purely aesthetic goals: Breasts can be enlarged or reduced, and some sagging can be corrected. However, all surgery carries some risk, and the results of cosmetic surgery are not always satisfactory. Therefore, consider all your options and your motives before deciding on cosmetic surgery.

- Since one in 11 American women will eventually develop breast cancer—most often between the ages of 45 and 55—it is essential to be alert to any change in the breast tissue. Examine your breasts monthly and see a doctor at the first sign of abnormality. And remember, many changes in the breasts are *not* caused by cancer.

- The surgical solutions for breast cancer are much less drastic than in the past, and postoperative breast reconstruction, or mammoplasty, can restore the look of the breast that has been removed or surgically altered. But breast cancer is a major event that can have lasting psychological effects as well. Be sure to seek counseling if necessary, as well as continuing medical attention, after breast surgery.

3
A Wrinkle in Time

"It's never too soon to start," proclaims an ad in a woman's magazine for a product called the "Age-Zone Controller." The copy goes on:

> Why wait? You may not even be aware of it now, it's so subtle. Those tiny, tiny lines. Barely noticeable today. Inevitable tomorrow. Until now.
>
> Used twice daily, a tiny drop of this remarkable complex gives vulnerable areas (where age shows first) the rich nourishing moisture they crave. Diminishes lines, accelerates cell renewal as it penetrates deeply.

The product, states its manufacturer, has been "proven in clinical tests to reduce facial lines by 37 percent on average in just 14 days."

There's nothing particularly remarkable about this ad. Women flip past such claims constantly, in magazines from *Vogue* to *Good Housekeeping*, from *Cosmo* to *Ms*. Every magazine aimed at women over 30 features advertisements for cosmetics that will make skin look "younger." But no cosmetic can get rid of wrinkles, age spots, or other facial imperfections that show up with age. The best it can do is plump up the wrinkles for a few hours, making them less noticeable. Cosmetics do not change less-than-perfect skin; they camouflage it.

The ad was right about *one* thing, though: The changes do begin subtly. Between the ages of 30 and 35, a woman notices her first real "laugh lines"—crow's feet around the eyes, lines on the forehead and between the brows, creases from the nose to the mouth. Most of these lines conform to the lines a face makes while talking, smiling, emoting. In other words, their presence or absence depends a good deal on how animated a woman is.

It will be another 20 years or so, until well into a woman's 50s or 60s, before she may notice the stereotypical hallmarks of old age: the droopy chin, the "wattles" on the neck, the crisscross wrinkles on the cheeks, the tiny "purse-string" wrinkles surrounding the lips.

These changes—the result of sun exposure, gravity, and loss of skin elasticity—are common, but they are not (no matter what the "Age-Zone Controller" ad says) inevitable. Dermatologists have proved with reasonable certainty that a 70-year-old woman's skin need not look 70 years old. If a woman begins preventive steps in her 20s and 30s—by limiting her sun exposure and using a good moisturizer—she can keep her skin looking relatively smooth and fresh throughout middle age and beyond.

Is Beauty Only Skin Deep?

It might seem superficial, so early in a discussion of aging, to describe what happens to the skin. After all, one can say, from the safety of the early 30s, skin is only an outer covering for the person underneath, and if you can keep your health, and your personality, throughout a lifetime, the skin changes are incidental.

But that is not how an aging woman experiences these changes. They can give pause to even the most self-confident of women. "I don't mind *being* older," confesses one 40-year-old woman to Elissa Melamed, author of *Mirror, Mirror: The Terror of Not Being Young*, "I just don't want to *look* older." [1]

Some women—especially those who stay fit and lean, and who look good in the same kind of clothes and youthful hairstyles they wore at 25—can quite comfortably deny their own aging. But they cannot deny it forever. The moment of truth comes when they finally look in the mirror and confront the wrinkles, sags, and lines that seemingly weren't there a few months before. "One day, a few weeks after my forty-fifth birthday, I looked in the mirror and said to myself, 'Joan, you look old!' " recalls Joan Israel, a Detroit psychotherapist, in an article she calls "Confessions of a 45-Year-Old Feminist." "The skin under my chin and neck suddenly sagged and wrinkled. . . . After I got over the shock of my neck, I examined my hands. Gee, they looked wrinkled. All of a sudden, there was a lot of gray in my hair. My skin was dryer and flabbier." [2]

Joan Israel says she hadn't thought of herself as the sort of woman to be so bothered by these superficial changes. She was, after all, a feminist —and a woman who had always been told, to her secret delight, that she looked far younger than her age. But in her terrifying, sudden intimations of mortality, Joan Israel is not alone. Her fear and worry are typical; almost universally, a woman's knot-in-the-stomach awareness that she really is aging occurs without warning one day in her middle years when she's looking in a mirror.

When the first wrinkle is noticeable, says Dr. Carol Nowak, a psychologist formerly at Penn State University, a woman usually begins a period of extreme concern with facial attractiveness. Unfortunately, she says, this concern about attractiveness—which an intelligent woman *should* be able finally to cast aside—is often transformed, in a woman between 45 and 55, into a more fundamental concern about self-worth. "It is as if their concerns about age-related changes in their looks interfere with how objectively they can judge themselves on other qualities and char-acteristics," Nowak says. "The mid-life woman who has begun to notice a new wrinkle or sag begins to worry about things like 'not being up on what's happening today,' 'being rather boring and unexciting lately,' 'having doubts about her husband's interest in her,' and 'not getting out and involved as much as she probably should.' "[3]

Interestingly, Nowak has found that this excessive concern with her aging skin seems to disappear after the age of 65—the age at which a woman really *does* look "old." Perhaps, she theorizes, the anticipation of losing one's youthful looks is far more distressing than the actual expe-rience. Perhaps by the 60s and 70s a woman's worries about appearance are overshadowed by a more pressing preoccupation with her own or her husband's failing health or approaching death. Concludes Nowak: "At no other time in a woman's life does there seem to be as high a concern with facial attractiveness as during middle age."[4]

Of course, this kind of neurotic vanity is not an inevitable part of how a woman ages. Nor is it inevitable that a woman's skin must start to look haggard and unpretty at a certain point in her life. If a woman begins and maintains a sensible skin care program in her 20s or 30s—one designed to avoid the hazards that usually confront skin over the years —she can, with luck, keep her skin looking good far beyond those high stress years of 45 to 55.

Wrinkling Factors

A wrinkle occurs when the deep layer of the skin, the dermis, loses moisture and elasticity. The process begins in childhood: A three-year-old girl's cheek or forearm bounces right back after a loving poke, but by age 18 or 20 her skin has become relatively slow to respond. The change is seen most dramatically on the back of the hand. Pinch this skin on a woman who is in her 20s, and the skin might pucker for a second or two before it flattens out again. On a woman in her 40s, it might take four or five seconds for the skin to resume its normal shape; on a woman in her 60s, six or seven seconds. This lack of elasticity doesn't mean anything by itself (after all, how quickly does anyone really *need* the skin on the back of her hand to return to normal after it's been pinched?), but it is a sign of the loss of elasticity and resiliency that has occurred in the deep layers of the skin throughout the body.

As the dermis shrinks, the skin's top layer, the epidermis, becomes

Anatomy of a Wrinkle

Wrinkles actually begin beneath the skin's outer layer in the dermis, a layer of living tissue rich in blood vessels, glands, and nerve endings. It is the stiffening of connective tissue in the dermis that causes older skin to become less elastic. Overall, the dermis shrinks and the epidermis therefore becomes too loose a covering, causing wrinkles to form. Decreased activity of the oil glands is another cause of dryer, less supple skin.

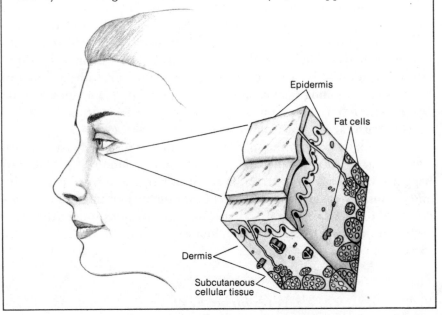

too loose for its purposes. The epidermis contracts irregularly, leaving behind tiny creases and folds. These are wrinkles.

Dr. Anthony Cerami of Rockefeller University has likened the process of wrinkling to the browning of a Thanksgiving turkey. Collagen, the protein that is the main component of the dermis, seems to bind together much as a turkey's skin does when it's been in the oven. Cerami theorizes that the skin's collagen is "cooked," too, in extreme slow motion, by an individual's body heat.[5] His theory is supported by the fact that collagen, which is white during youth, turns yellowish-brown with age.

The extent and timing of wrinkling are determined by many factors. Some of these are not in a woman's control.

Her genes. Women born with "good skin," usually thicker and a little oiler than normal, will have fewer wrinkles and sags as they age.

Whether she had acne. Opinion is split on just how acne affects subsequent skin aging. According to Dr. Albert Kligman, a dermatologist at the University of Pennsylvania, many drying acne preparations, combined with the presence of acne scars, can cause wrinkling ten or 20 years after the condition has been controlled. But Dr. Sherrell J. Aston, a plastic surgeon at New York University, says the constant inflammation of acne increases the amount of connective tissue in the dermis, which makes skin less likely to sag in later years.[6]

Her facial habits. Your mother was right; if you perpetually grimace and contort your features, your face really will "stay that way." This explains, in part, why stage actresses—who use their faces far more expressively than most—seem to wrinkle earlier. And it explains, in part, why stroke victims who experience paralysis on one side of the face have baby-smooth skin on that side.

But many factors known to cause wrinkling *can* be controlled. And preventive steps can be begun early in a woman's life. Some of the most important determinants of later wrinkling are listed below.

Sun exposure. "All the change we think of as aging—the wrinkling, the blotching, the bumps—isn't aging at all. It is sun damage," says Dr. Barbara Gilchrest, professor of dermatology at Harvard Medical School. Exposure to the sun's ultraviolet rays makes the skin grow tougher, more leathery, and more wrinkled. It causes the skin to pigment unevenly, leading to the brown "age spots" that show up on the faces and hands of women over 60. And it is responsible for 95 percent of all skin cancer—which now numbers about 400,000 new cases a year, the third most common cancer in women (after breast cancer and cancer of the reproductive organs).

To keep the skin "looking young," doctors recommend protecting it from the sun. This involves wearing protective clothes—hats, sun visors, long-sleeved tops—and using a high-SPF sunscreen (see box, page 51) for any sun exposure, however brief. Sunscreens are now available not only as separate creams or gels, but even in makeup foundation. These precautions must be started early. "Eighty percent of the damaging effect of the sun occurs before the age of twenty," says Albert Kligman of the University of Pennsylvania. "We have to teach mothers not to get their kids undressed and let them run around in the sun and get tan."

Adults have to learn, too, that "getting tan" at any age isn't necessarily a good idea. Madison Avenue tells us that a deeply sun-bronzed face and body are incredibly sexy and attractive. Indeed, the tanner we are, the healthier we think we look. That image has got to change—and, slowly, it *is* changing. Barbara Gilchrest says that at least one leading woman's fashion magazine has decided, as a matter of policy, to run photos only of untanned or lightly tanned models in the interest of the public health.

Exercise. Experts agree that the more vigorous the exercise, the healthier the skin. Brisk aerobic exercise—the old standbys like walking, jogging, bicycling, swimming, and dancing—stimulates blood flow to the skin, which in turn keeps the skin's collagen fibers well-nourished. Collagen is a protein that helps give shape and smoothness to skin tissue, and it must be "fed" with proper circulation to keep fresh.

Smoking. Actually, there are enough good reasons to quit smoking without adding skin wrinkling to the list. But some physicians believe that smoking does cause wrinkles—possibly by cutting off the very flow of blood to the skin that exercise enhances.

Moisturizing. To be most effective, moisturizers should be applied twice a day to still-damp skin, since all they do is lock in whatever water is already in the dermal cells. The brand is not really important; more expensive does not necessarily mean better, although it might mean more pleasant-smelling or easier to blend in. Kligman recommends Vaseline, or at least a product that contains large amounts of petrolatum: Albolene, Eucerin, and Nivea. Petrolatum, he says, is better than a more absorbable moisturizer at sealing in wetness in the deep layers of the skin.

Tones and Textures

Wrinkling isn't the only change found in aging skin. Many other changes can be expected in the skin's texture, tone, and quality over time. Age spots, which we have mentioned, are only part of the pigment changes a woman is likely to notice. The color of her face may become generally more blotchy and uneven, the result of broken blood vessels, sun exposure, and hormonal ebbs and flows. During pregnancy, for instance, many women develop brown spots on the face called chloasma that are caused entirely by hormonal changes. After menopause, comparable changes occur on the face, arms, and hands.

Skin damage from sun exposure is most severe for the fairest women. Blue-eyed or green-eyed blonds or redheads suffer the most damage; black women suffer the least. Black women also benefit from their thicker skin layers; in combination with their higher degree of pigmentation, their skin reflects rather than absorbs the sunlight and the dam-

The Sun and Your Skin

There are a few benefits of the sun: It can help dry up acne, heal scars, and relieve aching joints, and it's a good source of vitamin D. However, these benefits cannot compensate for the potential dangers and aging effects of the sun on the skin. It's essential to protect yourself.

Learn about sunscreens. The active ingredients in them are, in order of their effectiveness: p-aminobenzoic acid, or PABA; benzophenone derivatives; and PABA derivatives like glyceryl and isoamyl. Don't use a product that does not contain at least one of these ingredients.

The best way to choose a product is by its SPF (sun protection factor). First, determine your skin type. Then buy a product in the range (they're numbered 2 to 20) that is right for you.

- **Skin Type I** people are very fair, tend to burn after ten to 15 minutes of exposure, and never tan. Use #15 on your body and the highest factor you can find on your face (products with factors above 15 are manufactured less—Clinique makes a good non-oily one for the face).

- **Skin Type II** people burn after 20 to 30 minutes in the sun. If they acquire a faint tan, it's after slow and gradual exposure to the sun. Use #15 to #20 on your face, even if you think you've primed your skin for the sun. Use #15 on your body during the first days out, then go no lower than #10.

- **Skin Type III** people usually burn after 30 minutes in the sun but eventually acquire a fairly dark, even tan. Use #10 to #12 on your face and don't drop lower than #7 or #8 on your body.

- **Skin Type IV** people almost never burn. Their skin is naturally dark or black, and exposure to the sun quickly makes it darker. A #7 or #8 should provide adequate protection for your face during your first days out in the sun. Always use some kind of protection on both your face and body. Even black people can develop skin cancer, or at least severely dry out their skin, if they spend time in the sun unprotected.

To determine how long you can stay in the sun without burning while wearing an SPF product, multiply the number of minutes it takes your unprotected skin to burn by the SPF number. For example, a Type II that burns in ten minutes can be in the sun 15 times longer, or about two and a half hours, when protected by a product of SPF #15. But remember that other factors may speed your sunburn: close proximity of the sun to the earth, or the rays reflected off water or snow.

One drawback to the SPF system is that people mistakenly believe that if they use the products diligently, they are immune to all sun damage. The best protection is to avoid sunbathing.

age is minimized.[7] In general, a black woman's skin will remain less wrinkled, less blotchy, and less weathered-looking than will the skin of a white woman of the same age.

Skin Changes over Time

Age 30: Her skin is taut, generally smooth. She may still have residual adult acne (which, paradoxically, might make her wrinkling worse), and she probably has a few horizontal lines across her brow, and laugh lines running from the sides of the nose to the corners of the mouth.

Age 40: By now she has a 50-50 chance of having developed at least one "liver spot." Crow's feet have developed around her eyes, and beneath her eyes she might have permanent dark circles.

Age 50: The wrinkling begins in earnest now. There are wrinkles on the forehead, around the eyes, at the root of the nose. The laugh lines are turning into "nasolabial folds." Cheeks hang more loosely on the bone, and the first hint of a jowl appears. On the neck, some loosening of the skin might be apparent, too.

Age 60: The underlying bone structure of the face becomes more prominent. In some women, especially those with beautiful cheekbones, this can be quite striking. Fat pockets may be forming under the eyes, skin around the jaw and chin may become slack, and the nose may seem longer and more drooping. The skin isn't just wrinkling; it's creasing, everywhere.

Age 70: Contours continue to change; the skull appears smaller, since the bone has actually shrunk. Around the cheek, delicate crisscross wrinkles appear, as they do in well-aged leather. The mouth may turn down at the corners; combined with the vertical "drawstring" lines around the lips, the woman may look stern and unhappy even when she's not.

Sometimes, "age spots" can be frozen off under local anesthesia by a dermatologist, but if they then recur most doctors advise against a second try at removing them. Over-the-counter fading creams, such as Porcelana, do not work on these age spots, nor do bleaches intended for lightening facial hairs. The best method is concealment with some carefully applied makeup.

Beginning in a woman's 50s, her skin tone will gradually lighten. This is usually caused by a less vigorous circulation. That's when it is most important for her to remember to recheck the shade of foundation, powder, and rouge she is wearing. Just because she has worn a certain shade all her life does not mean it's the appropriate shade now. The nice thing about this lightening skin color is that it is part of a newly softened package. Her skin now blends better with her hair, which is also fading and turning lighter, and even with her eyes, which may subtly change to a lighter tone.

The skin texture will change as well. In her 40s, a woman might start to notice that the pores on her nose and cheeks are larger than they used to be. This is part of the "weathering" of the face, when the skin becomes tougher and thicker. At the same time that some skin thickens, however, other regions might become thinner. The delicate skin under the eyes thins early, beginning in a woman's 30s. This explains the dark circles that often appear there; the circles are really just blood vessels that can now be seen through thinner, more transparent skin.

If this catalogue of age-related skin changes sounds like a catalogue of decay, take heart; many of the changes the skin undergoes can actually help *improve* a woman's looks over the years. The lines a woman acquires can make her face look more interesting, more animated, more full of character. Wrinkles can help camouflage some of the blemishes and imperfections that have always been there. And the slackness of skin tone that might occur can bring out a woman's cheekbones, focusing new attention on the slope of her eyes and brow. In fact, the middle years can easily be a time when some women, who were fairly ordinary-looking in youth, become truly beautiful.

Body Skin

A woman's body skin tends to age more slowly than her skin above the neck, because it is more protected from the sun. "If you look at buttock skin with the naked eye," Barbara Gilchrest says, "you often cannot tell whether the skin is 80 years old or 20 years old." But superficial changes do occur. The skin of the body will become thinner and drier, and it will need some extra care to stay soft. This is not merely a matter of appearance, but of comfort, too. The extreme dryness of some women's skin makes itchiness a frequent companion, especially in the winter when cold winds and overheated rooms rob their skin of what little moisture it has.

In other regions of the body, the skin also becomes thinner, almost parchment-like. This thin, loose skin, commonly called crepe, is found most prominently around the chin, neck, and upper arms. Crepe is the result of extreme weight fluctuations combined with loss of moisture, loss of elastin, and the lifelong pull of gravity. Besides avoiding extreme weight gains or losses, a woman can do little to prevent crepe. But it usually will not show up until a woman is well past 60.

Stretch marks are also relatively common with age. Any rapid weight gain or change in body contour can cause stretch marks, including the development of the breasts and hips during puberty. The most common cause of stretch marks is pregnancy. The skin on a pregnant woman's breasts and abdomen is forced to expand enormously in just a few months, and sometimes the skin tissue can tear. A series of shiny lines, like rivers on a topographical map, may result, pulling across regions where the skin was stretched. Ordinarily, stretch marks begin as bright pink lines, and they gradually fade to white. Eventually they seem to disappear, although they will become more prominent if the nearby skin becomes tanned; the stretch marks do not tan and are always a little shiny. Home preparations recommended for avoiding stretch marks, such as cocoa butter for pregnant women, are usually ineffective. The best way to prevent stretch marks is to keep weight in a normal range. But many women, especially those with fair skin, simply cannot avoid them.

Skin ordinarily rejuvenates by a simple mechanical process. New skin tissue is produced at the base of the epidermis, and it gradually makes its way to the surface, where it is sloughed off by friction. In a young person, this cycle takes an average of 30 days to complete. But the cycle slows down over time; the average "epidermal turnover rate," according to Barbara Gilchrest, decreases by about 50 percent between the ages of 20 and 60.[8] The result: The older an individual is, the farther along in its life cycle is his or her epidermal skin.

When surface skin is "older," in terms of how long ago it was produced, it has a different look—duller, perhaps scalier, altogether less fresh. That is why methods to hasten the scraping off of this skin can have dramatic effects on an individual's appearance. In men, the surface skin is scraped off each morning by a razor blade. Women can speed the cycle also by shaving ("All women shave in Japan," asserts Albert Kligman, "and they have gorgeous skin there") or by using abrasive skin cleansers.

Facial scrubs made with apricot kernels, sold in drug stores and at cosmetic counters, are helpful in hastening the skin-sloughing process. So are home facials concocted with gritty ingredients like oatmeal or crushed almonds. Body skin, like face skin, can also benefit from a good scrub. Elizabeth Martin, a former model and author of *The Over-30 6-Week All-Natural Health and Beauty Plan,* recommends rubbing with an inexpensive sponge called a loofah. Originally used in Europe, the loofah, a natural vegetable sponge available in most drug or department stores, is said to "polish" the skin and "help prevent cellulite." As Martin describes the routine: "Stroke the loofah upward on your body, always going in the direction of the heart. Use a firm, constant pressure as you cover the entire surface of your arms and legs; use a rotating, circular motion on your buttocks, abdomen, upper chest, and shoulders. Soon you will note that your circulation is much better, and that your skin is more resilient, more even in tone, and more satiny in texture. . . . The loofah is a nice preventive skin care method to teach a daughter at an early age."[9]

To Lift or Not to Lift?

When Betty Ford had her face lifted in 1978—after she was out of the White House and presumably out of the public spotlight—she seemed to unleash a horde of women just waiting for permission to do the same. "We've had more calls than we know what to do with," the receptionist for a California plastic surgery clinic told *Time* magazine shortly after Ford announced her surgery. Ford's reason for the face-lift, which she underwent four years after a mastectomy and just months after recovery from drug and alcohol addiction: "I'm sixty years old and I wanted a nice new face to go with my beautiful new life."[10]

For some people, a face-lift can mean the difference between giving in to aging and conquering aging head on; it can be an affirmation of the spirit, the spunk, that's still left inside their wrinkling skins. These are the plastic surgery candidates generally considered most likely to succeed. They don't expect to become different after a face-lift; they simply want to look a little better.

But others do not do as well, physically or psychologically. These are the women who approach the surgery as a last chance to get a job, get a husband, get their kids to love them, get all the things that they think their lives are missing and that they attribute to the fact that they're not as pretty as they used to be. For these patients, surgery is often a disappointment—not only because it doesn't make them look 30 years old again, as they had hoped it would, but also because the surgeon's knife doesn't deliver any of the changes they had been counting on.

A decision to have a face-lift is not one to enter lightly. The procedure involves a certain amount of risk in terms of the surgery itself and in terms of cosmetic result. Adverse effects are rare, but they can occur; most likely are excessive bleeding at the incision, infection at the suture site, or severing of a facial nerve. Other complications include hair loss, bleeding behind the eyes (which can lead to blindness), inability to close the eyes, skin perforation, earlobe misplacement, and flap necrosis (death of the lifted skin).[11] And, cosmetically, no one knows with certainty what might happen after the skin heals. Individuals heal differently, and some hazards of the healing process can interfere with the aesthetics of the results. Incisions might pucker, scars might pull, or keloids—thickened, raised red scars at the site of trauma, most common in black skin—might form. Smokers should be extra wary about seeking facelifts. A recent study of face-lift patients in Manhattan found that 10 percent of them experienced "skin slough" (the death of skin from inadequate blood supply) after surgery and that 80 percent of those patients smoked more than a pack a day.[12]

Although many physicians perform plastic surgery, not all of them have been certified by the board that oversees physician qualifications. According to the American Medical Association, in 1981 there were 3,245 physicians who described themselves as plastic surgeons. Of these, only 62 percent had been certified by the appropriate board. Of the others, 12 percent were board-certified in subspecialties other than plastic surgery, and 26 percent were not board-certified at all.[13]

The face-lift itself is relatively straightforward. In the typical face-lift, known in the trade as a rhytidectomy ("wrinkle removal"), the surgeon makes an incision along the patient's hairline and gently pulls the skin back toward the incision to smooth it out against the face. This creates the effect of smoothing out the wrinkles, at the same time that slackening skin around the jowls, chin, and cheeks is made more taut. (A neck-lift is not included in a typical face-lift package, although it might be ordered separately.) Excess skin is cut away at the hairline, where the skin is stitched down. The operation usually takes three to four hours, and stitches are usually removed within a week.

This kind of operation certainly does make a woman look fresher. But it will not make her look 20 years younger. And it will not last for very long. Within a few years, the aging effects that had been at work to create the wrinkling and sagging in the first place will make their mark again. It is not uncommon for a woman to feel she "needs" a second face-lift three to eight years after her first.

In general, the younger the face-lift patient, the better the result. Younger skin heals more easily, has more superficial wrinkles to smooth out, and will not continue to age as rapidly after the operation. Perhaps because of our current obsession with youthfulness, or perhaps because the sun-worshiping baby-boom generation is feeling the effects of age sooner, a surprising number of women in their 30s are asking for face-lifts these days. But few can find doctors willing to operate, at least for full face-lifts; most plastic surgeons like to work on patients between the ages of about 45 and 55, when the wrinkling is advanced enough to make the procedure worth it, but the skin is still resilient enough to heal well.

Other surgical "treatments" for aging skin—all of them temporary—are less extreme than a face-lift. These are the ones generally recommended for younger women, or for those who cannot afford the $3,000 to $6,000 price tag for the whole works. For women who are noticing dark circles under their eyes, several procedures are available to remove them, including cauterization (burning with an electric needle), chemical peeling (destroying the top layer of skin with a controlled chemical burn), or cryosurgery (freezing of the skin surface), which is also useful for removing other age-related skin spots.

Collagen injections have been used for the past five years to plump up certain superficial wrinkles, acne scars, and other skin irregularities. They are said to work best on the lines running from the nostrils to the corners of the mouth, and the frown line between the brows. The injections are very temporary, though, and might need reapplication within six months. In addition, many individuals are allergic to the collagen; sensitivity tests before treatment are mandatory.

Dermabrasion is another skin-smoothing technique that mid-life women often turn to. This procedure involves the mechanical scraping away, with a wire wheel, of the top layer of the skin. Two weeks after the raw skin forms a thick, gooey crust, the crust peels away, leaving a new epidermal layer that is presumably less wrinkled and less scarred than the original. This is a risky business, though, because a plastic surgeon, no matter how skilled, cannot know for sure how an individual's skin will heal. Cases have arisen of epidermal layers that grew back shiny, too pink, unpigmented, or with abnormal ridges and valleys that came from planing to uneven depths. Research is now under way to use computers rather than a surgeon's hand to guide the dermabrasion tool, and to use a laser beam—which is associated with far less bleeding and crusting—to scrape off the epidermis.

A blepharoplasty, a sort of mini-face-lift confined to the eyes, can also be useful for younger women for whom a complete face-lift is unnecessary. Excess skin and fat pads on the eyelids and under the eyes are snipped away, and the skin is redraped with an invisible suture line. For a woman troubled by tired-looking eyes, this procedure is often enough to brighten up her whole face.

Why go through these extravagant procedures, at any age? Each one is expensive—and not covered by medical insurance; each one carries some risk; and each one involves the surgical invasion of a normal, healthy body. But women engage in it, to the tune of 2 million face-lifts a year in America alone.

Psychotherapist Elissa Melamed thinks women turn to cosmetic surgery to fulfill an almost tribal need. She views the face-lift as Western society's closest approximation of a menopause ritual, a rite of passage into the last stage of life. "Cosmetic surgery has all the earmarks of a rite of passage," she writes in *Mirror, Mirror.* "It is usually undertaken at a time of transition. As in primitive tribes, a sacrifice must be made. The ritual involves a period of withdrawal. There are ordeals to endure with courage: the facing of pain, social disapproval, possible medical complications. The anesthesia and analgesia produce an altered state of consciousness. There are scarification ceremonies. And the doctor is the shaman who leads us through it all." [14]

Whatever the source of its appeal—an individual denial of mortality, an aspiration for prizes beyond the reach of the woman who looks old, a social rite of passage—cosmetic surgery is a popular and dramatic way to turn back the clock on the aging face. At least for a while. Other methods of skin care, careful eating, exercise, and posture might work as well, or nearly as well, but they are not done to the woman; they are things she must do herself.

These skin-preserving steps can make a difference in how a woman feels about herself, especially if they are begun early enough. But perhaps the most important step comes from within. Once a woman can finally accept what she sees in the mirror, wrinkles and all, as looking good, her very bearing will say, "This is the woman I am—not someone who looks younger than her age, or someone who looks good for her age, but someone who *is* her age and is proud to show it!"

Any woman who has made it into her 40s or 50s having lived a full, rich life will have some signs to show for it—some wrinkles, lines, furrows, and spots that were not there 20 or 30 years before. If she can carry those signs boldly, they will become so much a part of her look that she would feel naked and bland-looking any other way.

The Hair

Eventually, everyone's hair turns gray. The process can begin early—in the 30s or even the 20s—or late—in the 60s or 70s—but begin it will. By the age of 50, according to Barbara Gilchrest of Harvard, graying "is pronounced in about half the population." [15]

Graying is caused by a decline in the production of pigment at the

Thinner, Lighter Hair

Although there are marked differences among women in the rate at which hair falls out or turns gray, there does seem to be a consistent pattern in the way individual hairs thin. A woman's hairs are thickest at about the age of 20; after that each hair shrinks, and by 70 her hairs are as fine as they were when she was a baby. According to information supplied by the Orentreich Institute for the Advancement of Science, the diameter of a single hair, measured in microns (millionths of a meter), changes like this:

Age 20: 101 microns
Age 30: 98 microns
Age 40: 96 microns
Age 50: 94 microns
Age 60: 86 microns
Age 70: 80 microns

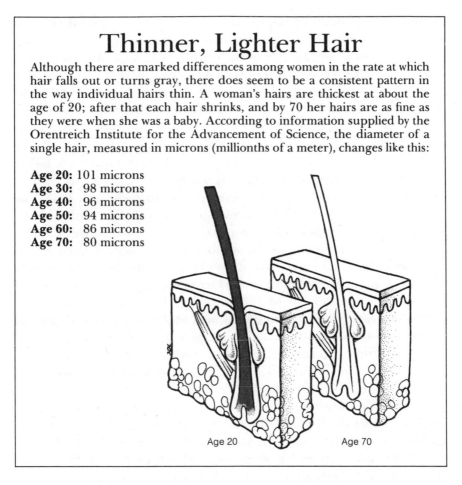

Age 20   Age 70

root of the hair follicle. A totally unpigmented hair is white; a hair with less-than-normal amounts of pigment is, depending on its original color, grayish, pinkish, or white with a tinge of yellow. Even pubic hair turns gray, but more slowly than scalp hair because it spends a smaller proportion of its growth cycle actually growing.

The pattern, timing, and extent of graying is determined largely by heredity. The same genes that told a woman's hair to be blonde at birth and brown in adulthood—just like her mother's—are telling it to be gray beginning at the age of 42—the age when her mother started to gray. But some scientists theorize that environmental influences might play a role. Deficiency of vitamin D, the "sunshine vitamin," has been blamed recently for hair graying, and some report that graying has been slowed by large doses of the vitamin. Large doses of some B vitamins have also been said to have similar miraculous effects.

Graying hair is not the end of the world. As more and more women refuse to cover up their natural hair color, the inherent beauty of gray hair—or even gray-streaked hair—is finally being recognized. As the hair's tone lightens, so does the complexion's, so that many women can grow to look softer, prettier, more ethereal over the years. And as graying comes to the baby-boom generation, we may reach a time when a woman's silvery locks will come to be viewed the way a man's are today: as striking, distinguished, and, yes, even sexy.

Color changes aren't the only hair changes that occur over time. The hair often changes in texture and consistency as well. Especially with the estrogen loss that comes with menopause, many women notice that their hair is thinner and more sparse. Middle-aged or older women almost never go bald to the extent that most older men do, but many women do notice a particular thinning of the hair in the regions most vulnerable to "male-pattern baldness"—the hairline and the top of the head.

"Within recent years," note the authors of *The AMA Book of Skin and Hair Care,* "complaints from women of more generalized hair loss at an earlier age appear to have increased markedly."[16] This has been attributed to a number of hair-styling techniques now in vogue, including bleaching, permanent waving, setting of hairs on tightly wound rollers, the use of nylon brushes with sharp bristles, and, perhaps most damaging, habitual styles with ponytails and buns that put great tension on the growing ends of the hair. This kind of hair loss is usually correctable. Hair loss from too-tight hairstyles—a condition called "traction alopecia"—usually corrects itself within a few months after the hairstyle is changed.

Hair also reflects hormonal shifts, particularly thyroid gland dysfunction, one of the most commonly diagnosed hormonal problems of older women. If the thyroid gland is overactive, the hair often becomes fine and oily; if it is underactive, the hair can turn brittle and dry. Temporary hair loss can also occur after childbirth, surgery, or a high fever.

Hair reflects a woman's nutritional status, too. If her diet is deficient in certain nutrients—which is a common hazard of age—her hair can become breakable, dry, and flyaway. And it can reflect the simple passage of time. Beginning in her 40s, a woman can expect her hair to become drier, duller, less shiny. Fortunately, such cosmetic changes usually can be corrected cosmetically: a good haircut, a new shampoo or conditioner, and a daily gentle brushing. But doctors advise against the long-heralded 100-strokes-a-day for hair care; that much brushing, they say, strips the hair of oils, the loss of which is already causing problems for aging hair.

Hair Dyes: The Cancer Scare

In the late 1970s, a report from the National Cancer Institute made millions of women take a new look at a widely accepted cosmetic measure: the dyeing of their hair. NCI researchers found that hair dyes made of coal tar derivatives—mostly dyes in the darkest shades—caused cancer in laboratory mice and rats. The offending chemical was known by the shorthand 4-MMPD. Even though hair dyes are used externally, they are known to be absorbed through the scalp and from there they can enter the bloodstream.

Some manufacturers have since tried to eliminate 4-MMPD from their hair dye formulations, and more than 30 million American women have continued to change their hair color in relative security. Government scientists at the Food and Drug Administration say the relative risk of cancer from hair dye is quite low—two orders of magnitude, or 100 times, *less* than the risk from saccharin—but women who dye their hair for ten years or more may nonetheless face an increased risk of cancer. "If a woman smokes ten cigarettes a day and is still concerned about the risk of hair dyes, I'd say she is misinformed," says Hans

Does She or Doesn't She?

According to Clairol, Inc., the nation's leading manufacturer of hair coloring, most women who color their hair do so to cover the gray. Accordingly, the percentage of women who use hair coloring increases with age. Only time will tell whether the baby-boom women—one-third of whom are *already* coloring their hair—will continue the trend.

Age	Percentage of women who color their hair
13–19	11
20–29	20
30–39	34
40–49	45
50–59	45
60–69	38

Source: Clairol, Inc., 1983.

Eyerman of the FDA. "But if she has never smoked, and stays away from diet soda pop and bacon because of the cancer risk, then another way for her to minimize the risk is to stay away from hair dyes."

Some scientists say lighter tones of hair dye may pose a relatively lower cancer risk, since brown and black dyes are the ones that contain the highest proportion of suspect chemicals. Retouches should be spaced as far apart as possible—about five or six weeks apart, if cosmetically acceptable—and the scalp should be rinsed thoroughly with water after the dye is used.

Body Hair

Women throughout their lives have a mixture of "male" and "female" hormones. The "male" hormones, androgen and testosterone, are present in very small amounts and are responsible, among other things, for a woman's hair growth and sex drive. After menopause, one feature of which is the cessation of estrogen secretion by a woman's ovaries, the male hormones begin to constitute a proportionally higher share of a woman's hormonal profile. The result: some "masculine" tendencies begin to become evident.

One of these masculine tendencies is excess body hair. A woman approaching menopause may begin to notice new patterns of hair growth on her face, chest, or abdomen, particularly if her mother exhibited excessive hair growth. Excess body hair, or hirsutism, is more common among women with Jewish, or southern Mediterranean heritages. After menopause, as before, white women are more hairy than blacks, and Oriental women are least hairy of all.

Excess body hair is a natural part of growing older.[17] It need not be disfiguring, however, because there are many good techniques available now for removing excess hair, temporarily or permanently.

Shaving. Even facial shaving is acceptable for women, although it needs to be repeated every day or two to prevent a bristly appearance of the regrowth. Contrary to conventional wisdom, shaving does not make the hair grow back thicker; this false impression came about because the hair that grows back is shorter, and therefore less flexible and stubbier looking, than the hair that was shaved off.

Tweezing. This is a good temporary method for removing occasional facial hair from the chin, upper lips, and sides of the face. It should be done on clean skin with clean tweezers.

Bleaching. This method does not remove the hair, but by making the hair lighter and therefore less conspicuous it may replace the need for shaving or tweezing. It is best used on the upper lip, arms, and legs.

Depilatory cream. Like shaving, the use of depilatory creams must be repeated relatively often. Creams are potentially less damaging to the skin than razor blades, which can nick and cut, but some women are allergic to them. A woman should test her own sensitivity first on a patch of skin and wait 24 hours before using the cream extensively.

Waxing. Because waxing removes hair from below the skin surface, regrowth is a little slower than it is after other methods of temporary hair removal. Waxing, often done in beauty salons, is a good method for removing hair from the upper lip, arms, legs, and "bikini line" on the upper thighs.

Electrolysis. This technique, done by a licensed electrologist, is the only way to remove unwanted hair permanently. A needle attached to an electrical impulse is used to kill the hair down to the root, and the hair is then plucked out. Usually two or three sessions of electrolysis are needed to remove all the hair in a region; for extensive hair growth, many more sessions are required. Electrolysis is expensive (about $20 for 15 minutes) and sometimes uncomfortable, but it is permanent.

Some changes in the skin and hair are inevitable with age. The skin will become thinner and drier; the hair will gray; the face, neck, and hands will wrinkle. But as we have seen, a change in a woman's looks is simply that—a change, *not* a decline. Lines in the face bring character, gray in the hair brings highlights, and a woman who shows in her bearing that she's proud of her appearance will outshine a self-conscious woman who is years younger.

Maintenance: The Skin

If a woman listened only to skin care advertisers, she would be convinced she needed dozens of products, many with bewildering names, all with glorious promises. The truth is that most of those skin care products are created to satisfy one of the four basic steps of a sensible skin care program. These essential steps are to *cleanse, slough, moisturize,* and *protect* the skin. Find a product you like for each one of the steps and you will be adequately equipped.

CLEANSING

Cleansing's first function is to remove the substances that accumulate on your face: dirt and pollutants, dead skin cells, excess oil, and makeup. Almost any cleansing product can accomplish that. Judge a cleanser on how it leaves your skin: It should feel supple and refreshed, not tight, or coated, or irritated. For older, dry skin, some dermatologists recommend cleansing only once a day—at night after the skin has been exposed to a day's worth of impurities. Try simply splashing your face with water in the morning. If it feels uncomfortably oily as the day wears on, your skin produces too much oil to skip the morning cleansing.

Cleansers come in three basic forms:

- *Cleansing bars, aka soap.* Deodorant soaps are too harsh and drying for the face, but if you have strong, rather oily skin, an unscented soap should work well for you. Choose one with a short list of ingredients: You're less likely to come in contact with an irritant. Neutrogena, and other clear soaps, and Basis (a superfatted soap) are good choices.
- *Cleansing creams.* Creams are good for drier skin and, because they contain some oil, are more effective at removing makeup. If your skin is very dry, choose a dense, highly emollient cream.
- *Cleansing lotions.* Because lotions tend to be lighter in oil, they are for normal-to-dry skin.

SLOUGHING

Sloughing is a process that goes by many names: Expect to find products for exfoliation, epidermal stimulation, and acceleration of cell renewal. The purpose of sloughing is to rid the top layer of skin of its dead cells through some form of friction. A washcloth is an acceptable slougher for young skin. As skin ages, however, new skin cells, produced at the base of the epidermis, come to the surface more slowly and tend to stick together more tenaciously once on the epidermis. An older woman must slough the dead skin cells more often in order to stimulate the growth of new ones and create a smoother, fresher-looking epidermis.

Sloughing can be accomplished with three types of products.

- *Sloughing pads* are soft and have a tighter weave than the loofah you use on your body. One brand is called Buf-Puf from 3M. Use with soap or cleansing lotion and circle the pad gently over your face.

- *Facial scrubs* are creams or rich, sudsy cleansers that contain a rough grain, or crushed apricot kernels or almonds. Use as directed for normal, not oily, skin.
- *Texturizing lotions* are the least abrasive method of sloughing because the lotions contain an ingredient that dissolves dead skin cells—there's no need to rub them away. Recommended for sensitive skin.

MOISTURIZERS

Moisturizers, when applied to still damp skin, trap the water and your skin's own moisture to keep the epidermis supple. Moisturizers are often credited with doing even more: "controlling" wrinkles and "hydrating" all layers of the skin, for instance. Moisturizers may indeed plump up tight, creased skin for a smoother look, but they can't eradicate wrinkles or penetrate beneath the epidermis. Nevertheless, moisturizers are crucial for women over 30 whether they have dry, oily, or "combination" skin. For oily or combination skin, find a light cream and apply it to the drier areas of your face, day and night. For dry skin, choose a cream that's light enough to blend in easily without leaving a greasy shine, but rich enough to last all day. If your face feels tight a few hours after application, try a heavier one. An effective night cream for dry skin will contain little water, and a good amount of petrolatum.

Some of the very effective, and most expensive, moisturizers contain collagen or elastin. Collagen is a substance found in the dermis, and researchers believe that when smoothed on the epidermis, it's quite successful at trapping moisture and leaving the skin with a fine, soft texture. It cannot, however, penetrate the dermis to supplement or rejuvenate the collagen in the dermis. Elastin works less at sealing moisture and more at filling in the tiny lines and creases for a smoother-looking face. Products with elastin should also contain some petrolatum, or another sealer, to be effective as moisturizers.

PROTECTION

Protection for your skin means protection from the elements, the sun in particular. See the box on page 51 for tips on how to avoid the sun's damaging rays. The wind and extreme cold can dry your skin, as can a winter's worth of indoor heating. For extremely cold, dry weather, find a makeup base with a moisturizer to apply over your moisturizer. When you're out in the sun, apply a makeup base with a sunscreen over your moisturizer for protection. And always adhere to these protective measures:

- Avoid sunbathing, and try to stay out of the sun between noon and 2 p.m.
- Apply all products at least a half hour before you go out, and reapply them every two hours—more often if you go swimming or are sweating heavily.
- Apply a sun block to the delicate areas that burn most easily: your ears, nose, and lips. Sun blocks are opaque, contain zinc oxide or titanium oxide, and are the most complete protection you can buy.

Maintenance: The Hair

Here are the changes that may come to your hair and ways to adjust your hair care regimen:

- An older woman's hair is thinner and more sparse, which is why shorter, blunter cuts are often the best choice.
- If you notice that your hair is increasingly dry and brittle, your diet could be at fault. For shiny, stronger hair, it's important to meet the recommended daily requirement for vitamins A, D, and E. Vitamins D and B are thought to have some effect on slowing the graying process as well.
- Dry hair can also be a symptom of hormonal shift, specifically thyroid gland dysfunction, a common problem of women as they get older. If the thyroid gland is underactive, hair dries out. Conversely, if it's overactive, hair becomes fine and oily. Tell your doctor about it.
- Women of all ages successfully combat the coarse, brittle look and texture of dry hair with conditioners. If your hair is dry, use one after every shampoo and your hair should become softer and shinier. Conditioners can not really "revitalize" or "fix" severely damaged hair.
- Limit your use of hot rollers, curling irons that require heat, and blowdryers. If you must use a blowdryer, do not dry hair completely.
- Cover your hair in the sun.
- Rinse your hair, and wash it if possible, after swimming in a chlorinated pool.

Perhaps the most dramatic age-related change that every woman will eventually experience is graying hair. For the most part, the patterns and timing of the loss of pigment in the hair are set by heredity. Gray and white hair can be beautiful, and many women choose to keep it that way. However, if you want to change the color of your hair, consider the following tips:

- Choose a softer, lighter shade in the same color family as your original natural hair color. As a woman ages, her complexion tends to lighten, and bright or dark hair can look harsh.
- Whether you color your hair at a salon or at home, try a temporary coloring process to begin with. Many salons use henna or vegetable dyes to highlight or color the hair temporarily. Temporary hair-coloring products for home use come in a foam or gel, can be shampooed in, and usually last about four to six shampoos.
- Remember that permanent coloring means that it cannot be washed out. Depending on how quickly your hair grows, you can expect the roots of your natural color to become noticeable after a few weeks, which means retouching at least once a month.

4

Teeth, Bones, and Joints

We'll call her Susan, a woman of 32, who is thinking a lot about how she will look in 20 or 30 years. And her thoughts often turn to teeth and bones. Her own teeth are white and regular and her back is straight, but she worries about whether they will stay that way. Susan's aunt, at the age of 50, underwent massive periodontal surgery and still lost six of her teeth. Will this happen to Susan too? Her mother, who is 55, has already begun showing signs of "dowager's hump." Will she eventually develop osteoporosis? And will Susan? Susan's paternal grandmother had a full set of dentures by the age of 40; her maternal grandmother broke both hips and a wrist before she died. How will Susan fare in keeping all her teeth, and all her bones, intact?

The toothless, humpbacked, swollen-jointed crone is a staple of Western literature—and of a young woman's darkest fears. But just because *many* women lose teeth, bones, and flexibility with age is no reason to think *every* woman must. As with so many "inevitable" declines of so-called normal aging, the cause—and possible prevention—of each condition has just come to light in the last 30 years.

Researchers have found, for instance, that periodontal disease—the single biggest cause of tooth loss in persons over 45—is by no means a "normal" part of growing older but is a bacterial infection that often can be prevented.[1] Similarly, osteoporosis—the thinning bone condition that causes humped backs and fractures of the wrist and spine—is not inevitable with age; it is probably caused by deficiencies of calcium, and might be prevented by a regimen of calcium supplements and exercise beginning early in life.[2] Finally, osteoarthritis—the swelling and stiffening of the weight-bearing joints of the body—affects almost every older woman to some degree, but its effects can be minimized by such lifelong habits as maintenance of normal weight and avoidance of jarring exercises like frequent jogging on cement.[3]

Periodontal Disease

Toothlessness is indeed rampant among today's aged. According to researchers at the National Institute of Dental Research, in 1971 an estimated 23 million Americans, most of them over 45, were missing all of their teeth.[4] Because of fluoridation and better dental care, this statistic should improve with time.

As a schoolgirl, the typical American woman most often went to the dentist because of cavities—to find them, to drill them, to fill them, to prevent them. During her teens, she might have added another mouth specialist to her routine: the orthodontist, who fit her for braces to straighten her crooked teeth. In her 20s, she typically encountered a new procedure at the dentist's, when her wisdom teeth were extracted, but even with this new twist the emphasis still was on the teeth themselves.

As she ages, however, this woman will find that the dentist's concentration will shift from the care of her teeth to the care of her gums.

The most common gum condition in women over 40 is periodontal disease, a bacterial infection of the soft tissues of the mouth. An estimated 100 million Americans have some form of periodontal disease. It is the single biggest reason for adult visits to the dentist.[5]

Bacteria accumulate in the mouth in the form of plaque, a thin sticky film that coats the teeth, especially at the gum line and in the spaces between teeth. Not everyone produces plaque at the same rate. A woman's tendency toward plaque (and, indirectly, her susceptibility to gum disease) probably depends on a combination of several factors, including the chemical makeup of her saliva and the general health of her immune system.

If plaque is allowed to accumulate (and it takes just 12 to 24 hours after a previous brushing for plaque to form), it can erode the tissue of the tooth and nearby gum and create periodontal "pockets" between the two. To combat the plaque, the body sends white blood cells and antibodies to the mouth. This creates a chronic inflammation and bleeding of the gums. This inflamed condition, called gingivitis, is the first step in periodontal disease.

Untreated, the infection can spread to the periodontal ligament (which holds the tooth to the gum) and the alveolar bone (which anchors the tooth). The result: abscesses, ulcers, the loosening of the tooth, and, eventually, the loss of the tooth.

What can stop the progression, in susceptible women, from gingivitis to periodontitis to edentulism (the dental term for toothlessness)? The first step is to eliminate the plaque. That's why dental checkups are especially important for adults; only a dentist can thoroughly clean the teeth of all plaque and its hardened relative, calculus. Depending on the rate at which plaque accumulates in her mouth, a woman will need to visit her dentist for a thorough cleaning—which includes a lot of time-consuming scraping—one to three times a year.

Between visits, a lot can be done to keep plaque at bay. A woman need only do what her mother told her: brush her teeth at least twice a day and floss at least once a day. Diligence is essential: One classic study of healthy-gummed volunteers found that it took just a few days of inattentiveness to create gingivitis.

Recently, scientists have hotly debated the value of the so-called Keyes (rhymes with "eyes") technique of dental hygiene in preventing periodontal disease. The method, devised by Dr. Paul Keyes, a retired researcher at the National Institute of Dental Research (NIDR), involves a daily ten-minute cleansing routine of massaging a baking-soda-and-peroxide paste into the gums, squirting on salt water through a Water Pik appliance, and then Water Pik-ing thoroughly with clear water. Regular toothpaste is unnecessary.[6]

The Diminishing Tooth

Eating gradually files down a tooth, but not enough to make any significant difference to anyone under the age of 200. The problem is keeping the tooth, and it is one problem a woman can control. Despite the fact that the amount of enamel on the surface will decrease with age and the layer of dentin underneath will become more translucent, most tooth and gum decay is a result not of aging but of neglect and disease. The average 70-year-old woman today has lost a third of her teeth; because of fluoridated water and better dental care, her descendants should fare better.

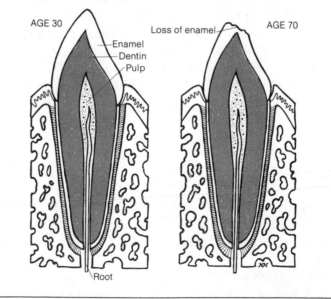

AGE 30   Loss of enamel   AGE 70

Enamel
Dentin
Pulp

Root

"There doesn't seem to be anything magical about baking soda and peroxide," says Dr. Martha Somerman, a periodontist at NIDR. "I haven't seen a situation where the Keyes technique produces any better result that good [conventional] home care. If you can get people to spend ten minutes every day carefully cleaning their teeth, whatever they use, they will be getting rid of plaque." The NIDR is currently supporting research at two universities to see whether the Keyes technique prevents periodontal disease under controlled experimental conditions.

Dental researchers have also investigated the possibility of using antibiotics to combat periodontal disease. But this course has several obstacles. First of all, no one has yet identified the particular bacterium responsible for the condition, so a targeted medication cannot yet be prescribed. Second, long-term antibiotic use carries hazards for the individual, such as an increased susceptibility to vaginal tract infections. Third, it carries social hazards as well: By changing the environment in which the bacteria must live, its use can lead, through natural selection, to the development of strains of "superbugs" that are resistant to those very antibiotics. And fourth, the studies that have been done so far using antimicrobials offer little solid evidence that they even work in preventing periodontal disease.

Because of the bone involvement, scientists at one time thought periodontal disease was an early sign of osteoporosis. Some scientists still think so[7]—but most consider the evidence far from convincing. "Periodontal disease is caused by plaque," says Martha Somerman. "It's an inflammatory, not a bone loss, disease. If you prevent the inflammation, you won't have this type of bone loss."

Certain changes do occur in the mouth that are the result of normal aging. Over the years, a person really does become, as the expression goes, "long in the tooth." This occurs because the gum line naturally recedes. It is only a few millimeters in the course of a lifetime, but it can make a subtle difference. Beginning at about age 40, a woman will notice that photographs of her smiling look somehow toothier. And the teeth themselves will be subtly different—though this will be hard to detect in a typical snapshot. The tooth's protective enamel coating becomes thinner and absorbs more dark pigmentation, while its inside layer—the layer known as dentin—becomes more translucent. After a lifetime of cigarette smoking, coffee or tea drinking, or other tooth-staining habits, teeth also will lose some of their youthful gleam. The result: a duller smile. (Incidentally, a nice side effect of the Keyes baking-soda-and-peroxide paste is that peroxide can bleach the teeth, sometimes masking this change in coloration.)

After the age of about 40, a woman will probably get fewer cavities on the surface of the teeth. But because more of her tooth root is exposed as her gum recedes, she becomes more prone to "cervical caries"—that is, cavities that eat into the root of the tooth.[8] Daily flossing and professional plaque removal are the best ways to prevent cervical caries.

Osteoporosis

The sad but familiar story of the older woman who falls and breaks her hip often has a surprising twist—the woman breaks her hip *first;* that's *why* she falls. In youth, a broken bone is caused by trauma, and it usually heals with relative speed. In old age, though, fractures can be the result of a painful condition of thinning bones called osteoporosis—and some of these fractures can never be repaired.

Osteoporosis (literally, porous bones) affects one in four white women over the age of 65.[9] It's a dreadful disorder, causing disfigurement, disability, and pain as the bones—especially the bones of the spine, wrist, and hip—become too thin to support their own weight and spontaneously break. *But it need not happen.*

As occurs over and over again in gerontology, osteoporosis is a condition that was once thought to be an inevitable result of aging, but which has now been traced to deficiencies of life-style—deficiencies that begin in childhood. The proper habits—including regular exercise, no smoking, sufficient calcium intake, and less red meat and soda pop consumption (they contain phosphorus, which interferes with calcium metabolism)—are essential if a woman's one-in-four risk of developing osteoporosis is to be minimized. This is especially important for women in the highest-risk group, particularly those who

> have close relatives (mother, grandmother, sister) with osteoporosis;
> are fair-skinned, slim, or delicately built;
> are heavy smokers;
> are heavy coffee drinkers; or
> have taken cortisone drugs for other diseases.

The sooner a woman develops an anti-osteoporosis life-style, the better. If she starts her regimen early enough—that is, in childhood and adolescence—she might even be able to prevent the condition from developing in the first place. If she begins by her 20s or early 30s, especially if it is before the birth of her first child, her efforts might have a similarly protective effect. But even if she waits until her 50s or 60s to increase her calcium intake and exercise level, she will still reap some benefit in terms of stronger bones and fewer fractures.[10]

Bone, composed primarily of the minerals calcium and phosphorus, is constantly being manufactured, broken down, resorbed, and manufactured again. In early life, when bone growth is fast and furious, a well-nourished child will experience bone growth that is far more rapid than bone resorption. The net effect, then, is overall growth of bone. This is the period in life when high levels of calcium can do the most good.

According to Dr. Myron Winick, director of the Institute for Human Nutrition at Columbia University, during childhood "the conditions for storing the maximum possible amount of calcium within the growing bones are ideal. Such perfect conditions will never again occur in a woman's life." Winick recommends that parents pay particular attention to the calcium content of their little girls' diets. Supplements are not necessary at this age, he says, but lots of dairy foods and dark leafy greens are.[11]

A woman's habits in youth can irrevocably determine her bone health in later years, says Dr. Morris Notelovitz, director of the Center for Climacteric Studies at the University of Florida. One of the major determinants of whether a woman will develop osteoporosis after menopause, says Notelovitz, is how much bone mass she has at bone maturity, which occurs at about age 35.[12] And one of the major determinants of her bone density at maturity is how well she's eaten and how well she's exercised during childhood, adolescence, and young adulthood.

Each bone comprises two kinds of tissue: cortical bone and trabecular bone. Cortical bone tissue is solid and dense, while trabecular bone tissue is porous. Every bone has some of each type of tissue, but bones differ in how much of each they have. On the dense extreme are arm and leg bones, composed almost entirely of cortical tissue with trabecular bone tissue at either end. At the porous extreme are spinal vertebrae, which are almost entirely trabecular bone encased in a thin cortical shell.

Beginning at about age 35, both women and men begin to lose more bone than they make, especially in trabecular bone. At first, the rate of loss between sexes is approximately the same. Dr. Stanton Cohn of the Brookhaven National Laboratory on Long Island, where bone mineral

The Shrinking Spine

One normal consequence of aging involves the spine and its support system. Over the years the back muscles weaken and the discs between the bones in the spine deteriorate, causing the vertebrae to move closer together, even in a woman free of osteoporosis. The result: a slumping back and a loss in height.

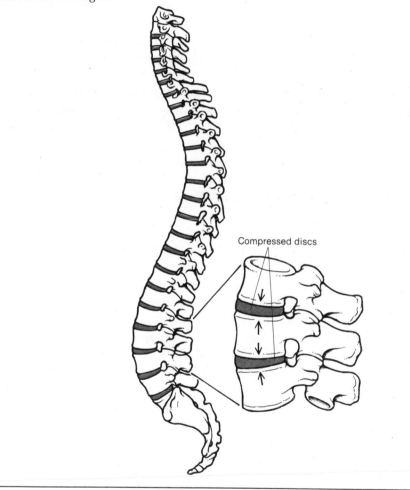

Compressed discs

content is measured through a nuclear technique called single photon absorptiometry, has calculated that women between the age of 35 and menopause lose bone mass at the rate of .3 percent a year—roughly the same rate of bone loss as is found for men in that age range.[13] But after menopause, women experience a definite acceleration of bone loss, probably because the loss of estrogen inhibits efficient absorption of dietary calcium. The postmenopausal woman loses bone at the rate of nearly 1 percent a year, while a man's annual rate of loss stays slow and steady at about .3 percent.[14] This difference, combined with the fact that women start out with bones that are less dense than men's, makes osteoporosis a woman's disease. (And mostly a white woman's disease: White women, for some unexplained reason, start out with less dense bones than black women.) Oriental women are also at relatively high risk, either because of a genetic predisposition or the lack of calcium in most Oriental diets.

A woman's years of most rapid bone loss occur between 50 and 65, especially the five or six years immediately after menopause. The bone loss is most extreme, once again, in trabecular bone, which starts off thinner and more porous; this is found most plentifully in the spinal vertebrae and the bones of the wrist and hip. The average 80-year-old woman today has lost about 47 percent of her trabecular bone mass—compared to just 14 percent in a man her age.[15] The effect of the process can be devastating. One report says that by the age of 50, one-quarter of all white women have had fractures of the spinal vertebrae caused by osteoporosis; by age 70, that figure has climbed to one-half.[16] (These fractures usually do not hurt the way a broken arm hurts a youngster; they may cause some pain or discomfort, but often the only sign of their presence is loss of height.) And fractures are only the last sign in the process of bone destruction. Far greater numbers of mid-life women are losing bone each day at a rate that puts them in imminent reach of the so-called "fracture threshold" of bone mass—the density below which a spontaneous fracture is most likely to occur.

While spinal fractures are not always painful, they can lead to a significant loss of height. Notelovitz has seen patients who have lost as much as eight inches from their height at maturity—and all of the height loss occurs above the waist. One such patient is Eve, now 67, whose height dropped from 5 feet 7 inches to 4 feet 11 inches over the past five years. "One of the hardest things is finding clothes," Eve confesses. "I can't get into anything anymore. . . . By the time I get something to fit around the hump and around my stomach, it's too big everywhere else. My legs are still long but I'm so short and wide on top." Eve says she has learned to bring cushions with her to restaurants so she won't "feel like a little kid who needs a booster seat."[17]

Hip fractures, the second most common fracture in osteoporosis, are no less painful than spinal fractures. And they are associated with even more morbidity and mortality. According to Notelovitz, fewer than half the women who fracture their hips will ever regain normal function. Fifteen percent will die shortly after the break, and 30 percent will die within one year, usually from a condition resulting from being bedridden, such as pneumonia, blood clots, or a fat embolism trapped in the lung. On the average, a hip fracture is estimated to reduce a woman's life expectancy by 12 percent.[18]

Diagnosis and Treatment

Osteoporosis is usually defined as bone loss sufficient to be diagnosed on X ray or to have caused at least one fracture. But by that time, the osteoporotic process is already so far under way that preventive efforts are fruitless. Bone loss cannot be seen on X ray until at least 30 percent of the bone is already lost; fractures do not occur until bone loss is even further advanced. Sophisticated medical technology such as single photon absorptiometry, double photon absorptiometry, computerized axial tomography (CAT scans) of the wrist, and photodensitometry have all been tried experimentally for earlier detection of bone loss, when it can still be arrested or perhaps even reversed. But so far, these techniques are either too costly, too risky, or too vague to be put to general use.

In the absence of an easy means of early detection, physicians have had to rely largely on inferences from the occurrence of related disorders. They look for the earliest signs of bone density loss, signs that occur before the disease process has become irreversible. While they disagree on just what these signs might be, many experts consider such indicators as decline in height, periodontal disease, and low back pain —especially when they occur in high-risk women—to be clues that some degree of bone loss is under way.

Significantly, a woman's fate regarding osteoporosis has already been all but sealed by the time she enters her middle years. According to Notelovitz, a woman's risk is determined by three things: how much bone she has at age 35, how quickly she loses that bone, and how long she lives.[19] That's why it is essential for young women to be aware of the risk factors, and to take preventive steps early.

To delay and minimize the rate of bone loss that comes with age, a woman can take the following precautions.

Take enough calcium. Women do not get enough calcium in their diet.

Keeping Limber

Stiffness of the muscles and joints can result from stress, inactivity, over-activity, injury, disease, and degeneration due to aging. In most cases, the best remedy for stiffness is exercise. Even women suffering from arthritis and other joint ailments have found that regular physical activity relieves pain and restores mobility. For minor complaints—a dull ache in the lower back or a tight hamstring—gentle stretching can work out tension and increase flexibility.

The seven exercises listed at right cover areas where kinks are likely to set in: the neck, shoulders, back, groin, fingers, knees, and ankles. The movements are relatively small, and simple to execute. You can do them in the morning before you start your day, or as a break from your work. You may also want to use them as a warm-up for the calisthenics described in Keeping in Shape (see pages 26–27), or for any strenuous exercise, such as aerobics. In aerobic dance classes, which put some strain on the ankles, knees, elbows, and lower back, instructors should incorporate a number of limbering-up movements into their workouts. The benefits of stretching go well beyond loose muscles and joints. With ten to 15 minutes of these exercises each day, you'll gain better posture, better circulation, and a freer range of movement.

The current Recommended Daily Allowance for calcium is 800 milli-grams. Many specialists feel the RDA is too low for women, but most women fall far short even of this low mark. According to Notelovitz, the

SEVEN DAILY STRETCHES

1

Fingers. Extend your arms to either side at shoulder level, hands in tight fists. Quickly flick the hands open, fully stretching all fingers and joints, and return to fists. Alternately open and close for 16 counts.

2

Shoulders. Keeping your rib cage lifted and your back erect, raise your shoulders straight up toward your ears, press backward and then down. This should be a continuous rolling motion. Try not to jut out your chin or tense your neck as you lift. Repeat 8 times pressing up and backward, 8 times pressing up and forward.

3

Ankles. You can do this standing or sitting, either on the floor or in a chair. Start with one leg extended, foot in a flexed position and toes pointing up. Circle your foot slowly to the left, point your toes down and around to the right, returning to flexed, toes-up position. Circle your foot to the right. Alternate left and right, 16 times, then repeat with other leg.

4

Knees. Lie flat on your back, legs extended and toes pointed. Draw one knee up toward your chest. With both hands clasped *underneath* the knee, pull your thigh in toward your chest and press gently. To get the best stretch, think of touching your heel to your buttocks as you press. Repeat left and right, 16 times.

5

Neck. Sit or stand with shoulders relaxed and arms hanging loosely at your sides. Drop your head forward until you feel a stretch in the back of the neck, then sideways as though you were trying to rest your ear on your shoulder, backward, side again, finishing front. Keep your abdomen and rib cage lifted. Gradually pick up the pace until the head motion is smooth and circular. Repeat 8 times to the right, 8 times to the left.

6

Groin. Sit with knees out to the sides and the soles of your feet pressed together in front of you. Keep your back flat and erect, even if you have to lean forward slightly, and shoulders relaxed. With your hands grasping either your ankles or your insteps—never the toes—gently press your knees toward the floor. It helps to keep the abdomen pulled in, and to think of lifting your torso up as you stretch. Repeat for 16 counts.

7

Back. This pelvic tilt is a good toning exercise for buttocks, abdomen, and lower back. Stand with feet parallel and hip-width apart, rib cage lifted, arms relaxed at your side. Allow the pelvis to release as you slightly arch the lower back; hold for 2 counts. Then drop the buttocks, tilt the pelvis forward and bring your lower back into proper alignment again; hold muscles tightly for 2 counts. Alternately release and contract, for a total of 16 times.

average American woman over 45 consumes only 450 milligrams of calcium a day.[20] Worse yet, after menopause a woman's calcium requirements actually increase, because she has become far less efficient at metabolizing the calcium she does eat. Notelovitz recommends the following levels of calcium intake for women:

age 20–35	1,000 milligrams per day
age 35–60	1,200 milligrams per day
age 60 and up	1,400 milligrams per day

The major objection of nutritionists to such high levels of calcium intake is that they can almost never be attained through diet alone. Four glasses of milk daily would do it—that would provide 1,200 milligrams of calcium—but few women are willing or able to drink this much milk. So some doctors recommend partial reliance on calcium supplements (or total reliance for those women who have lactase deficiency, a digestive problem that makes them unable to tolerate dairy products). Calcium lactate and calcium carbonate are the most readily absorbed forms of the product. Stay away from bone meal (dolomite), which was found recently to contain high levels of lead. The supplements should be taken before meals, on an empty stomach, and it helps if they also contain some vitamin D to aid in absorption. It is especially useful to take some calcium at bedtime, because bone loss is accelerated at night.

Exercise. Not only does exercise help prevent bone loss, it actually stimulates the production of new bone. Exercise works by placing stress directly on the bones (which, like muscles, become bigger and stronger when stressed) by stimulating blood flow to the bone, and by shifting the body's hormonal balance so that it stimulates new bone formation. Aerobic, weight-bearing exercises—walking, bicycling, jogging, dancing —are the best bone-builders.

At the University of Florida, Morris Notelovitz advises his sedentary patients to engage in some pleasant form of moderate aerobic activity for at least one-half hour three times a week. Indeed, he tells his patients, whatever their age, that the best way to avoid osteoporosis in their *daughters* is to get them moving beginning in childhood. For his more active patients, Notelovitz recommends continuation of their exercise program or—if their bone density warrants it—an acceleration of activity. He often suggests that his patients begin with walking, since it is cheap, effective, and has a low injury rate. The goal: a regular, thrice-weekly walk of two or three miles.

Reduce phosphorus intake. Phosphorus, a major component of bone tissue, must also be consumed in sufficient quantities to prevent the loss of bone. But too much phosophorus can actually inhibit the absorption of calcium. Experts recommend trying to keep the calcium-to-phosphorus ratio of the diet at about one to one—but that's not so easy to do. The typical American consumes two to four times as much phosphorus as calcium every day.[21]

The major contributors of phosphorus to the diet are packaged cereals and baked goods (which contain phosphates as preservatives), nuts and legumes, and animal protein—fish, poultry, eggs and, especially, red meat. Canned soda, especially colas, contains a high amount of phosphorus—up to 60 milligrams in every 12-ounce can. Processed foods are also high in phosphorus. One ounce of natural Swiss cheese contains 226 milligrams of calcium and only 160 milligrams of phosphorus; but one ounce of processed American cheese contains 198 milligrams of calcium and 219 milligrams of phosphorus—actually *more* phosphorus than calcium per serving.

Eat less animal protein. Red meat especially interferes with the absorption of calcium because of its high phosphorus content. That is why Myron Winick recommends waiting one or two hours after consuming a meat-rich meal before ingesting calcium supplements or foods. But there's more to the relationship than phosphorus itself. Meat has a high acid content, and some scientists believe the body tries to neutralize this acidity by dissolving bone tissue.

Studies have found that vegetarians lose significantly less bone with age than do meat eaters, even though their calcium intake may be no higher. One study of white women between the ages of 50 and 89 found that the meat eaters had lost 35 percent of their bone mass while the vegetarians (who ate eggs and dairy products but no meat) lost just 18 percent.[22] Another study found that vegetarian men and women in their 70s had an average bone density greater than that of meat eaters in their 50s.[23] Morris Notelovitz suggests that women concerned about developing osteoporosis go vegetarian, or at least limit their red meat consumption to two or three meals a week.

Stop smoking. Preventing bone loss is just one more of the dozens of good reasons to stop smoking. The association between smoking and osteoporosis was established in the 1970s, when a study of women with osteoporotic fractures of the spine found that 76 percent were smokers, and 68 percent of them heavy smokers (more than a pack a day).[24] Morris Notelovitz says that smoking might impair the activation of vitamin D in the liver, which in turn decreases calcium absorption and results in a loss of calcium from the bones. But other relationships, he says, are also possible: Since smokers go through menopause about five years earlier than nonsmokers, they may simply experience a longer period of rapid bone loss; and since smokers are less likely to be over-weight than nonsmokers, they may as a group be lacking the extra protection from osteoporosis that obesity provides. The exact mechanism is yet to be described, but, as Notelovitz says, "why wait around for the bad news?"

Cut down on caffeine. Heavy coffee drinking also has been associated with a greater risk of osteoporosis. One study found that heavy coffee drinkers (four cups of coffee or more a day) made up 31 percent of a group of postmenopausal women with bone loss, and only 19 percent of an age-matched group of women with normal bone density.[25] As with smoking, the exact mechanism of this association is unclear, but it might be prudent for a high-risk woman at least to limit her coffee consumption.

Get pregnant. Pregnancy is a time when a woman absorbs calcium at the most efficient rate she has since childhood. If she enters pregnancy in good calcium balance and maintains a high level of calcium intake during pregnancy—about 1,200 milligrams a day—she can actually emerge from pregnancy with a net *increase* in bone density.

During pregnancy, all her hormones are on a woman's side. She produces high levels of estrogen throughout pregnancy, which in turn promotes calcium absorption and inhibits bone breakdown. The goal of all this activity, of course, is to maintain the fetus's health during a time when bone growth is faster than it will ever be again. If the pregnant woman does not ingest sufficient calcium, that is when her bones will suffer. "For every child, a tooth" is an old wives' tale that dates to the time when nature had to rob a woman's calcium stores—that is, her teeth and bones—to meet the needs of the fetus. But in the United States, where prenatal care generally includes the advice to drink four glasses of milk a day, women who have had children are actually protected from severe bone loss. One study found that among women with osteoporosis, two-thirds had never had children.[26]

Similarly, long-term use of the birth control pill, which mimics the hormonal changes of pregnancy, has also been associated with increased bone density in later years.[27]

And, maybe, take estrogen. The relationship between pregnancy and bone density helps make it clear that estrogen is the good guy in maintaining bone mass and preventing osteoporosis. When estrogen production falls off at menopause, bone loss accelerates sharply. This raises the question: Would estrogen replacement therapy (ERT) be a useful way to prevent, or even to treat, osteoporosis? The answer is a political and medical hot potato.

Morris Notelovitz likes ERT. He points to the several studies that have shown a beneficial effect of ERT in terms of postmenopausal bone loss and the incidence of fracture. "Compared with untreated women," he points out, "estrogen-treated menopausal women have a sixty percent lower incidence of wrist and hip fractures and a ninety percent lower incidence of vertebral fractures. Women beginning estrogen therapy within five years of their menopause are four times more likely to remain free of wrist and hip fractures than women who do not take estrogen."

To be effective, the therapy must be continued, Notelovitz says, "until the natural slowing down of bone loss occurs"—usually around age 65. Until then, the dose can be kept quite low, and the cancer-causing potential of the hormone can be minimized by administering it in tandem with another female hormone, progesterone. More on the pros and cons of ERT appear in Chapter 5.

Arthritis

Osteoarthritis, the most common joint complaint in older women, has been called the "wear-and-tear disease." It arises largely because of the way joints were used in young adulthood. Persistent misuse or overuse of certain joints can cause arthritis. According to Dr. James F. Fries, director of the Stanford Arthritis Clinic in California, exercise can be a two-edged sword. On the one hand, certain forms of strenuous exercise may make one prone to arthritis, particularly weight lifting, push-ups, football, and baseball. But on the other hand, most mild to moderate forms of activity—basketball, biking, jogging, handball, soccer, swimming, tennis, walking—can actually help prevent arthritis by keeping the bones, ligaments, and cartilage in good working order.[28]

The back, the neck, the hips, and the knees are prone to arthritis, especially after a lifetime of sports injury, trauma, or even just bad posture. Ballet dancers tend to get arthritis in their feet; tennis players tend to get it in their elbows; joggers tend to get it in their knees. Obesity has been linked with arthritis, too, since it burdens the joints with excess weight to bear. And in women, for reasons not yet understood, one additional region is especially sensitive to arthritis—the first joints of the fingers.

Five Steps to a Healthier Back

1. Be aware of your posture. Keep chest lifted, shoulders down, abdomen in, buttocks dropped. Move as though a string were pulling through the top of your head.
2. Avoid bending over or reaching with a rounded back. Even the simple act of pulling off a boot can wrench a muscle. In general, curvature makes for weakness. So in all your movements, whether it's typing, mopping a floor, or lifting a suitcase, try to keep your back straight.
3. When you lift heavy objects, rely on your hips and legs for strength. The safest approach is to bend your knees, squat to the floor, and, keeping your back straight, lift up slowly.
4. The correct way to roll out of bed is, literally, to roll out of bed. Shift your weight to one side, place your feet on the floor, and you're up. Never sit up suddenly from a flat-back position. This also applies to exercise classes. After floor routines, roll over to one side, sit flat on your bottom, then stand up.
5. Exercise. The only way to support your back is to strengthen the muscles of your torso. Calisthenics that work the abdominals are particularly important.

Osteoarthritis results when the spongy cartilage, or gristle, of the joints grinds away, leaving the joint bones raw and unpadded. It is surprisingly common—and it can arise at a surprisingly early age. The majority of persons over the age of 40 show some evidence, on X-ray examination, of arthritic changes in one or more joints. Sometimes the changes are observed only in the fingers, where bony nodules, or spurs, develop around the first joint; these are unsightly but seldom cause any pain. Sometimes they are located in the spine, with bony growths around the neck or lower back associated with wear and tear on the disks between the spinal vertebrae; once again the symptoms are mild or nonexistent. And sometimes they occur in the weight-bearing joints, such as the hips and knees; this form of osteoarthritis is the one that causes stiffness, swelling, and pain.

According to Dr. Frederick McDuffie, senior vice-president for medical affairs of the Arthritis Foundation, by the age of 75 about 85 percent of people show X-ray evidence of arthritis of the hands or feet. But even more surprising is how little the X-ray findings predict about the subjective experience of pain. Only 50 to 60 percent of persons with severe or moderate X-ray changes, says McDuffie, report having pain; of those with less severe changes, 40 percent have pain; of those with borderline changes, 18 percent have pain; and of those with no changes, 8 percent nonetheless have pain they attribute to osteoarthritis.

"The most interesting group," McDuffie says, "is the forty to fifty percent of individuals with severe arthritic findings on X ray who experience no pain." He thinks these are individuals with sufficiently well-toned muscles surrounding the arthritic joints to allow for continued motion and flexibility despite the worn cartilage. In other words, those who feel the changes least are those who are most physically fit.

The best way to prevent osteoarthritis is to stay slim. Obesity, which adds to the weight-bearing burden on the joints, can cause osteoarthritis, especially of the hips and knees. The best way to prevent *pain* from osteoarthritis is to stay fit. Joint problems, once they occur, usually can be minimized if the nearby muscles are strong.

James Fries says that smooth, easy, regular exercise is the best treatment for osteoarthritis. "If you start getting some osteoarthritis," he writes in *Arthritis: A Comprehensive Guide*, "it is not a signal to begin to tone down your life, but rather to develop a sensible, regular exercise program to strengthen the bones and ligaments surrounding the affected joints and to preserve mobility in joints that are developing spurs."[29]

A few experts advise against stressful exercises, such as jogging, as a way to prevent osteoarthritis, particularly for women over age 35 who are not in good physical condition. Dr. Barbara Edelstein, author of *The Woman Doctor's Medical Guide for Women*, is especially emphatic in her criticism of jogging for women in this category.[30] Like many other authorities, she prefers to see such a woman embark on a program of regular swimming or sustained, brisk walking.

But not everyone advises mid-life women to avoid jogging. Frederick McDuffie, for one, is a marathon runner who sees no reason for stopping himself or for advising anyone else to stop. James Fries says vigorous exercise is the only way to keep cartilage well-nourished. The cartilage of the joint does not have its own blood supply; it can get oxygen and get rid of waste only by being used. Every time a joint is bent, the spongy cartilage squeezes out fluid and waste; every time it is relaxed, the joint fluid in which it is bathed, which carries nutrients and oxygen, is squeezed back in. For this reason, Fries says, exercise is a way to *prevent*, not cause, cartilage destruction: "Marathon runners and others who subject their cartilage to great stress throughout life tend not to have excessive degeneration of the cartilage."[31]

For a woman who wants to be conservative about osteoarthritis, or who is bothered as she ages by shin splints or other discomfort after jogging, there are less potentially traumatizing ways to tone up. Among the most heartily recommended: swimming, walking, yoga, t'ai chi, and gentle stretching. (It must be remembered that of these exercises, only swimming and walking carry any aerobic benefit. A woman who chooses a routine of stretching exercises should combine or alternate them with a more vigorous workout that gets her heart pounding.)

Rheumatoid arthritis is a wholly different disease than osteoarthritis. It is a disorder of the immune system, not a result of normal aging. The people it affects are younger, usually in their 30s, 40s, or 50s. And it is even more often a woman's condition; women are twice as likely as men to get osteoarthritis, but three times more likely than men to get rheumatoid arthritis.

Rheumatoid arthritis is an autoimmune disease; something goes haywire in the body's immune system so that it begins to recognize its own body cells as foreign invaders, and mounts a misguided attack. While osteoarthritis usually affects the major weight-bearing joints (hips, knees, and spine), rheumatoid arthritis is more likely to occur in the small joints of the knuckles, toes, ankles, wrists, knees, and neck.

One of the most common symptoms of rheumatoid arthritis, and one that does not appear in other kinds of joint problems, is morning stiffness. Even a relatively brief period of motionlessness can make a patient's muscles feel stiff and difficult to move. The only treatment for morning stiffness is motion; gradually the joints loosen up and movement becomes easier.

Rheumatoid arthritis often can be diagnosed with blood tests, most commonly the test for the rheumatoid factor, present in about 80 percent of rheumatoid arthritis patients. An individual in whom the rheumatoid factor is present is most likely to have the chronic form of the disease (there are other forms, characterized either by one brief acute episode or by several episodes relieved with periods of remission). But even the chronic form of rheumatoid arthritis is not necessarily debilitating or crippling. While it is the most severe form of arthritis, its progression can often be arrested by a careful program combining moderate exercise, moderate rest, and cautious use of such anti-inflammatory drugs as aspirin, Motrin, Indocin, or—if these are insufficient— chloroquine (an antimalarial), gold salt injections, or penicillamine (an experimental drug).

Fibrositis is a condition that has been called "the I-ache-all-over disease."[32] It refers to pain and tenderness in the fibrous tissues and muscles surrounding a joint. Fibrositis seems to be a complaint primarily of women, especially women in their 40s or 50s. The symptoms: generalized aches and pains, tenderness without joint swelling, and stiffness after prolonged activity. It is most likely to occur in the knees, lower back, shoulders, and hands.

The cause of fibrositis is a mystery. Although its incidence does seem to increase with age, the consensus is that fibrositis is not simply the result of normal aging. Recently, physicians have recorded the brain wave activity of fibrositic individuals during sleep and have found a jerky pattern characteristic of the sleep patterns of healthy volunteers after they are kept awake for two or three nights.[33] This pattern, in which slow wave brain activity is decreased, signifies a chronic deficiency of the kind of sleep known to be the most restful to the muscles. (Significantly, individuals who are well-trained athletes never experience this sleep pattern, even after sleep deprivation.) According to James Fries, persons with fibrositis may be unable to relax their muscles totally while asleep, creating an abnormal strain on the tendons at night that in turn causes inflammation and pain on arising. The source of it all might be tension. "Fibrositis," he concludes, "is similar to tension headache, but it affects many parts of the body."[34]

The best preventives for fibrositis: staying in shape, maintaining normal weight, avoiding tension (relaxation exercises and long warm baths in periods of stress are always useful), and maintaining good posture. The best treatment: exercise. "We use exercise as practically our only therapeutic modality," Fries reports. "When a patient is able to walk extensively and to swim, hike, or bike regularly, we have seen gradual resolution of the syndrome after a few weeks to a few months."

Maintenance: Teeth, Bones, and Joints

Building healthy teeth, bones, and joints is almost entirely a matter of maintenance. With proper hygiene, diet, and exercise, women have a much better chance of avoiding such age-related conditions as periodontal disease, the single biggest cause of tooth loss in persons over 45; osteoporosis, the thinning bone condition that causes humped backs and fractures; and the effects of osteoarthritis, the swelling and stiffening of the weight-bearing joints of the body. At any stage of a woman's life, the following recommendations are bound to yield benefits.

TEETH

- The culprit is plaque, a sticky, bacteria-filled film that coats the teeth and can lead to periodontal disease. The only way to eliminate it is through professional dental cleaning, anywhere from one to three times a year. Between visits, brush twice a day and floss at least once a day.

- Be aware that the gum line naturally recedes with age, making for a toothier look and exposing the roots to cavities. After about age 40, a woman will probably get fewer surface cavities.

- Cigarette smoking and coffee and tea drinking will stain teeth, a fact that becomes more noticeable in later years when the tooth's protective enamel coating becomes thinner and absorbs more dark pigmentation. Brushing with the baking-soda-and-peroxide paste advocated in the Keyes regimen of dental hygiene (see pages 71–73) can bleach the teeth, sometimes masking a change in coloration.

BONES

- Be sure to get enough calcium. A woman between the ages of 35 and 60 needs 1,200 milligrams per day, or four glasses of milk, to maintain bone mass and prevent osteoporosis. If you're unwilling to consume this much milk (or are unable to because of lactose intolerance), take a calcium supplement. It's especially useful to take some calcium at bedtime, as bone loss is accelerated at night, while the body is at rest.

- Exercise. Not only does it help prevent bone loss, it actually stimulates production of new bone. Aerobic, weight-bearing exercises—walking, jogging, bicycling, dancing—are the best bone-builders.

- Reduce your phosphorus intake. Phosphorus is a major component of bone tissue and must also be consumed in sufficient quantities to prevent bone loss. But too much phosphorus can actually inhibit the absorption of calcium. Foods to limit: cereals and baked goods that contain phosphates as preservatives, nuts and legumes, animal protein (particularly red meat), canned soda, and processed foods.

- Stop smoking. The exact relationship between smoking and osteoporosis is not yet known, but studies clearly link the two.

- Limit your consumption of caffeine. Heavy coffee drinkers (four cups or more a day) are at high risk of developing osteoporosis.

JOINTS

- Exercise is the best treatment for stiff and aching joints. It restores mobility and strengthens the muscles and bones surrounding the affected area. As a woman ages, she may want to limit participation in those sports that put great stress on the weight-bearing joints—the knees, hips, and ankles in jogging, for instance—while increasing her daily quota of light stretches (see the Keeping Limber box on pages 78–79).

- Stay trim, stand tall. Several joint disorders have been linked to obesity, which is especially burdensome to the hips and knees. Also, poor posture can throw the body out of alignment, distorting joints and musculature. Practice standing with your rib cage lifted, shoulders square, abdomen pulled in, buttocks tucked.

- Protect your joints. Avoid sudden, jerky movements. Don't exercise without first warming up. After strenuous activity, take a warm bath or shower.

5
Babies and Beyond

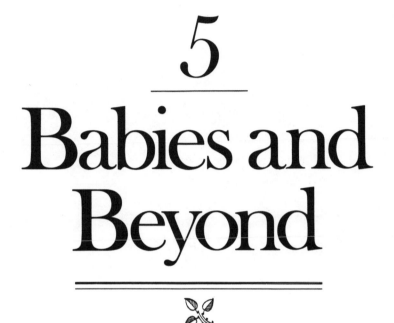

The organs of a woman's reproductive system—the ovaries, the uterus, the vagina—take on an importance in a woman's life that far outstrips their size. The ovaries are crucial to a woman's sense of herself during her childbearing years, secreting hormones that keep her looking and feeling "feminine" and that keep her reproductive cycle in working order. The uterus is the vessel for the next generation, and its healthy functioning is proof that a woman can fulfill her unique (and, to some, ultimate) role, that of becoming a mother. The vagina, into which sperm are deposited and out of which the newborn emerges, is a sexual organ as well, and a woman comes to focus on it as an ambiguous and much-valued symbol of both sexual and reproductive prowess.

A woman who must deal with changes in any of these organs—atrophy of the ovaries or vagina at menopause, removal of the uterus or ovaries at any age, slackening of the vagina or uterus after childbirth—must deal with profound changes in her self-image as well. But, as with most other systems, age need not mean deterioration. Over the years, the reproductive system will show the changes of time, but those changes are not always for the worse. And a woman who keeps herself in good health, and who has a realistic attitude toward her body, will better be able to face those changes, and to maintain a satisfying level of sexual activity and a positive self-image far into her 60s, 70s, or beyond.

Menstruation

Menstruation seems to be one of the few physical constants in a woman's life. From the time of her first period—about the age of 12—until her menopause—about age 50—a woman can count on three to seven days of bleeding every four weeks or so. Unless she is pregnant, she knows she will almost invariably menstruate this month, and next month, and the month after that.

But while the fact of menstruating is constant, the quality of the menses changes imperceptibly from decade to decade. The duration of the bleeding tends to become shorter, with longer stretches in between, over the years. And the kinds of menstrual irregularities most frequently encountered are different at different stages. Women in their teens and 20s, if they have difficulties with menstruation (which, by the

The Reproductive Organs

Menarche, pregnancy, childbirth, and menopause are the milestones of a woman's reproductive life, each marking major changes in her system. Minor changes also occur in a woman's middle and later years: the cervix, uterus, and ovaries decrease in size; the walls of the vagina become thinner and lubricate slower, and the vagina itself may become smaller and lose some elasticity; the muscle tone of the pelvic floor slackens and the pelvic organs relax. These changes don't mean deterioration. A healthy woman with a realistic attitude about her body won't necessarily feel a lessening of her sexuality and femininity.

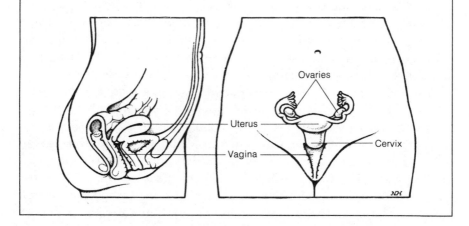

way, most women do *not*), will tend to have cramps in the first day or so after the flow begins.[1] Women in their 30s and 40s, especially after they have had children, will experience far fewer cramps but may encounter a new set of problems that arise in the week or so before the onset of bleeding: premenstrual syndrome.[2]

In order to understand the menstrual disorders that can occur, it helps to be reminded that menstruation is the culmination of a complicated hormonal cycle.[3] Each month a woman's body prepares itself to receive a fertilized egg for implantation in the uterus. If no fertilization has occurred that month, the uterine lining (the endometrium) is sloughed off in the form of menstrual flow. Several female hormones, all regulated by the hypothalamus at the base of the brain, rise and fall in predictable fashion during the cycle, which averages 28 days in length. Beginning with the release of the follicle-stimulating hormone (FSH), about 20 of the hundreds of thousands of egg follicles in the ovary begin maturing. As they mature, they release more and more estrogen. Once the estrogen level reaches a certain point, all but one of the follicles atrophy. A new hormone, called the leutenizing hormone (LH), is released, stimulating the remaining follicle to mature fully and finally to burst out of its ovarian sac. That bursting is called ovulation.

With ovulation, which occurs 14 days before the onset of menstruation, a scar is left on the ovary that turns into a new, temporary gland, the corpus leuteum. The corpus leuteum secretes vast amounts of the hormone progesterone, which thickens the womb lining into a plush, nutritive bed in which the fertilized egg may implant and develop into an embryo. If the implantation does not occur, the production of hormones will cease abruptly, and a day later the thickened lining of the womb is sloughed off in the form of menstruation.

Dysmenorrhea

In the year or two immediately after menarche (the time of the first menstrual period), most girls do not menstruate regularly. Ovulation has not yet begun, which means that progesterone, the regulator of the system, is secreted in levels that are still too low to impose any rhythm to the cycle. Once a girl begins ovulating, though, she is prone to a particular hazard of the early reproductive years—cramps.

Cramps are part of a menstrual disorder called dysmenorrhea, which in its most severe form affects about 5 percent of girls aged 15 to 25. Dysmenorrhea is not restricted to cramps; it can include nausea, vomiting, backaches, and diarrhea. And, no matter what the old wives say, dysmenorrhea is not "all in your mind." Careful research over the past few years has found that women with dysmenorrhea have higher-than-normal levels of a hormone-like substance called prostaglandin.[4] This chemical, or an as-yet-unidentified "circulating factor" in the blood that stimulates prostaglandin production, is so potent that it is capable of inducing dysmenorrhea in a woman who does not suffer from it—even if that woman has no uterus.[5]

In an earlier generation, a physician was likely to send a woman with cramps home with a prescription for Darvon (an expensive painkiller usually no more effective for cramps than aspirin) and leave her to her hot-water bottle and raspberry tea. Today, the doctor is likely to take the complaint seriously, and to offer medications that have been shown to have an effect: antiprostaglandin drugs (similar to aspirin but 30 times stronger), estrogen (usually in the form of the birth control pill), or dietary supplements (such as calcium pills).

Menstrual cramps do not affect every woman, nor do they affect any one woman forever. In a telephone survey conducted in 1981 by Tampax Incorporated, a leading manufacturer of tampons, only one-third of female respondents said their last periods were painful. Of those, only 39 percent sought relief from their physicians.[6] Dysmenorrhea is most likely to occur among younger women, between 15 and 25, and usually eases, disappears, or changes in character after childbirth or when a woman is on the Pill.

The conventional wisdom is that dysmenorrhea tends to disappear after the age of 25. For a woman who has gone through a full pregnancy, the permanent enlargement of the postpregnant uterus counteracts menstrual pain; as a less compact muscle, it now seems to react less strenuously to the cyclical effects of hormones. But a woman in her 30s who has not borne children has a uterus that is as tight as ever. This fact, complicated by an increased likelihood over the years to suffer from uterine abnormalities known to be associated with cramps (particularly fibroids and endometriosis, which will be described in the following section), can make period pain for non-mothers in their 30s as bad as it was for them in their teens.

The important thing for a woman of any age to remember is that pain during menstruation can—and should—be treated. The pain is not all in her head, and it is no longer something that a woman simply has to grin and bear.

Premenstrual Syndrome

Premenstrual syndrome (PMS) was first recognized as a clinical entity only about five years ago. Today it is said to affect severely an estimated 10 percent of women, the great majority of them over age 35. For some women, the symptoms first appear after childbirth, when the levels of hormones are elevated and never quite return to their prepregnancy state. Other women, however, have been suffering from PMS, probably because of a genetic predisposition, since their late teens.

The syndrome encompasses such a grab bag of symptoms—abdominal bloating, acne, aggressiveness, asthma, back pain, breast tenderness, clumsiness, constipation, craving for sweet or salty foods, depression, epileptic-like seizures, headache, irrational outbursts, irritability, lethargy, migraine, tiredness, weepiness, weight gain—that it has been difficult for the medical profession to pin it down. For any symptom to qualify as part of the PMS picture, though, it must reappear cyclically, month after month, in the week or so before menstruation, and it must disappear once menstrual flow begins.

The condition has been traced to a deficiency of progesterone in the second half of the menstrual cycle, and has been treated successfully with natural progesterone (usually administered in the form of injections or pills inserted into the vagina) beginning soon after ovulation.[7] Other less drastic forms of treatment, effective in milder cases of PMS, include dietary changes such as reduction or elimination of caffeine, sugar, alcohol, and salt; frequent small meals to avoid low blood sugar; and vitamin B_6 supplements.

Now, with greater recognition of PMS on the part of both women and their doctors, PMS sufferers are getting the treatment they need. No longer are they told that the violent mood swings they experienced each month are evidence of a psychological problem; no longer do they feel "crazy" for lashing out at their families or falling into inexplicable depressions. Another bright note: These women can look forward to relief of symptoms with menopause, after which PMS seems to disappear.

Fertility Changes over Time

As her biological clock ticks on, a woman will be more and more likely to encounter problems conceiving, carrying, and delivering a healthy baby. The first time a mid- to late-30s woman might really *feel* her age is when she has trouble conceiving a child, and is told by her doctor— either directly or by implication—that she has waited too long. While she was busy getting her degrees, establishing her career, playing the field, and finding the right mate—all the while scrupulously using birth control—her fertility was declining imperceptibly. When this woman finally gets around to starting her family, she finds that she has fertility problems—and she wonders why she and her peers ever believed they could have it all.

"I realized in my early to mid-thirties that my time clock was running out," says Mary Jo Eheart, 37, a single woman, vocational counselor, and part-time folk singer in Washington, D.C. "The problem is that even if I met someone in the next three months, the relationship developed real quickly, and we got married next summer, I would probably want to spend at least a year married to that person before I thought about children. If I was to have a child, it would have to be no later than 40—that's my cutoff."[8]

Advanced age in the potential father can complicate things, but, in terms of age-associated difficulties in conceiving, the woman is the critical partner. Men, it seems, either can make enough healthy sperm or cannot; sperm count declines somewhat with age, but age alone is not sufficient to turn a once fertile man into a man who cannot father children. But women can lose fertility simply with the passage of time. "A woman's chances of conceiving at forty are about half those of a woman thirty-five or under," says Dr. Shepard Aronson, an infertility specialist at New York University Medical Center. "Anatomically and physically speaking, the mature woman produces either no more eggs or essentially infertile ones. After forty-five, the chances of conceiving are very low indeed."

For years, experts believed a woman's fertility stayed relatively high until about the age of 35. But in 1982, a worrisome report from France seemed to imply that fertility in women dropped sharply even earlier than that—at about the age of 30. Using a sample of 2,193 women undergoing artificial insemination, the French researchers concluded that after the age of 30, the incidence of infertility jumps by about 50 percent.[9] The study has been criticized by some American researchers, but its message cast doubt in the minds of many women who were putting off children until after their careers and their marriages were well established.

"Nobody should have to tell a woman that she ought to get pregnant before she's 30 years old," Dr. Wayne Decker, executive director of the Fertility Research Foundation, says flatly. "My practice is made up of people who waited too long." (Decker admits, by the way, that his own daughter ignored his warnings and did not have her first baby until she was 32.) Dr. Marcia Storch, an infertility specialist in New York City, is somewhat milder in her approach. "Most of us tell our patients, the sooner the better," she says. "Not that they should mortgage their souls, but that if this year is as good as next year, by all means do it this year."[10]

No one is sure why women encounter more fertility problems with age. One possibility is that, having lived a longer time, they are more likely to have developed some of the age-associated changes in the reproductive system that are linked to infertility, especially endometriosis and uterine fibroids.

Endometriosis occurs when some of the uterine lining dislodges from the uterus and turns up at various sites in the pelvic cavity—behind the uterus, on the ovaries, or, less often, in the Fallopian tubes, the vagina, the intestines, even the skin of the vulva. With each period the endo-metrial tissue swells, just as it would inside the uterus, and it can cause pain, scarring, and hormonal irregularities that interfere with ovulation and fertilization. Its incidence increases significantly with age: Endo-metriosis is rare before the age of 20, and the average age of diagnosis is 37.[11] The typical woman with endometriosis is childless—either by choice or because of difficulties conceiving—or has at most two chil-dren, usually beginning her childbearing after the age of 25.

Fibroids are benign tumors of the uterus that usually cause few symp-toms—except infertility—and almost never become cancerous. They occur in 25 to 35 percent of all women, and tend to run in families. Occasionally, the fibroids grow so large that they can lead to pain and excessive menstrual bleeding, and then the growths, or the uterus itself, must be removed. More often, though, the fibroids stay small and self-contained. But fibroids do tend to interfere with implantation in the uterus of the fertilized egg, much as an IUD does. Like endometriosis, the growth of uterine fibroids is an age-associated condition: Virtually no one under 20 has fibroids, and they become progressively more common after age 30, with the highest incidence in women between 35 and 42.[12] After menopause, when estrogen output diminishes, fibroids tend to shrink and may even disappear.

Of course, there are always stories about women who remain incred-ibly fertile until far into their 30s—and beyond. Infertility specialist Storch recalls one 39-year-old patient who assumed that, because of her age, it would take her nearly a year to conceive. So she started trying to get pregnant long before she was really ready—at a time when she had a business to sell and a household move to make—and she got pregnant right away.

The occasional appearance of so-called "menopause babies" also gives the lie to the image of failed fertility in a woman's 40s. Menopause babies are born to mothers who stop using birth control because the infrequency of their periods convinces them they are unable to conceive again. Although the availability of legal abortions means fewer women are carrying these surprise pregnancies to term, women who do so are —along with their husbands and teen-agers—often thrilled with the new baby. As Meg, who had her fourth child at 40 (when her youngest was 18), is quoted as saying in *Growing Older, Getting Better* by Jane Porcino: "Despite the admonitions of most of our friends, this little one is the joy of all of our lives. There is simply no comparison between those hectic early days of child rearing in my 20s and the leisurely way Jennine is growing up now. She is three years old today, and I feel I've never been happier." [13]

Not every woman could adjust so well to an unexpected pregnancy at age 40 or more. Many women look forward to the freedom of the "empty nest"; others are uninterested in starting child rearing over again 20 years later, or feel that a new baby would present too many emotional and financial strains on their marriages. These women must follow birth control measures as scrupulously at 40 as they did at 20 or 30. Because of the uncertainty of precisely when ovulation stops during the premenopausal years, physicians define menopause as the complete cessation of menstrual periods for a full year. A woman must use contraception until she misses 12 periods in a row.

Age-Related Changes in Pregnancy and Childbirth

In the 20s. The years between 18 and 25 are considered the best time to have a baby—at least from a physiological point of view. In the 20s, a woman's hormonal, digestive, and cardiovascular systems are geared to producing the healthiest possible baby with the least possible stress on the mother's body. In later years, as in earlier years, one or the other side of the balance will suffer at least a little—either the mother or the baby will show the effects of a less than perfect union.

One advantage occurs in terms of fertility. As we have seen, not every menstrual cycle involves the release of an egg. Even after a young girl begins ovulating, one or two years after menarche, she cannot expect to release a mature egg every month of her reproductive life. Over the next 30 years, just over one-half of an average woman's menstrual cycles will be "ovulatory"—that is, accompanied by the release mid-cycle of an egg from the ovary. The proportion of cycles that are ovulatory is at its lowest before the age of 20, reaches a high of about 80 percent between 26 and 35, and declines to about 70 percent after age 40 and about 50 percent after age 45. [14]

Everything clicks during the early 20s. The pregnant body in its 20s is most efficient in rerouting nutrients and oxygen from the mother's system to the baby's without doing damage to either. Dozens of chores must be accomplished during the course of a pregnancy; a woman's blood volume, for instance, will just about double, the placenta will be created and maintained, and a whole new system of muscles, bones, and tissue will be created in the course of a few months.[15] A body that can do these chores well will provide an optimum growing environment for the fetus without depleting energy from or jeopardizing the future health of the mother.

Postpartum (after birth) recovery is also thought to be easier for women in their 20s. Many physiological changes occur immediately after delivery, when the high estrogen level that had been maintained throughout pregnancy suddenly falls drastically and the humming machinery of fetal nourishment is shut down. The younger the system, the better able it is to respond to this abrupt change. Even the more obvious changes of pregnancy—stretch marks, pigment changes, widening of the chest and hips, loss of abdominal muscle tone, increase in proportion of body fat, weight gain—are easier to erase in a woman who is relatively young.

In the 30s. A younger woman might have more energy, goes the new wives' tale, but an older woman has more patience. So which woman makes the better mother? More and more women are choosing patience over energy, waiting until their mid-30s or beyond to begin their families. If pregnancy itself is harder, they reason, so be it; the rewards of parenting will be sweeter for the delay.

For the first time in history, the over-35 new mother is becoming almost commonplace. In its survey of first-time mothers, the National Center for Health Statistics reports that the proportion of women over age 35 increased by 30 percent between 1975 and 1980. In the 1980s, the proportion will increase further still; the Census Bureau estimates that the proportion of women giving birth past the age of 35 (either for the first time or for later children) will increase by 37 percent by the end of the decade.[16]

Social trends notwithstanding, there is at least one individual (in addition, perhaps, to her mother-in-law) who thinks any woman having a baby past 30 is "elderly." That individual is her obstetrician. Obstetrics texts still refer to a woman over 30 who is pregnant with her first baby as an "elderly primigravida"; unfortunately, this can translate into a negative attitude toward the supposedly "older" patient.

A woman in her 30s will instantly recoil from the term "elderly," implying as it does that she is over the hill and has waited too long for a child. But is there, perhaps, some medical justification for treating over-30s differently during pregnancy, labor, and delivery? Expert opinion is split as to just how dangerous it is to conceive, carry, and deliver a baby in one's 30s, and just how old one has to be to be considered obstetrically geriatric in the first place.

Two problems are known to be associated with advanced maternal age per se. One we have already discussed: fertility problems. The other is perhaps more worrisome: a greater tendency on the part of older mothers to bear children with chromosomal abnormalities.

Little girls are born with all the eggs they will ever have, some 2 million altogether. By adolescence only about half a million eggs are left. These are the eggs that will mature, one by one, into a follicle and emerge from the ovarian sac for a chance to be fertilized. They are freshest at sexual maturity, about age 18, and subsequently get progressively more stale. As the years go by, a woman's eggs are more and more likely to make mistakes at some point during the process of maturation, fertilization, and cell division.

By common consent, the age of 35 has been pinpointed as the age at which the risk of some mistake occurring becomes significant. But there's nothing magical about 35. A woman of 30 is more likely to encounter a chromosomal disorder than a woman of 28, and a woman of 32 is likelier still. This has been shown again and again in studies of the relationship between a mother's age and the incidence of Down's syndrome. Down's syndrome, which comes about from an extra dose of chromosome 21, leads to a characteristic "mongoloid" appearance of the child as well as mental retardation and possible physical abnormalities. It is the most widely studied chromosomal disorder because it creates such obvious changes that it is unlikely to be overlooked. But it is by no means the only chromosomal problem for which babies of older mothers are at risk. Of the 15,000 babies born each year with a chromosomal abnormality, just 3,000 of them have Down's syndrome.[17] The others have a variety of conditions—Trisomy 18, Klinefelter's syndrome in males, Turner's syndrome in females—all of which have been shown to increase with the age of the mother. A woman of 30 runs a one in 885 risk of bearing a child with Down's syndrome; by 33 her risk increases to one in 592; by 35 to one in 365.

This is where prenatal genetic testing comes in. Since the 1970s, older mothers have had access to a sophisticated medical technique that takes a sample of fetal cells during pregnancy to check for chromosomal abnormalities. The technique, called amniocentesis, involves insertion of a large needle into the mother's abdomen around the sixteenth week of pregnancy. Using an ultrasound picture of the fetus to guide the needle's point of entry, the physician withdraws a bit of the amniotic fluid in which the fetus floats and sends it to a laboratory for culturing. In about four weeks, the few fetal cells included in the fluid sample have grown into a colony large enough for chromosomal analysis. If the cells look normal—as they do in about 95 percent of cases studied—the fetus gets a clean bill of health for some 60 genetic abnormalities that can be detected in this way.

Amniocentesis involves some risk. The injection into the uterus carries a very slight chance of causing the uterus to contract and expel the fetus—a risk estimated at less than 1 percent at most good medical centers. It is this risk that has helped enshrine the "after-35" rule regarding amniocentesis. Physicians will not perform the procedure, or any other one, unless the potential benefit of the technique seems to outweigh the risk. (That is why ultrasound itself is only recommended for certain conditions of pregnancy, such as abnormal growth patterns, that can only be explained after peering directly into the womb.) And it is not until after age 35, when a woman's chance of carrying a child with a detectable genetic abnormality rises to more than 1 percent, that the potential benefits of amniocentesis start to outweigh the risk of miscarriage.

In 1983, a new method of fetal cell sampling was introduced in the United States that might replace amniocentesis as the method of choice. Chorionic villi biopsy can be done far earlier in the pregnancy—about eight to 11 weeks after the last menstrual period—and, because fetal cells grow so much more rapidly during this stage, results can be reported within 24 hours. This allows the mother, if she so chooses, to have a first-trimester abortion, instead of the far more traumatic (both physically and psychologically) second-trimester abortion necessitated by the timetable of amniocentesis. The risk of chorionic villi biopsy, which is still in the experimental stages, now appears to be higher than that of amniocentesis, but further studies are needed to separate the risk of the procedure itself from the rate of spontaneous miscarriages, which are always most likely to occur during the first trimester.

Chorionic villi biopsy involves the aspiration of a few of the hairlike projections (villi) of the chorion, the preplacental structure that surrounds the developing embryo during the earliest stages of implantation. Once again guided by ultrasound imaging, the physician removes the villi with a delicate probe through the vagina. Each villus is composed of cells from the embryo, which can be cultured quickly and analyzed for chromosomal abnormalities. The technique can detect all disorders now detectable through amniocentesis with the exception of spina bifida, which is detectable only through certain proteins present in the amniotic fluid. Some genetics-testing experts expect that chorionic villi biopsy will replace amniocentesis in the next decade.

Motherhood in one's 30s carries other hazards, to both the mother and the baby, beyond the chromosomal risk. Many of these can be traced not to age itself, but to preexisting conditions that are more likely to be found in women the older they get. These conditions—known to complicate the course of a pregnancy, or to be aggravated by pregnancy—include diabetes, epilepsy, fibroid tumors of the uterus, hypertension, kidney disease, and tumors of the breast. Older women are at statistically higher risk of these diseases simply because they have lived more years. But new research shows that an older mother who takes care of herself runs the same risk of fetal complications as the population as a whole. According to the National Natality and Fetal Mortality Survey, first-time mothers between 30 and 34 tend to be better educated, and are more likely to exercise, seek early prenatal care, and refrain from smoking. Because of their better health habits, these mothers as a group run a risk of fetal death, birth defects, or low birth weight that is no higher than normal. It is only after the age of 34, when age-related changes cannot be so easily compensated for, that first-time mothers face a significantly greater risk of encountering these problems.[18]

Women in their 30s are also the most likely group of women to give birth to twins. (Many women consider this a *benefit* of later pregnancy:

Twins, Triplets, and More

The incidence of multiple birth increases with age, generally peaking for mothers in their mid- to late 30s. This is especially true for blacks; a pregnant black woman in her 30s has a 3 percent chance of giving birth to more than one child.

RATIO OF MULTIPLE BIRTHS
(Number of multiple births per 1,000 live births)

Age of mother	White	Black	All races
25–29	20.4	29.6	21.4
30–34	23.9	32.9	24.6
35–39	26.1	32.0	26.6
40–44	19.1	23.5	19.6
45–49	14.3	17.8	15.8

Adapted from Bureau of the Census, *Statistical Abstract of the United States 1981* (Washington, D.C.: Department of Commerce, 1981), p. 62.

It allows for an instant, one-shot family!) The rate of identical twins—
who come about when one fertilized egg splits into two separate embryos early in cell division—is just slightly higher for women in their
late 30s, about four sets per 1,000 births, than for women under 25,
about 3.5 sets per 1,000 births. But the rate of fraternal twins zooms for
older mothers. For a white woman, the chance of bearing twins is lower
the younger she is—about 6.4 sets per 1,000 births occur in mothers
under age 20—and steadily increases until the age of 37, when it peaks
at 16.8 sets per 1,000 births.[19] Other factors increase a woman's likelihood of bearing fraternal twins—her race (black women have more
twins than white women; Oriental women have fewer), whether fraternal twins run in her family (it is a tendency inherited through female
ancestors), and whether she has already borne twins (the mother of
twins has a four-times-greater chance of bearing twins again, no matter
what her age).

The theory is that at the age of 37 a woman's secretion of the hormone
gonadotropin is at a lifetime high. This hormone, secreted by the pituitary gland, controls the timing and release of the egg during the menstrual cycle. When it is released in large amounts, more than one egg
might mature and emerge from the ovary within one cycle. Another
complicating factor is that women in their 30s are more likely to be
under treatment for infertility, and the most popular infertility drugs—
Clomid and Pergonal—often stimulate more than one egg at a time to
mature and get fertilized.

In the 40s. In the early 1970s, doctors at the University of Iowa studied
26,000 women who delivered between 1962 and 1972; 293 of them were
over 40 at the time of delivery. (The national figure today is about 3
percent, and growing.) Pregnancy and birth were normal in two-thirds
of the patients over 40 studied, but a significant number encountered
problems. About 20 percent of the women had medical problems—
hypertension, diabetes, kidney disease, heart disease, breast cancer, cervical cancer—that were probably aggravated by pregnancy. The women
experienced a twice-normal rate of Cesarean deliveries; a twice-normal
rate of congenital abnormalities, mostly Down's syndrome and heart
defects; and a three- or four-times normal rate of perinatal death. According to Dr. Steven Craig Johnson, who conducted the study, "There
is a definite high risk for both the mother and infant in patients over
the age of 40."[20]

A pregnant woman in her 40s encounters many of the problems of a pregnant woman in her 30s—and then some. As we have seen, a woman in her 40s encounters a significant decline in fertility, especially as she approaches menopause. And, like her slightly younger sister, she faces a high risk of bearing babies with chromosomal abnormalities. The incidence of Down's syndrome escalates rapidly after a woman turns 40—one in every 39 births.

And Down's syndrome is not the only disorder to worry about. According to Dr. Jane Porcino, director of gerontology at the State University of New York at Stony Brook, 7 percent of all human fetuses are chromosomally abnormal, but for a mother over 40 this figure approaches 24 percent.[21]

Women past 40, Porcino adds, are also more likely to encounter problems with pregnancy, labor, and delivery. They are four times as likely as younger women to miscarry in the first trimester. They are more likely to experience difficult labor, Cesarean births, hypertension, and diabetes. They are more likely to encounter toxemia and hemorrhaging before or during childbirth.

Toward a Healthy Pregnancy

Nevertheless, even though the risks of childbirth increase with age, a woman can still improve her chances of bearing a healthy baby after a normal pregnancy and a stress-free delivery. As with so many other aspects of aging healthily, the groundwork for a good pregnancy, at any age, is laid early in a woman's life.

A woman in her 20s or early 30s who wants to have a child "some day" must start taking care of herself *now*. The fitness of the body with which she goes into pregnancy will determine how well her body gets through it—and, more important, it may even determine the health of her baby. The major health factors that can be controlled by a woman before she becomes pregnant are as follows.

Smoking. Because it restricts the flow of oxygen to the growing placenta, which must be well-nourished to establish and maintain a healthy pregnancy, cigarette smoking has been associated with an abnormally high incidence of miscarriage and premature labor. And because it restricts the flow of oxygen to the growing fetus, cigarette smoking also inhibits the baby's rate of growth. Smokers are statistically more likely than nonsmokers to give birth to low-birth-weight babies (weighing less than five pounds), who are at higher risk of developing a host of complications in the months immediately after birth—lung infections, lung hemorrhages, inadequate sugar or calcium levels in the blood—and perhaps for years afterward. So doctors advise, strenuously, that a woman stop smoking when she becomes pregnant—or, better yet, long before.

Subtle changes occur in the reproductive apparatus that make a change in smoking habits at conception a change that is almost too late. The most significant of these results in a pregnancy complication called placenta abruptio, the premature separation of the placenta from the uterine wall that necessitates delivery of the fetus. This condition, which endangers the life of both mother and child, is fortunately quite rare, but it is significantly more common among smokers than among lifelong nonsmokers.[22] Minimizing this risk is especially important for women who will wait until their 30s or later to get pregnant, because older women run more than twice the normal risk of placenta abruptio no matter what their smoking history.

Weight. The healthiest babies, says Dr. Myron Winick, director of the Institute of Human Nutrition at Columbia University, are born to mothers who weigh 10 percent to 20 percent *above* their ideal weight immediately after delivery. Therefore, a woman who is too thin before becoming pregnant will have a lot of weight to put on if she wants to give her baby the statistically best start in life. And most thin women are unable, physiologically and psychologically, to gain 40 or 50 pounds in nine months. The reducing diet orientation of many thin women, and their dislike of excess fat on their bodies, will usually prevent them from eating the high-calorie meals such a weight gain would require.

This is not to say that *overweight* is any protection. A woman who starts out her pregnancy with a lot of extra fat could also harm her fetus, Winick says. "The body of an overweight mother," he writes in *For Mothers and Daughters,* "is not as efficient in dividing available nutrients between her and her fetus as that of an underweight mother."[23] And pregnancy is not the time for a woman to take off her excess weight. For the health of the fetus, a woman, no matter how overweight before pregnancy, must gain at least 15 pounds between conception and delivery. A woman of normal prepregnancy weight should gain at least 25 to 35 pounds. All in all, it's better for a woman to weigh the right amount, and get her body metabolism humming at a healthy level, before she starts trying to nourish an unborn baby.

Drug use. Many recreational drugs, including marijuana, are probably damaging to the fetus. A fetus is most prone to drug-induced damage in the earliest days of pregnancy—when a woman might not even realize yet that she is pregnant. According to the March of Dimes, the majority of birth defects occur before an embryo is eight weeks old.[24] The most prudent course, then, is to give up drugs before even trying to conceive. Some conservative physicians recommend staying off all drugs, alcohol, and medications—even birth control pills—for three months before attempting unprotected intercourse, to be sure all drug residues have been flushed out of the system. And the abstinence applies to the father as well; habitual use of marijuana, for instance, has been shown to diminish sperm count in users and to increase the proportion of damaged sperm.

Nutrition. During pregnancy, the placenta tends to take everything the fetus needs from the mother's bloodstream, and if it cannot find what it needs, it moves on to the mother's reserves. The fetus must draw iron and folic acid for its developing blood system; calcium for its developing bones; protein for its developing organs. If a woman is not ingesting sufficient quantities of these nutrients every day, the fetus will draw upon what she has stored away. Iron is stored in the red blood cells, calcium in the bone marrow, protein in the muscle. The fetus will get it somehow. (The one exception to this rule is folic acid, a vitamin that is not stored. The fetus will get whatever folic acid the mother consumes, even if her intake is low. As a result, folic acid deficiency is rare in fetuses—but occurs in up to 16 percent of pregnant women.[25])

The quantity of a woman's iron, calcium, and protein stores depends on the quality of her prepregnancy diet. If, before her pregnancy, a woman consumed a diet rich in essential nutrients—especially iron and calcium—she will have a rich supply from which the placenta can draw. This is better insurance for her than simply starting to eat well after the baby is conceived. When her reserve is well-stocked, she will not deplete her stores simply for the sake of the baby, and she can draw on them later when her own body needs an extra boost.

Pregnancy is a time when metabolism of these essential nutrients is more efficient than ever before, and a woman with healthy stores beforehand can actually emerge from pregnancy with a *better* supply of iron and calcium than she had going in. This affords her extra protection against the development, later in life, of iron-deficiency anemia or osteoporosis (see Chapter 4).

Exercise. It's a good idea, for several reasons, to begin an exercise program before becoming pregnant. First, and perhaps most important, it establishes a healthy habit to be continued throughout pregnancy, at a time when most women are more amenable to change. Second, it

Kegel Exercises:
The All-Around Preventive

In the 1950s, Dr. Arnold Kegel, a surgeon at UCLA, devised a series of exercises he hoped would put him out of business. Kegel specialized in repair of flabby vaginal muscles, prolapsed bladders, and prolapsed uteri —in other words, organ changes caused by poor tone of the pubococcygeal (PC) muscles between the vagina and the anus. This area, known as the "pelvic floor," slackens during pregnancy and childbirth. But good muscle tone can be restored and maintained, Kegel found, through faithful adherence to a set of simple exercises.

Pelvic-floor exercises, now known as "Kegel exercises," can help keep a woman's pelvic organs functioning well her whole life. Kegel exercises have been reported to improve sexual functioning, promote perineal muscle tone, relieve hemorrhoids, correct stress incontinence, and prevent prolapse of the uterus. For maximum effect, they should be repeated 50 to 100 times a day. Kegels can be done anywhere, at any time, while sitting, standing, eating, driving, even making love.

To perform a Kegel exercise, tighten the muscles of the pelvic floor, hold for a count of five, and then slowly release. A good way to find which muscles to tighten is to try to stop the flow of urine while urinating. Try to get into the habit of performing your Kegels in groups of ten or 20, at least five times a day.

builds up muscles that will come to your aid in later months, particularly abdominal muscles (which, if strong enough, can help support the uterus and prevent backache in the third trimester) and muscles of the pelvic floor (which will prevent hemorrhoids, vaginal tears, and stress incontinence that all can result from pregnancy and delivery). And third, exercise at all stages of life improves a woman's circulation, lung power, muscle-to-fat ratio, and mental attitude—all things she will come to rely on during the physiological and psychological stress of pregnancy and parenthood.

Menopause

As a woman ages, her definition of who is truly "old" changes with the decades. Take a woman who is now in her 30s. When she was a girl, she knew that girls over 16 were old; after all, couldn't they all drive cars? In college, she knew she would never trust anyone over 30, that mystical point at which a woman leaves the realm of the politically enlightened and culturally young-at-heart. But after she herself passed 30, and began to conclude that the 30s really weren't so old after all, she still retained one date that seemed to signal the *true* beginning of old age: menopause.

Will her definition of "old" change once more when she herself goes through menopause? Probably. Because even though her reproductive life will sputter to a definite end, this woman is likely to discover, to her surprise, that she's as energetic, as attractive, as sexual, and as open to new experiences during and after menopause as she was at 25 or 35. The "change of life," she'll find, is not the end of life. All it is is the beginning of another stage.

One or two generations ago, menopause really was the beginning of the end. In 1900, when the average age of menopause was 46 years, the average life expectancy for women was just 51.[26] But in the 1980s, when the average age of menopause is 50 years,[27] women can generally expect to live another one-quarter century—fully one-third of their life-spans —beyond it.

This is not to minimize the trauma a woman might encounter as she goes through menopause. After all, it's not called "the changes" for nothing. During the five years or so before her periods end, and the five years or so afterward, a woman faces a hormonal upheaval that is as powerful, and as disturbing, as the one she underwent during puberty. If she is not prepared for the physiological changes she will experience, she might think that all her internal turmoil is just a sign of her own craziness. That is why a well-informed woman is better braced to face the onslaught of menopause than is her blissfully ignorant peer.

Hot Flashes and Other Signs

The medical definition of menopause is the complete cessation of menstrual periods for 12 consecutive months. Therefore, a woman doesn't know for sure when she really is going through menopause; she only knows she's been through it once it's passed. During the perimenopausal period—the five to ten years before and after menstruation finally stops, also called the "climacteric" (from the Greek for "top rung of the ladder")—a woman will experience many symptoms to let her know menopause is imminent. Among these are sporadic periods, often skipping two or three months at a time; scanty periods or, in some women, heavier-than-normal periods; hot flashes; breast enlargement; vaginal dryness; insomnia or other sleep disturbances; headaches, anxiety, depression; and an increase—or decrease—in sex drive.

The range of what is "normal" during the climacteric is maddeningly wide. Some women, for instance, have scanty periods every two or three months, while others might menstruate in the same pattern they always did and then stop abruptly. (A woman in this latter group is apt to rush for a pregnancy test when her periods stop. But she should be aware that during menopause, urine tests for pregnancy have a high "false-positive" rate; that is, they often come up positive *even when she is not pregnant*. A blood test for pregnancy, rather than a urine test, is therefore recommended for women in their 40s or 50s.)

The most common symptom of the climacteric is the hot flash. One recent study found that at least 75 percent of menopausal women go through it. A "flashing" woman feels a distressing rush of heat to her chest, neck, face, and arms; her skin reddens, her pulse quickens, her breathing becomes shallow, and she breaks out in a sweat. Then, as fast as it came, the flash is over, often leaving the woman chilly and breathless. Each flash usually lasts no more than a few minutes, although some women report flashes of as long as half an hour.

Some women get hot flashes a few times a day; some get them only at night; some get them five or ten times an hour. The condition can begin as early as age 42, and in some cases can continue for years.

Hot flashes arise when the blood vessels in the skin enlarge. As the ovaries secrete less estrogen, the pituitary reacts by secreting more of its hormones. When this happens, the body's internal thermostat goes awry. Recent research suggests that hot flashes occur because the hor-

---

The Timing of Menopause

The average age of menopause is 50, but no woman is average. Menopausal symptoms can begin as early as age 35 or as late as age 55. Past the age of 55, though, menstruation is rare indeed; only 5 percent of American women have not gone through menopause by then.

Age of women	Percent who have passed menopause
47	25
50	50
52	75
55	95

Source: The Diagram Group, *Woman's Body: An Owner's Manual* (London: Paddington Press), p. F-02.

mone shifts make a woman's body think it is cooler than it is, mistakenly sending it into its get-warm mode.[28] The flashes usually cease within one or two years, when the hormonal upheaval slows down. But some women continue to have them for as long as five years after menstrual periods have stopped.

The Timing Question: Early or Late?

The climacteric can begin as early as the age of 40. Many factors help determine exactly when it occurs. Conventional wisdom once had it that the healthier the woman, the later her menopause, and the later the menopause, the healthier the woman. This is not really true. In fact, some illnesses—particularly breast and endometrial cancer, which have been linked to the prolonged presence of high levels of estrogen—are associated with *later* menopause.

Women who are overweight tend to have later menopause. Upper-class women, who, presumably, are better nourished, tend to have later menopause. Women who have children after the age of 40 tend to have later menopause.[29] On the other hand, smokers tend to have *earlier* menopause—perhaps because in smokers nicotine changes the functioning of the endocrine system.[30]

Another old wives' tale is that the earlier the menarche (the age of a girl's first menstrual period), the earlier the menopause. In fact, the exact opposite is true. A woman who begins menstruating early (before age 12) is likely to stop menstruating late (after age 50); one who begins menstruating late is likely to stop menstruating early.[31] The reason for this is unclear.

When menopause occurs before the age of 40—as it does in an estimated 8 percent of women—it is called "premature" menopause. The most common reason for premature menopause is surgical removal of both ovaries; if a woman, no matter what her age, has no ovaries, she cannot produce estrogen and cannot menstruate. Surgical menopause tends to create more severe symptoms than natural menopause, because the abrupt cessation of estrogen production can seriously disrupt a woman's hormonal system. For a young woman whose ovaries are removed, a gynecologist will almost certainly prescribe estrogen replacement therapy (ERT). The ERT, usually administered in combination with progesterone to minimize the risks of uterine and breast cancer, can be expected to continue until the woman's mid-40s or 50s. At that time, the estrogen can gradually be tapered off in a way that mimics natural menopause.

Recently, researchers have theorized that other conditions can lead to ovarian failure—and therefore cessation of menstruation and loss of reproductive capacity—at an early age. Some scientists have reported instances of autoimmune reactions in young women, in which the woman produces antibodies to her own ovarian tissue. Others have found that a mumps infection can cause ovarian failure many years later. And a few reports have been issued recently of former birth control pill users who, after discontinuing the pill, fail to begin ovulating again, instead experiencing menopause at a very young age.[32]

How can a woman in her 30s tell whether she is going through a temporary episode of amenorrhea—cessation of menstrual periods—or is really experiencing menopause? A simple blood test will give the answer. The test measures the level of FSH (follicle-stimulating hormone) and LH (leutenizing hormone) in the blood. Both are elevated after menopause.

Other than these extreme cases of premature menopause, it probably does not really matter at what age a woman goes through menopause. Normal variations in age stretches from about 40 to about 55. And menopause seems no different at age 41 than at age 53.

The physical symptoms of menopause—hot flashes, night sweats, vaginal dryness—occur in roughly the same proportions among women in their early 40s, in their late 40s, and in their early 50s. Two generalizations can be made, however. Physiologically, a later menopause does place a woman at somewhat higher risk of developing breast cancer or uterine cancer, because of the extra years of exposure of these organs to high levels of estrogen. And psychologically, women who begin menopause at an unusually young age may find themselves unprepared for its emotional component.

One woman who began experiencing menopausal symptoms at age 42 recalls in the book *Eve's Journey:* "About two years before my period ended, strange moods seemed to come over me. Like a vapor. I had been blue or down before, but this was different. I can date it exactly from one night when I awoke and felt empty, as if my insides had disappeared. I was 42 and had never thought about menopause or expected it so soon. I began having terrible headaches and I started having hot and cold flashes. . . . I really wasn't ready for what menopause was doing to me."[33]

In fact, because of our automatic definition of menopausal as "being old," and our insistence that "old" is always a few years older than our current age, a woman never feels 100 percent ready for menopause. Another woman quoted in *Eve's Journey,* who underwent menopause at the age of 53—an age by which at least 75 percent of women have already stopped menstruating—was just as surprised by it as the 42-year-old. "I never really connected the idea of menopause with me," she says. "When I began to miss my period I did what I had always done—go to a clinic for a pregnancy test!" [34]

The "Senile Vagina Syndrome"

With the withdrawal of estrogen that is part of menopause, the vagina tends to revert to its prepubertal state, thinner and once again vulnerable to trauma and infection. Thus the reproductive tract seems to have come full circle. But there is a difference between the vagina of a ten-year-old and that of a 60-year-old: the way it is used.

Sexually, a menopausal woman is quite different from a preteen. After a lifetime of sexual experiences, she still has sexual urges, sexual capacities, and means of sexual expression that are as profound as they've ever been in her life. For this reason, a vagina that is anatomically similar to a preteen's will not service her adequately, and the mature woman must take pains to avoid the "senile vagina syndrome."

At puberty, a young girl undergoes a dramatic increase in estrogen production. This hormonal change creates a tough outer cell layer and a thickened vaginal wall that helps prepare her vagina for the new environmental stresses of sexual intercourse, pregnancy, and childbirth. The added protection remains in place throughout her reproductive years.

At menopause, a woman undergoes an equally dramatic *decline* in estrogen production. In response, the lining of the vagina becomes thinner, and it loses the protective layer of extra cells. Thus, the vagina is more vulnerable to injury and infection. The vagina may also become smaller and lose its elasticity. The clitoris, too, diminishes in size, as does the thickness of the labia.

These changes can all have effects on sexual behavior. With the loss of the protective cell layer of the vagina, a woman may experience dryness, burning, itching, and pain. These symptoms can be heightened during sexual intercourse—resulting in a condition known as dyspareunia, or painful intercourse—but they can occur as well in women who are sexually inactive.

Recent research has found, however, that the best way to avoid the "senile vagina syndrome" is to remain sexually active throughout life. One study of 52 postmenopausal women, for example, found that women who had intercourse three or more times a month were less likely to suffer vaginal atrophy than those who had intercourse less than ten times a year.[35] Other studies have found that orgasm itself, rather than intercourse, is the significant variable; a woman who achieves orgasm through any means at least once a week significantly reduces her risk of vaginal atrophy.[36]

The Pros and Cons of ERT

Many young women believe that after menopause everything in the body shuts down, at least as far as femininity and estrogen production are concerned. But that is not what happens. In fact, an estimated 50 to 75 percent of postmenopausal women continue to excrete at least small amounts of *natural estrogen* for ten to 15 years after their periods have stopped.[37]

Where does this postmenopausal estrogen come from? To answer this question, we must first back up a bit and talk about estrogen itself. Throughout a woman's life, she manufactures three forms of estrogen: estradiol, estrone, and estriol. The difference from one phase to another occurs in what form of estrogen predominates. Estradiol is the most potent of them, and is secreted by the ovary during the reproductive years. Estriol, the next strongest, is manufactured by the placenta during pregnancy. And estrone, the least potent, is characteristic of the estrogen found in women after menopause. According to Dr. Morris Notelovitz, director of the Center for Climacteric Studies at the University of Florida, the relative potency of the three forms of estrogen, determined primarily by how long they remain in the target cell, is 100 to ten to one.

Estrone, the relatively weak menopausal estrogen, comes from various sources. The ovaries are one source, and they continue to produce estrone for many years after menstruation has stopped. The adrenal glands, which also produce estrone throughout a woman's life, are another. In addition, the ovaries, like other components of the endocrine system, continue to manufacture the male hormone androgen in the same amounts they have always produced it. (Women always produce some male hormones, just as men always produce some female hormones. The difference between the two sexes is in the balance.) After

Should You Take Estrogen?

The risk-benefit equation of estrogen replacement therapy (ERT) can only be computed by an individual woman and her physician. To some, any increased cancer risk is too great; to others, the slight risk of developing cancer 15 years hence is worth the benefit of greater comfort today.

Given the known risks and benefits of ERT, the following guidelines can be offered:

- A woman should discuss ERT with her doctor if she needs relief from
  hot flashes;
  osteoporosis;
  vaginal atrophy.
- A woman should *not* take ERT to correct the symptoms for which it has not been shown to be effective, such as
  wrinkling;
  leg cramps;
  depression;
  insomnia.
- A woman should *not* take ERT if she has the following conditions:
  personal or family history of breast, uterine, or ovarian cancer;
  fibrocystic breast disease;
  large fibroid tumors of the uterus;
  circulatory disorders such as phlebitis or severe varicose veins;
  severe chronic illnesses such as heart disease, kidney disease, diabetes, or hypertension.
- If she and her doctor agree that she can benefit from ERT, she should take the drug
  in the lowest possible dose,
  in combination with progesterone, and
  for as short a time as possible.
- Periodically, with her physician's guidance, she should try to wean herself from ERT and stay off the drug if the symptoms do not recur.

menopause, androgen is converted into estrone in a woman's fat cells. This explains why the more obese a woman, the more estrone she has.

But estrone is far less potent than estradiol, and a woman past the menopause will eventually begin to feel the effects of reduced levels of female hormone in the target cells. The result: an increased tendency toward hot flashes, vaginal dryness, decreased muscle tone, and osteoporosis. A tendency, of course, is not a sealed fate; a woman can avoid these symptoms with some life-style changes—and, if her situation warrants it, with estrogen replacement therapy.

In 1966, gynecologist Robert Wilson published a popular book called *Feminine Forever*. How could a woman stay "feminine" her whole life?

By taking estrogen replacement therapy at the first sign of menopause and continuing it, literally, forever. It was no coincidence that the use of estrogen zoomed after this book hit the stores. In 1965, just before publication, 8.5 million American women were taking estrogen. Ten years later, that number had tripled—to 26.7 million.[38]

But in the mid-1970s, the dark side of estrogen use began to receive equal time. In 1975, the first reports appeared linking estrogen to cancer of the endometrium (the lining of the uterus). In 1976, more studies linked estrogen to cancer of the breast in animals. In 1980, a relationship between ERT and breast cancer in humans was quantified: Women between the ages of 50 and 75 who had taken estrogen were twice as likely to get breast cancer as those who had not been on ERT.[39]

These medical pronouncements, coupled with a growing assertiveness on the part of women "health care consumers," led to a sharp fall-off in estrogen use during the late 1970s. Even if gynecologists weren't alarmed by the drug's potential hazards—and many were not—their patients were. "Estrogen replacement therapy is a dangerously overused treatment," warned Dr. Cynthia Cooke and Susan Dworkin in *The Ms. Guide to a Woman's Health,* a feminist health care book published in 1979. "Avoid it if at all possible." For perhaps the first time, gynecologists were facing resistance when they tried to prescribe ERT as a routine "treatment" for menopause.

In the 1980s, however, the pendulum has begun to swing in the other direction. Today, many well-respected bodies of scientists, led by the National Institutes of Health and the American College of Obstetricians and Gynecologists, advocate the use of ERT in the treatment of several conditions that accompany the menopausal years (see box, opposite). ERT has been found useful in the treatment of only a few carefully studied conditions, but for hot flashes, vaginal atrophy, and osteoporosis, it is now considered the most effective medication. (A few physicians are also trying ERT as a means of *preventing* osteoporosis, but the success of such use is less well established.)

At the same time, it now seems that ERT might actually be less dangerous than was thought a decade ago. The amount of estrogen used in a typical dose has decreased significantly, and many doctors are now prescribing it in combination with progesterone, which more accurately mimics the menstrual cycle. The use of progesterone means a woman on this treatment will menstruate each month; her ovaries are not functioning—she cannot conceive—but she does bleed. That is the idea:

When her uterine lining is sloughed off each month, the estrogen has less chance to accumulate.

Besides improved methods of ERT administration, new epidemiological studies report that ERT might not carry as great a cancer risk as originally thought. One surprising study of more than 2,000 women, for instance, concluded that postmenopausal estrogen users actually had lower risks of heart disease *and lower death rates from all causes* than women of the same age who did not take estrogen.[40] And another, smaller study, while finding that the risk of endometrial cancer is higher than normal for women on ERT, reported that the risk of ERT is decreased for women who had used the birth control pill during their reproductive years.[41]

The question then becomes not whether estrogen can reverse some of the symptoms of menopause, but whether a potentially risky drug is warranted in the treatment of an essentially mild problem that might be managed in other ways. Hot flashes, if they are not severe, can be minimized by dressing in loose, comfortable layers of natural-fiber clothing that can be removed, layer by layer, if a woman gets too hot. Some women swear by ginseng extract or vitamin E; in other cases, a mild tranquilizer may be helpful. Vaginal dryness can be minimized by regular sexual activity and the use of lubricating creams (*not* estrogen creams, which carry the same cancer risk as oral estrogen) before intercourse. The risk of osteoporosis associated with loss of estrogen (see Chapter 4) can be minimized by increasing calcium intake and exercise levels, and perhaps by restricting the intake of caffeine, protein, and red meat.

Even its proponents do not say that ERT can "treat" menopause. Menopause is a natural stage of life, not a hormone-deficiency disease, and as such it needs no "treatment" unless it is accompanied by severe symptoms. Remember that nearly 80 percent of menopausal women experience no symptoms, or experience symptoms so minor that they never bring them to a doctor's attention. And many of the symptoms that might trouble mid-life women, such as insomnia, depression, and irritability, have no relation to loss of estrogen and have not been shown to benefit from ERT.

Cancer of the Reproductive Tract

The most common cancer of mid-life women, after breast cancer, is cancer of the reproductive tract. One in 11 American women will de-

velop breast cancer (see Chapter 2), and the rates for various gyneco-
logic cancers are not much more encouraging: about one in 100 for
endometrial cancer and about one in 50 for cervical cancer. But the
good news is this: Endometrial cancer has a cure rate approaching 90
percent, and for cervical cancer the cure rate is even better, about 95
percent. Unfortunately, the other cancers of the reproductive tract—of
the ovaries and the vagina—are, while rare, also far more resistant to
treatment. A woman with ovarian cancer has only a one in four chance
of recovery.[42]

The first step in diagnosing cancer early is to have regular checkups.
Women over 35 are advised to have a Pap smear every year. This simple
procedure, which involves scraping off a bit of tissue from the cervix
for microscopic analysis, detects cervical cancer in its earliest, most treatable stages. Some experts, including those at the American Cancer Society, say that women between 35 and 45 need to have Pap smears only
every two years if two previous Pap smears have been normal. But many
doctors prefer an annual Pap smear, since it gets a woman into the
office for a pelvic exam. (Pap smears, while they are excellent at detect-
ing cervical cancer, can detect only about 40 percent of endometrial
cancer, and cannot detect ovarian or vaginal cancer at all. For early
detection of these malignancies, a complete pelvic exam is necessary.)

After the age of 45, all women need Pap smears every year. Sometimes Paps are ordered even more frequently for women in high-risk
groups: women whose mothers took the hormone DES while they were
pregnant with them; women who have had abnormal Pap smears in the
past; women who have had cancer.

While nothing but a complete examination can determine the existence of cancer, a woman should be aware of certain statistically proven
risk factors. These are:

> *for cervical cancer:* early sexual activity; early first pregnancy; multi-
> ple sexual partners; low socioeconomic status; history of genital
> herpes.
> *for endometrial cancer:* history of infertility; failure to ovulate; child-
> lessness; abnormal uterine bleeding; obesity; metabolic or endo-
> crine imbalance such as diabetes or hypertension; estrogen
> replacement therapy for more than three years.
> *for ovarian cancer:* advanced age (average age of occurrence is 50).
> *for vaginal cancer:* advanced age; exposure in utero to DES.

Most of these risk factors are things over which a woman has no

Catching Cancer Early

A woman with any of the following Seven Warning Signals of cancer should see her doctor even if she has recently had a checkup:

1. A change in bowel or bladder habits.
2. A sore that does not heal.
3. Unusual bleeding or discharge.
4. Thickening or lump in the breast or elsewhere.
5. Indigestion or difficulty in swallowing.
6. Obvious change in a wart or mole.
7. Nagging cough or hoarseness.

The American Cancer Society has issued a set of guidelines for early detection of cancer in women without symptoms. A woman without symptoms should follow the schedule below for examinations. (These are ACS guidelines only; some physicians may prefer a different timetable for their patients.)

AGE 20 TO 40

Breast self-examination every month
A cancer-related checkup *every three years* to include:
Breast examination
A base-line mammogram (breast X ray) after age 35
Pelvic exam
Pap test
(after two initial negative tests spaced one year apart)
Exam for cancer of the thyroid
Exam for cancer of the mouth
Exam for cancer of the ovaries
Exam for cancer of the skin
Exam for cancer of the lymph nodes

AGE 40 AND OVER

Breast self-examination every month
A cancer-related checkup *every year,* to include:
Breast examination
A mammogram (breast X ray)
Pelvic exam
Pap test
Endometrial biopsy at menopause for women at risk
Digital rectal exam
Exam for cancer of the thyroid
Exam for cancer of the mouth
Exam for cancer of the ovaries
Exam for cancer of the skin
Exam for cancer of the lymph nodes

AGE 50 AND OVER

Cancer-related checkup *every year,* to include all of the above *plus:*
Test for occult blood in the stool every year
Rectal exam with a proctoscope every three to five years
(after two initial negative tests spaced one year apart)

control. But she should see her doctor when significant changes occur that could signal a problem. The warning signs that should send a woman to her physician are:

>*for cervical cancer:* bleeding after intercourse; other abnormal bleeding; abnormal vaginal discharge.
>*for endometrial cancer:* abnormal spotting or bleeding; any bleeding after menopause; heavy discharge of mucus from the vagina.
>*for ovarian cancer:* sudden or recurrent pelvic pain; abnormal pressure on the bladder; abnormal pressure on the rectum; gastrointestinal complaints.
>*for vaginal cancer:* unusual soreness or itchiness of the vulva; vaginal discharge or bleeding.

Hysterectomy

Recent estimates have been made that if present trends continue, more than one-half of all American women will have had a hysterectomy by age 65.[43] A hysterectomy is the surgical removal of the uterus, with or without removal of the cervix, Fallopian tubes, and ovaries as well. Strictly speaking, there are only four reasons to have a hysterectomy:

1. cancer of the reproductive tract;
2. large uterine fibroids;
3. excessive bleeding that does not respond to D&C (dilation and curettage, a means of cleaning out the uterus); or
4. severe disease or infection of the tubes or ovaries for which other treatments have failed.

But these conditions account for only 12 percent of the hysterectomies performed.[44]

Of the more than 800,000 hysterectomies done each year, perhaps as many as 40 percent are unnecessary. Why? One explanation often given is the profit motive. Hysterectomy rates are higher among surgeons in private practice than for those in prepaid health plans, whose fees do not depend on the number of procedures done. And hysterectomy rates are four times higher in the United States, where fee-for-service predominates, than in Sweden, where medicine is socialized.[45]

Another explanation is attitudinal. Gynecologists often think that, since the reproductive organs are breeding grounds for cancer, they should be removed at the first sign of trouble. For women who have completed their childbearing, these doctors might be quick to recommend removing the uterus—and, just to be safe, the ovaries as well—for such conditions as pelvic pain, small fibroids, prolapse of the uterus, or vaginal bleeding, each of which can be treated with a less invasive procedure. The operation has even been suggested for treatment of backache or depression, which are unrelated to the uterus, and as a means of surgical sterilization, rather than the safer and far less traumatic method of tying the Fallopian tubes.

But taking out a uterus is not like taking out a spleen. Even a woman who has completed her childbearing is likely to feel somehow defeminized when her uterus is removed. And if the ovaries are removed as well, she is literally defeminized, and usually requires estrogen replacement therapy (especially if she is under 50) to prevent the sudden onset of menopausal symptoms.

With today's generation of women taking better care of their bodies from young adulthood onward, and insisting on taking an active role in medical decision-making, the hysterectomy rates of tomorrow might actually go down. Women and their doctors are learning a good deal about ways to prevent deterioration of the reproductive organs over time, and women now can look forward to keeping those important organs healthy, and intact, their entire lives.

Maintenance:
The Reproductive System

From the onset of menstruation through menopause, a woman's reproductive system undergoes profound, often unanticipated changes. The key is knowing what to expect from each cycle.

Menstruation. Over the years, the duration of the menstrual periods tends to become shorter, with longer stretches in between. Women in their 30s and 40s, particularly those who have had children, will experience far fewer cramps than those in their teens and 20s, but may encounter discomfort due to premenstrual syndrome (PMS). Physicians may prescribe natural progesterone in severe cases; dietary changes—such as the elimination of caffeine, sugar, alcohol, and salt—in milder ones.

Pregnancy. No matter what your age, if you're planning to get pregnant, prepare for it now with good health and fitness habits:

- Don't smoke. Smoking has been associated with miscarriage, premature labor, low birth weight, and a host of other complications for the newborn.

- Don't diet, unless instructed to by your doctor. Even if you're overweight when you conceive, you should gain at least 15 pounds before delivery. A woman of normal prepregnancy weight should gain at least 25 to 35 pounds.

- Avoid drugs, alcohol, and medications. Some doctors even recommend staying off birth control pills for three months prior to attempting unprotected intercourse.

- Get plenty of iron, calcium, and protein. Since the fetus will draw on the mother's reserves, if necessary—even to the point of depletion—it's important to follow a diet rich in these nutrients before conception, as well as during pregnancy and lactation.

- Exercise. You'll want to be in top physical condition to carry and deliver a baby. In addition to your normal fitness routine, consider exercises that strengthen the muscles of the abdomen and pelvic floor.

Menopause. For some persistent and severe conditions that may accompany the menopausal years, estrogen replacement therapy (ERT) is a widely used, albeit hotly debated, form of treatment. Before you agree to take a potentially risky drug, ask yourself whether or not the problems you wish to treat might not be managed in less drastic ways. Vaginal dryness, for instance, can be remedied by achieving orgasm regularly; the use of lubricating creams before intercourse will also help. Before, during, and after menopause, you should maintain a diet high in calcium, and exercise regularly, to reduce the risk of osteoporosis.

Cancer Detection. The most common cancer of mid-life women after breast cancer is cancer of the reproductive tract. For early detection, women over age 35 are advised to have a Pap smear and pelvic exam every year. Women of all ages should know the warning signs: unusual bleeding or discharge, sudden or recurrent pelvic pain; abnormal pressure on the bladder or rectum; excessive soreness or itchiness of the vulva.

6
The Heart of the Matter

The dull ache in the chest after a heavy meal; the skipped heartbeat that interferes with a four-mile run; the deep pain that seems to begin in the neck and to radiate down the left arm all the way to the fingers. These are symptoms of heart irregularities, and for years the majority of women never experienced them. Women stayed at home, less exposed to the excesses of life-style—overeating, drinking, smoking—that seemed to help make heart disease epidemic among men. And, at least until menopause, their high estrogen levels were thought to provide their hearts with an extra measure of protection.

In early adulthood, women seem almost immune to all forms of cardiovascular disease. But this protection does not last forever. By the time a woman is 55, she is more likely to die of heart disease than of any other cause. (Yet, significantly, she is still less likely than a man her age to die of a heart attack: Between the age of 55 and 64, heart attacks kill 791 men for every 100,000 in that age group, compared to 280 women per 100,000. After the age of 65 the ratios even out, but women maintain a slight advantage: 2,813 heart attack deaths for every 100,000 men over 65, versus 2,001 for every 100,000 women.[1])

Heart attack, angina (chest pain), stroke, high blood pressure, high cholesterol levels, and the buildup of plaque on the vessel walls known as atherosclerosis have traditionally been the fate of the middle-aged male. The new conventional wisdom is that women will soon experience their share of cardiovascular disease as they join the work force and suffer the same stresses of the rat race that men do. But to date, this theory is not supported by data. According to figures from the National Heart, Lung, and Blood Institute, both men and women have experienced an identical decline in coronary heart disease deaths—about 33 percent—between 1965 and 1980, the period when women flooded the marketplace in record numbers.

If the sexes seem destined to approach equality in their risk of heart disease, it will be because of hormones rather than life-style. When women lose most of their natural estrogen after menopause, they have lost their prime protection against heart disease. At the same time that estrogen levels go down, levels of other body chemicals are changing, too. This is especially true of the lipoproteins, the proteins that circulate in the bloodstream on which cholesterol from the diet must hitch a ride. After menopause, levels of HDL—the "good guy" lipoprotein that carries dietary cholesterol to the liver for excretion—go down, while levels of LDL—the "bad guy" lipoprotein that delivers dietary cholesterol directly to the cells and blood vessels, where it accumulates as plaque—go up. And other risk factors for heart disease, particularly obesity and hypertension, go up, too.

The mystery is that estrogen does not always offer protection against heart disease. Consider women who ingest artificial estrogen—women on the birth control pill, or women who, after a hysterectomy, are put on estrogen replacement therapy. Some studies show that these women actually have *more* heart disease than their peers who are not taking artificial estrogen [2]—although, to complicate the picture, other studies contradict these results. [3] And men with heart disease present another puzzle: They usually have *more* estrogen in their bodies than do age-matched men without heart disease. Further, men who take estrogen as treatment for prostate cancer prove later to be at higher risk of heart attacks. [4] So while estrogen, in its natural state, might help protect women from heart disease, estrogen in its unnatural state might be downright dangerous.

The best evidence available for cardiovascular functioning in old age is the well-known Framingham Study, in which the adults of one Massachusetts town have been examined regularly since 1949, when most participants were 30 to 60 years old. The Framingham researchers have found that women—of whom they have examined 2,400—lag ten years behind men in the incidence of all heart disease, and lag 20 years behind men for the more serious forms of heart disease such as heart attacks. This protection holds true even for women with as many risk factors as men. In other words, women who smoke are less likely to develop heart disease than men of the same age who smoke; women who smoke and have high blood pressure are less likely to develop heart disease than men of the same age who smoke and have high blood pressure; and so on. The Framingham women have been followed so far to age 84, and they seem to maintain their advantage even then. [5]

But advantage is not the same thing as immunity, and a mid-life woman should not become too smug in thinking that heart disease is something that happens only to men. Women get heart disease, too, with one important difference that actually stacks the deck against them: Women don't seem to benefit from preventive measures undertaken *after* the disease has already progressed.

Coronary artery bypass surgery, the much-heralded surgical treatment to route the blood flow around blocked vessels near the heart,

Heart Health Hazards

A woman at risk of cardiovascular disease—which includes not only coronary heart disease but also angina, stroke, high blood pressure, high cholesterol levels, and atherosclerosis—is one who

- has a strong family history of cardiovascular disease, especially when it occurred in immediate relatives (parents, siblings, children) before the age of 60;
- smokes cigarettes (deaths from coronary artery disease among 35- to 45-year-olds are five times more common in smokers than in non-smokers);
- is sedentary, or engages in moderate aerobic exercises only occasionally;
- took oral contraceptives past the age of 35;
- is more than 10 percent overweight;
- has diabetes (female diabetics are five times more likely to have heart disease than female nondiabetics);
- eats a diet rich in animal fat, saturated fat, and cholesterol, or a diet low in fiber, or both;
- drinks more than five alcoholic drinks a day;
- has elevated levels in the bloodstream of serum cholesterol and serum triglycerides; or
- has a blood pressure higher than 140/90.

The Coronary Risk Factors Test, pages 130–131, can help you see how you stack up against these risk factors.

does not seem to be as beneficial for women as it is for men. And women who experience "little strokes"—transient ischemic attacks—which tend to foretell a tendency toward a bigger stroke are not helped, the way men are, by the prophylactic use of aspirin.

This means early prevention, by means of life-style improvement *before* the years of prime heart disease risk, is that much more important for women. And the ways to minimize the risks of heart disease have been well-documented, because the risk factors have been so clearly delineated. Fortunately, a woman can correct almost all the established risk factors for heart disease (except for a genetic susceptibility to heart disease) with significant effect. And young women today, who are eating and exercising in ways that the American Heart Association recommends, are even more likely than their mothers to avoid cardiovascular disease altogether.

A family history of cardiovascular disease is one of the most signifi-

Coronary Risk Factors: A Self-Test

Circle the points that reflect your age, health, and family history. Add up the circled figures to find your overall risk category.

I.   Factors over which you have no control   points

    A. Age

10–20 years old	1
21–30	2
31–40	3
41–50	4
51–60	5
61 or over	6

    B. Sex

Female under 40	1
Female 40–50	2
Female after menopause	3

    C. Heredity

Number of relatives in immediate family (parents, siblings, children) with cardiovascular disease

After age 60

none	1
one	2
two	3

Before age 60

one	4
two	5
three	6

II. Factors over which you have control

    A. Weight (see weight table, Chapter 2)

More than 5 pounds below average	0
5 pounds below to 6 pounds above average	1
6–20 pounds above average	2
21–35 pounds above average	3
36–50 pounds above average	5
More than 51 pounds above average	7

    B. Cigarette smoking

None	0
Less than 10 cigarettes daily	2
10–20 cigarettes daily	4
21–30 cigarettes daily	6
More than 30 cigarettes daily	10

    C. Exercise

Intense work and intense play exertion	1
Moderate work and moderate play exertion	2
Sedentary work and intense play exertion	3
Sedentary work and moderate play exertion	5
Sedentary work and light play exertion	6
Completely sedentary	8

D. Cholesterol

Low blood cholesterol; diet excludes all saturated fats and eggs	1
Medium/low blood cholesterol; diet excludes most saturated fats and eggs	2
Borderline blood cholesterol; diet includes some saturated fats and eggs	3
Mildly elevated blood cholesterol; diet includes moderate saturated fats and eggs	4
Markedly elevated blood cholesterol; diet includes excessive saturated fats and eggs	5
Extremely elevated blood cholesterol; diet includes excessive saturated fats and eggs	7

E. Blood pressure

Systolic pressure (first figure given) under 119	1
Systolic pressure 120–139	2
Systolic pressure 140–159	3
Systolic pressure 160–179	4
Systolic pressure 180–199	6
Systolic pressure over 200	8

Scoring

6–16	Below average
17–24	Average
25–31	Moderate
32–40	Dangerous
Over 41	Urgent—get to a doctor as soon as possible

Adapted from *The Sports Doctor's Fitness Book for Women* by John L. Marshall with Heather Barbash. Copyright © 1981 by John L. Marshall with Heather Barbash. Reprinted by permission of Delacorte Press.

cant risk factors for heart disease in any individual. But that is just about the only risk factor that cannot be changed. Almost everything else that places a woman at high risk for heart trouble—exercise habits, dietary excesses, estrogen use—are life-style decisions that can be undone. The benefits of adopting habits for a healthy heart can be significant. As the Framingham researchers discovered,

A woman who reduces her . . .	*will lower her risk of . . .*
blood pressure by 10 mm Hg	cardiovascular disease by 30 percent
serum cholesterol level by 10 percent	coronary disease by 30 percent
weight by 10 percent	coronary disease by 20 percent
cigarette smoking entirely	coronary mortality by 50 percent[6]

Blood Pressure and Hypertension

"There's no doubt that the lower your blood pressure, the less risk you run of developing heart disease," says Dr. William Kannel, professor of medicine at Boston University and an investigator in the Framingham Study. According to Kannel, there's no such thing as blood pressure that is too low: "If you have low blood pressure, below about 120/80, you're just about immortal."

Although cardiovascular disease is more common in men than in women, high blood pressure—one sign of cardiovascular disease, and a significant risk factor in developing other complications—affects more women than men. Hypertension, the medical term for high blood pressure, affects 30 percent of women in their late 50s and early 60s, compared to 28 percent of men. After 65, the sex gap widens: 36 percent of women have high blood pressure, and only 32 percent of men.[7]

Hypertension has been called "the silent killer" because it creates no symptoms yet does relentless damage. It is the most significant risk factor for the development of stroke, and one of the most important risk factors for heart attack. A person with high blood pressure is three times more likely than someone with normal blood pressure to have a heart attack, five times more likely to develop congestive heart failure, and eight times more likely to have a stroke.

Hypertension: A Woman's Problem

Women may be relatively immune to coronary heart disease, but they are not relatively immune to high blood pressure. In fact, after the age of 55 a woman runs a higher risk of developing hypertension than a man does. The first steps in blood pressure control: weight reduction, exercise, and a high-fiber, low-fat, low-salt diet.

INCIDENCE OF HIGH BLOOD PRESSURE
(Number of persons per 100 with blood pressure over 160/95)

Age	White Males	White Females
35–44	16	9
45–54	24	17
55–64	28	30
65–74	32	36

Source: U.S. Bureau of the Census, *Statistical Abstract of the United States 1981* (Washington, D.C.: Department of Commerce, 1981), p. 121.

A blood pressure reading is usually considered to be borderline when it is above 140/90 ("one forty over ninety") and high when it is above 160/95 ("one sixty over ninety-five"). In each reading, the first number is the systolic pressure, the pressure in the vessels (expressed as millimeters of mercury on a barometer-like gauge) when the heart is pumping. The second is the diastolic pressure, the pressure in the vessels when the heart is at rest. The more significant reading, in terms of risk of heart disease, has generally been thought to be the systolic reading. But some physicians now believe that a very high diastolic reading, even if the systolic reading is in the normal range, can be a danger sign, too.

At one time, high blood pressure was believed to be the inevitable result of normal aging. This was based on the observation that blood pressure almost invariably rose in any individual with each passing decade. The older an individual, the more likely he or she was to have high blood pressure: About one in six Americans of all ages have hypertension, but the rate jumps to one in three for those over 65.[8] For many years, researchers, physicians, and the lay public took it for granted that almost anyone would develop hypertension just by living long enough.

Conventional wisdom says that a "normal" systolic blood pressure reading is "100 plus your age"; in other words, as your age increases, so should your blood pressure. But Kannel calls this "a very serious misconception," which came about by the observation that blood pressure almost always rises with age.

"One theory is that this rise, since it occurs so often, must be normal," Kannel explains. According to this theory, "older people must require higher blood pressure to perfuse [flow] through vessels made tighter by atherosclerosis. But the incidence of coronary disease also goes up with age. That's normal?" Just because it *does* occur does not mean it *should* occur, he says. According to Kannel, high blood pressure is as dangerous—in terms of its contribution to the risk of heart disease—for an older person as it is for someone younger.

Cross-cultural studies have provided some clue to the reason for the observed increase of blood pressure with age. In some primitive cultures where salt is rarely consumed—such as those found in New Guinea, East Africa, West Malaysia, and the Cook Islands—blood pressure stays normal throughout a lifetime. But in some industrialized countries where salt consumption is far higher than that in the United States—in northern Japan, for example—blood pressure increases with age even more rapidly and to a greater extent than in the U.S.[9] (The incidence

The Antihypertension Diet

The sodium-potassium ratio in the cells is what regulates water content, which in turn determines the amount of pressure exerted on the vessels. The goal for a woman with high blood pressure is to *lower* the ratio of sodium to potassium; this can be done by decreasing the amount of sodium in her diet and increasing the amount of potassium.

CUT DOWN ON FOODS HIGH IN SODIUM

Buttermilk	Pickled foods
Canned tuna fish	Prepared salad dressings
Canned vegetables	Salted crackers, pretzels
(Read label)	Sausages
Cheese and cheese	Seasoning salts
spreads	Smoked foods
Cold cuts	Soy sauce
Ketchup	Soups—canned, dehydrated
Mustard	

EAT MORE OF FOODS HIGH IN POTASSIUM

Apricots and apricot	Milk (regular, skim,
juice	and low sodium)
Asparagus	Oranges and orange juice
Bananas	Peaches
Broccoli	Pears
Brown sugar	Potatoes
Carrots	Prune juice
Eggs	Tomatoes and tomato juice
Grapefruit juice	

Adapted from *For Mothers and Daughters* by Myron Winick, M.D. Copyright © 1983 by Myron Winick, M.D. By permission of William Morrow & Company.

of hypertension in northern Japan is 60 percent, about twice the rate of the United States.)

Salt intake is not the only determinant of whether a culture will develop high rates of hypertension. Obesity is an important factor as well. Although the data for obesity are less conclusive, they tend to run in the same direction: Where obesity is commonplace, blood pressure rises with age, and where it is rare, it does not.

That is not to say that either salt intake or obesity causes hypertension. The truth is far more complicated than that. Nor does it say that doing away with either will eliminate hypertension—although it can help. Studies show that about one-third to one-half of individuals with high blood pressure can significantly lower their pressure by reducing their salt intake to about four or five grams a day. (The current American average is about ten grams a day; a very low-salt diet, which can only be adhered to in a hospital setting, contains about one-half a gram.) Similarly, a 10 to 30 percent loss of weight in overweight hypertensives has been shown to bring about a significant reduction in blood pressure.

The controversy now arising about hypertension is twofold. First, is it worth cutting down on salt intake in a normotensive (person with normal blood pressure) in her 30s, 40s, or 50s, just to *prevent* hypertension? Only an estimated one-third of the population is salt-sensitive; for the rest, salt intake seems to have little or no relationship to blood pressure.[10] A normotensive individual cannot tell whether she is salt-sensitive until she develops hypertension and tries a low-salt diet for a few weeks. As a preventive measure, then, salt restriction is ordinarily something of a shot in the dark. Most experts generally recommend at least moderate salt restriction as a way to hedge one's bets; it cannot hurt, and it might help.

Second, once hypertension is established, how aggressively should it be treated? The catch in this question is that hypertension causes no symptoms in and of itself—but the treatment for lowering blood pressure usually does. In treating asymptomatic hypertension, then, a doctor must prescribe medicine that *creates* symptoms to treat a condition that has none—an awkward resolution to the risk-benefit equation that all doctors take into account before prescribing any drug. The only justification for such action would be if it helped prevent the serious consequences—including heart attack, stroke, and kidney disease—associated with high blood pressure. The issue boils down to what the risk really is for a "borderline hypertensive"—say, a 52-year-old woman with a blood pressure of 150/90—and whether the risk can be reduced with medication.

Most doctors would start by trying to lower this woman's blood pressure by changing her life-style. If she is overweight, the physician would try a weight-reduction diet. Taking off excess fat is often all that is needed to bring a relatively high blood pressure down to normal.

If she is sedentary, the physician would recommend vigorous, heart-pounding exercise—brisk walking, jogging, bike riding, swimming—for one-half hour sessions three times a week. Exercise not only has a direct effect on lowering blood pressure, it also reduces the overall risk of developing heart disease.

If she eats a lot of salt, the physician would advise cutting down on salt consumption, not only in cooking and table use but in prepared and smoked foods. Excess sodium (the guilty ingredient in table salt) can directly raise blood pressure by causing the cells to retain fluid; the higher the fluid content, the greater the pressure in the blood vessels needed to push the excess fluid through. This step, as we have seen, will lower blood pressure in about one-third of hypertensive individuals. For best effect, a reduction in sodium intake should be combined with an increase in the intake of potassium. See page 134 for a listing of foods that are rich in each mineral.

A final change in life-style revolves around a sort of "mind over matter" approach to hypertension. Relaxation exercises and biofeedback control have been shown, in some people, to reduce blood pressure. This is not to say that high blood pressure is caused by "excess (hyper) tension." Hypertensive individuals are no more tense, driving, or highstrung than the population at large. But for *some* persons, relaxation does indeed help counteract some of the underlying mechanisms of blood pressure regulation.

If life-style measures fail and the woman's blood pressure still hovers around 150/90, many doctors might then try some antihypertension medicines. This is a controversial step with borderline hypertensives, but recent research shows that aggressive treatment of even mildly elevated blood pressure can reduce death rates by 20 percent.[11]

The first drug to be tried is usually a diuretic, which makes an indi-

---

The Relaxation Response

Training the body to relax may be one of the best things you can do for your heart. According to Herbert Benson, a Boston Cardiologist and author of *The Relaxation Response,* this lessening of tension can be achieved in just 20 minutes of uninterrupted concentration. Those who have practiced meditation will recognize the technique. Here's what you do:

1. Find a quiet area, a comfortable chair, and sit down;
2. Close your eyes;
3. Relax your muscles, starting from your toes and working up to your neck and head;
4. Breathe through your nose and—becoming aware of your breathing—begin speaking the word "one" (or another simple, neutral word) as you exhale;
5. Continue the pattern for about 20 minutes. It is all right to open your eyes occasionally to check the time, although a timer shouldn't be used. After the 20-minute period has elapsed, you should stay seated, first with your eyes closed, then open for a few minutes, before carrying on with your daily routine.

vidual excrete more water through the kidneys and thus reduces the amount of fluid that must flow through the blood vessels. The two major side effects of diuretic therapy are frequent urination and potassium deficiency. The first can be handled by staying withing easy access of a bathroom, at least until the proper dosage is arrived at. The second can be handled by eating bananas, oranges, and other foods that are rich in potassium or, if that fails, by taking a potassium supplement.

More direct-acting antihypertensive drugs are available if diuretics do not sufficiently lower blood pressure. It is now that the really unpleasant side effects can come about. Some of these drugs can cause depression, fatigue, dry mouth, stuffy nose, headaches, reduced sex drive, and visual problems. Several inhibit the body's normal response to sudden postural changes, creating faintness or even blackouts when an individual stands up suddenly. Reserpine, a widely used antihypertensive, has recently been shown to increase the risk of breast cancer. It is important for patient and physician to work together to try to find the right medication, in the right dosage, that can lower blood pressure effectively with a minimum of side effects.

Cholesterol and Heart Disease

The good old American breakfast of bacon and eggs has gone from hero to villain in the past generation. In the 1950s, mothers pushed such a breakfast on their children because it was full of protein. By the 1970s, those children had become young adults who shunned bacon and eggs for their artery-clogging cholesterol. Now, in the 1980s, the children of the 50s have grown up—and they are just not sure about what to feed *their* children for breakfast. Now it seems the new conventional wisdom is that bacon and eggs, and other dietary sources of cholesterol, might have gotten a bum rap.

Scientists disagree about just what the relationship is between the amount of cholesterol you eat and the amount of cholesterol that accumulates in the bloodstream. It might all depend on what an individual's particular body does with the cholesterol. Some people, evidently, can eat eggs to their heart's content, and it passes right out of the body. Still others compensate for the excess of dietary cholesterol by producing less cholesterol of their own. But the unlucky few—about one-third of us, by most estimates—seem to send any cholesterol they consume straight to the point where it will do the most damage—to the walls of the blood vessels.[12]

Who Dies from Heart Disease?

By the time a woman is 55, she no longer seems immune to heart disease. Probably because of the loss of estrogen after menopause, she suddenly encounters a risk of heart attack death that is almost as high as a man's—especially over the age of 65.

DEATHS FROM HEART DISEASE, MALES VERSUS FEMALES
(Number of heart disease deaths per 100,000)

Age	White Males	Females
25–44	37	12
45–54	209	85
55–64	791	280
65 and over	2,813	2,001

Source: U.S. Bureau of the Census, *Statistical Abstract of the United States 1981* (Washington, D.C.: Department of Commerce, 1981), p. 76.

To understand this confusing situation, we have to know just what cholesterol is. Cholesterol is a fatty substance manufactured in the liver. It has an important role in the body; it is needed to strengthen cell membranes, protect nerve fibers, and produce vitamin D, sex hormones, and bile acids.

But while some cholesterol is necessary, too much can be dangerous. The liver can make all the cholesterol the body needs out of fats and carbohydrates in a cholesterol-free diet; any added dietary cholesterol is therefore extraneous. The liver makes about 1,000 milligrams of cholesterol a day to service the body, but the diet typically supplies another 600 milligrams of cholesterol a day that go straight to the bloodstream —and can clog it up.[13]

Too much cholesterol leads to a buildup of thick, fatty tissue on the blood vessel walls; eventually, it forms a mass called an atheroma (from the Greek for "porridge tumor"). Too many atheromas can lead to the total closure of one part of a vessel. The result, depending on where the closure occurs, can be a blood clot (thrombosis), kidney failure, chest pain (angina), stroke, or heart attack (myocardial infarction).

When atheromas accumulate, the condition is called *atherosclerosis.* The severity of atherosclerosis increases with age, but atherosclerosis is not the inevitable result of aging; it is the result of a lifetime of dietary and physical indiscretions. Autopsy studies of young GIs killed in the Korean War, whose average age was 22, revealed significant atherosclerosis even at this early age.[14] Autopsies of automobile accident victims have even shown atheromas in children.[15] But some individuals, especially lifelong vegetarians and long-distance runners, can reach an advanced age with blood vessels that are relatively fat-free.[16]

The term atherosclerosis is often used interchangeably with *arteriosclerosis,* but the two conditions are quite different. Atherosclerosis can worsen the effects of arteriosclerosis, which is no more than the narrowing, loss of elasticity, and increasing brittleness of the arteries that come about with age. The changes in the blood vessels that characterize arteriosclerosis—literally, "hardening [sclerosis] of the arteries"—are similar to the changes we have noted elsewhere in the body, particularly the skin. But they need not cause any problems. In an individual with few or no atheromas on the vessel walls, hardening of the arteries can create relatively few symptoms.

The most crucial matter, then, is to minimize the formation of atheromas. Scientists generally agree that atheromas come from cholesterol —but only from one type of cholesterol. Cholesterol cannot travel solo; it must hitch a ride on a special fatty protein called a lipoprotein, of which there are two kinds. High-density lipoproteins (HDLs) escort some cholesterol to the liver, through which it is excreted from the body. HDLs have been called the "good guy" lipoproteins because they actually help clear excess cholesterol from the bloodstream. Persons with high levels of HDL in their serum (blood) are at very low risk of cardiovascular disease.

Low-density lipoproteins (LDLs), on the other hand, are the "bad guys" of the system. When a cell needs cholesterol, it can grab some off the back of the LDL. But when there is more cholesterol available than the cells are likely to need, the LDL keeps it handy anyway, right in the bloodstream—where it can do its dirty work. Persons with high levels of LDL in their serum are at high risk of cardiovascular disease.

Women have higher HDL levels than men of the same age—but only before menopause. After menopause, a woman's protective level of HDL is likely to drop, which is why the incidence of heart attack and other cardiovascular disease increases in women past the age of 50. On average, the majority of cholesterol in the bloodstream (about 70 percent) is carried on LDLs. In persons who consume large amounts of saturated (as opposed to polyunsaturated or monounsaturated) fats, or who are obese, the percentage of LDL can be even higher. But an individual can actually increase the proportion of HDL in her body by making some life-style changes. HDL levels increase with consumption

Pressures on the Heart

As the level of cholesterol in the blood increases with age, the cholesterol accumulates on the artery walls, which are themselves thickening—the net effect of which is to force the heart to work harder to pump blood.

Although the connection between dietary cholesterol and serum cholesterol is not yet firmly established, one thing is clear: Women run a higher risk than men of developing high levels of cholesterol in the bloodstream. And no matter where those high levels come from —whether it be the diet itself or an inherited tendency to accumulate blood fats—everyone agrees that they place a person at a higher risk of developing coronary heart disease.

Free blood flow

Coronary arteries

Blood flow diminished by build-up of arterial plaque

HIGH SERUM CHOLESTEROL
(Serum cholesterol above 260 mg/100 ml, per 100 persons)

Age	White Males	White Females
35–44	25	14
45–54	31	32
55–64	29	46
65–74	29	50

Source: U.S. Bureau of the Census, *Statistical Abstract of the United States 1981* (Washington, D.C.: Department of Commerce, 1981), p. 121.

of more polyunsaturated fats, vigorous exercise, and weight loss in someone who is overweight.

The big question in medical circles is precisely what the relationship is between cholesterol in the diet and cholesterol in the bloodstream. The general consensus is that the more cholesterol an individual eats—

in the form of eggs, red meat, and high-fat dairy products like whole milk, butter, cheese, and cream—the higher the person's serum cholesterol levels will be. But some experts believe that serum cholesterol is determined more by heredity, body makeup, and exercise patterns than by foods. If you are born into a lucky family, they say, in which dietary cholesterol is converted easily into HDL, you can eat all the eggs and ice cream you want. But if you are born into an unlucky family, in which dietary cholesterol is converted easily into LDL, no amount of sacrifice in the diet will protect you from excesses in the blood vessels.

A recent study from Norway provides a surprising link in the diet-cholesterol connection: coffee. Women who drink more than nine cups of coffee a day (even black coffee) were found to have significantly higher levels of LDL and significantly lower levels of HDL than women who drank less than one cup a day. This connection held true even when all other risk factors for heart disease—overweight, age, exercise patterns, and cigarette and alcohol use—were held constant.[17]

Other Heart and Circulatory Problems

Heart attack. The symptoms are familiar: a crushing pain in the chest, often after a heavy meal (which is why some people confuse it with indigestion), that may radiate to the neck, jaw, arms, and stomach. Occasionally, the symptoms include chills, dizziness, fainting, nausea, shortness of breath, and sweating. A heart attack is a blockage of blood flow to the heart caused by a blood clot (thrombus) in the coronary artery. It is always accompanied by death of some of the heart muscle, and its severity depends on how extensive—and where—the heart damage is.

A woman headed for a heart attack may first experience several weeks of angina, chest pain that occurs in a similar pattern *but that disappears with rest.* Or she may have no reason to believe there might be anything wrong with her heart. The element of surprise is what makes a heart attack so scary.

Women under 60 are half as likely as men of the same age to suffer heart attacks, but after age 60 heart attack is the leading killer of both women and men. And a woman who recovers from a heart attack—as the majority of victims do—is in somewhat worse shape than a man: She runs a two to three times greater risk of having a second heart attack in the next five years.[18]

Although many heart attack victims die before they ever reach the hospital, those who make it there are usually assured of a good recovery. Eight out of ten heart attack patients in the hospital will go home, most of them to jobs, sports, and sex lives that are as vigorous as they were before the attack. But there's nothing like a heart attack to whip a person into shape, and heart attack survivors are among the most enthusiastic proponents of dietary and exercise programs designed to keep that crucial muscle pumping healthily for many, many years.

Stroke. Stroke is a big killer of women—Number Three for women in middle and old age. A stroke is a sudden blockage of blood flow to the brain, just as a heart attack is a sudden blockage of blood flow to the heart. Depending on where the blockage occurs, it can cause few permanent problems or can lead to paralysis, inability to speak, or death. A blockage in the right side of the brain will affect motion on the left side of the body, and vice versa. In addition, a left-brain stroke might impair an individual's ability to speak, think, or understand. Many of the functions lost right after a stroke can be relearned through therapy designed to train new parts of the brain to take on the tasks of regions that were destroyed.

Often, a stroke is preceded by a series of small blackouts called transient ischemic attacks (TIAs). A TIA most often occurs after a sudden shift in position, as when a person stands up quickly. Men with TIA can be greatly helped by taking aspirin; a man with TIA who takes aspirin four times a day is only half as likely to develop a stroke as a man with TIA who does not take aspirin. But for women with TIA, aspirin has no such effect. "No one has explained this finding satisfactorily," says Dr. Jerome Fleg, a cardiologist at the Gerontological Research Center of the National Institute on Aging. "It may relate to a different mechanism causing the stroke in women, but no one can say for sure."

The risk factors for stroke are the same as for all cardiovascular disease—smoking, overweight, a sedentary life-style. These are itemized in the Coronary Risk Test on pages 130–131.

Blood clot—thrombus and embolism. Women who take estrogen—either as postmenopausal estrogen replacement therapy or as oral contraceptives—are at increased risk for developing a blood clot in the deep veins of the legs, lower abdomen, or elsewhere in the body.[19] The risk is increased even further for women on estrogen who smoke. The blood clot itself is usually not dangerous, unless it breaks off and enters the bloodstream. A clot in the bloodstream is called a thrombus; if it stops blood flow entirely, it is called an embolism.

A leg in which a thrombus occurs is usually red all over, painful, and extremely swollen. A physician may prescribe blood-thinning drugs, called anticoagulants, to help dissolve the clot.

The best way to prevent blood clots is to follow the same life-style changes recommended for preventing atherosclerosis (see following section). And, especially important for women, stay away from birth control pills after the age of 35, and stay away from estrogen replacement therapy after menopause if you have any risk factors for blood clots—if you smoke, if you have diabetes, or if you have a family or personal history of blood clots or cardiovascular disease.

Varicose veins. Any woman over the age of 40, or any woman who has been pregnant, has an idea of what varicose veins are; if she has not noticed them in herself, she's at least seen them in her peers. They may begin as small blue spidery marks just beneath the skin surface and may sometimes lead to swelling and twisting of the surface veins. More than half of all adults have at least minor varicosities, and the condition is four times more common in women than in men.

Varicose veins usually occur below the waist, in the legs or anus (where they are called hemorrhoids). Women who must stand all day are more likely than others to develop them, as are women whose mothers have varicose veins. There seems to be a hormone component to their development: Varicosities often appear in early pregnancy, long before the weight of the baby could have had an effect on the flow of blood from the legs; and symptoms of varicose veins (cramps and aching in the legs) tend to worsen premenstrually.

While essentially harmless, varicose veins do tend to predispose a woman to other vascular disorders, particularly thrombophlebitis (blood clots in the legs, ten times more likely in a woman with varicosities than in one without), ruptures, and ulcers. Occasionally, the veins themselves become so swollen that they must be removed, or "stripped"; the work of the lost veins can be taken over by veins nearby. In the great majority of cases, though, the most distressing symptom of varicose veins is leg fatigue.

A woman with varicose veins can minimize her discomfort by taking a few simple steps:

- Wear support stockings, and put them on even before getting out of bed (this is when veins in the leg are most empty).
- Avoid standing in one place as much as possible.
- When seated, prop up your legs so that your feet are higher than your chest.

· Engage in moderate exercise of the legs, such as walking or swimming.

To prevent varicose veins, most physicians recommend a balanced diet (nutritional deficiencies, such as a lack of vitamin C, have been associated with varicosities[20]), weight reduction (if overweight), and regular exercise (especially leg exercises).

Mitral valve prolapse. This heart valve irregularity, first described as Barlow's syndrome, is a relatively common diagnosis among adult women, affecting an estimated 15 percent of all women over 30. In this condition, one of the heart's two valves, the mitral valve, does not close properly after each beat, leading to an irregularity in blood movement detectable as a faint "whoosh" to a doctor listening with a stethoscope. Mitral valve prolapse is most often diagnosed with echocardiography, a

Fighting Varicose Veins

More than half of all adult women encounter some varicosities, most frequently in the legs or anus (where they are called hemorrhoids). A woman is at high risk of developing varicose veins if she

- is pregnant,
- is on the birth control pill,
- has a mother, aunt, or sister with varicose veins,
- has an inadequate intake of fiber and vitamin C in her diet,
- is tall,
- is overweight,
- is sedentary and spends much of her time sitting, especially with her legs crossed at the knee,
- wears restrictive clothing, such as girdles or tight boots or pantyhose.

The main hazard of varicosities is cosmetic, but they can also cause symptoms including leg fatigue, leg ulcers, night leg cramps, and blood clots.

To prevent varicose veins, try the following measures:

- Eat a high-fiber diet, with lots of citrus fruits and vegetables.
- Exercise your legs with swimming, walking, jogging, or bicycle riding.
- Wear elastic support stockings during pregnancy, putting them on before getting out of bed each morning.
- Avoid sitting or standing still; move around occasionally or stand on your toes.
- Do not sit with crossed legs, and whenever possible elevate your feet so they are above your hips.

technique that bounces sound waves into the chest cavity to obtain a clear image of the heart with virtually no risk to the patient.

The condition is usually quite harmless, although it can cause some chest pain, heart palpitations, or shortness of breath after exertion. The most important reason for knowing whether one has mitral valve prolapse is that it can predispose to heart infection in certain situations. A woman with mitral valve prolapse is advised to tell her dentist about it so she can take antibiotics before and after any procedure. Most dental procedures, even a good cleaning, can release large amounts of bacteria into the bloodstream, and when a heart valve protrudes, as it does in mitral valve prolapse, it tends to attract those bacteria and act as a fertile breeding ground for infection.

Reducing the Risk

Women who are genetically prone to cardiovascular disease, or who have other conditions, particularly diabetes, that place them at higher risk, must be especially concerned about risk reduction through the only route available to them—life-style modification. But modifying one's life-style—be it through diet, exercise, stress management, or by cutting out smoking—almost always requires a great deal of motivation. It's not easy to change one's way of living *today* for some unseen —and unsure —benefit in the future.

One way to get the motivation needed to adapt to some of these changes is to measure just how much of a heart disease risk you really are. Women who can see, in cold, hard numbers, that their time may be limited are far more likely to try anything to keep their tickers ticking. One technique, which must be done in a doctor's office, is the measurement of forced vital capacity.

The forced vital capacity is an individual's ability to exhale a certain quantity of oxygen in one breath. Gerontologists have found that, in general, vital capacity declines with age even in the healthiest research subjects. In the Baltimore Longitudinal Study of the National Institute on Aging, for example, an average decline in vital capacity of about 50 percent was noted between the ages of 30 and 80.

But not everyone's vital capacity declines in the same way. And research has shown that persons with the greatest decline in vital capacity are also those at greatest risk of cardiovascular disease. This is an important finding, because vital capacity changes may occur long before any other symptoms of cardiovascular disease (angina, transient ischemic attacks, minor heart attacks) have occurred. Indeed, they may occur so early in the disease process that life-style changes can really be effective in reducing a woman's overall risk.

"For reasons that are not clear," says William Kannel of Boston University, the vital capacity test "provides more striking predictions for women than for men." The test, he adds, identifies women who urgently need to change those cardiovascular risk factors that can be changed. And, as we have already pointed out, it is especially important for a woman to begin risk-reduction steps early, years before any sign of heart disease is evident. Life-style modifications do not have much effect on women once the disease is established, which usually occurs between the ages of about 45 and 65.

Diet is perhaps the most important way for a woman to reduce her chances of developing heart disease. Despite the current controversy over just how important dietary cholesterol is in the development of atherosclerosis, the majority of physicians believe there is evidence enough to advise Americans to adopt a "prudent diet" aimed at reducing the chance of heart attack and other heart or blood vessel problems. The prudent diet, as recommended by the American Heart Association, is one low in fats and high in complex carbohydrates.

One dietary technique for lowering blood cholesterol that is now gaining some scientific attention is fiber—specifically, the fiber that forms a thick, gummy substance, which can actually take cholesterol out of the bloodstream. The most promising of these substances are oat bran, now marketed as a hot cereal by the Quaker Oats Company of Chicago, and guar gum, currently available only in England as a crisp cracker.

William Kannel says obesity promotes cardiovascular disease more in women that it does in men. But the fact is that being overweight puts a strain on *anyone's* heart, elevates blood pressure, and increases the odds of developing disorders known to complicate the course of atherosclerosis, particularly diabetes. The wisest move for an overweight woman, especially if she is at high risk of cardiovascular disease because of other factors, is to go on a reasonable reducing diet to help her lose one or two pounds a week over a long period of time. Persons who are at or below "ideal" weight (see page 36) are those at lowest risk of heart disease.

Among the other significant risk factors for cardiovascular disease are cigarette smoking and lack of exercise. For a view of how these and other life-style factors play into heart disease, take the Coronary Risk Test on pages 130–131.

Maintenance: The Heart

To avoid heart disease, a woman should eat right and exercise throughout her lifetime. And, perhaps most important, she should stay away from cigarettes. Smoking has been called the single most significant risk factor for heart disease. Cigarette smoke damages the blood vessel walls, making them prime targets for the buildup of atheromas. In addition, smoking makes the heart beat faster, reducing its supply of oxygen and putting an extra strain on it. A woman who is at risk of heart disease for any other reason should eliminate smoking entirely. A woman who is otherwise at low risk of heart disease but who continues to smoke should at least cut down.

As for eating and exercising, the American Heart Association advises all individuals (including children) to take the following precautions:

- Reduce the proportion of fat in the diet to 30 percent of total calories.
- Divide the types of fat consumed equally among saturated fat (10 percent of total calories), polyunsaturated fat (10 percent of total calories), and monounsaturated fat (10 percent of total calories).
- Limit cholesterol intake to 300 milligrams a day.
- Reduce salt intake to five grams (one teaspoon) a day.
- Reduce protein intake to 15 percent of total calories.
- Increase the intake of complex carbohydrates (fruits, grains, and vegetables) to 55 percent of total calories.

It is difficult to prove that exercise has a direct beneficial effect on the functioning of the heart. But there is no doubt that it at least has an indirect effect. Brisk aerobic exercise at least three times a week (see Keeping Aerobically Fit, pages 158–159) has been associated with an elevation of the level of HDL in the bloodstream. And exercisers find it easier than nonexercisers to keep their weight down.

7

Breathing Easy

Little girls and teen-agers dash up and down the stairs dozens of times a day. With each passing decade, the flight of stairs seems a little steeper, a little more difficult. A woman might first notice that she is having trouble with the stairs when she is pregnant. She might even have to pause midway to catch her breath. Such breathlessness is easy to shrug off as harmless. After all, it just reflects the fact that the growing uterus is rearranging the lungs; it will pass.

By the time a woman is in her 40s, though, a different sort of breathlessness might show up—difficulty in speaking, for instance, after racing upstairs to pick up an extension phone, or trouble catching her breath after running a block for the bus. "Age has finally caught up with me," the woman might think—but she'd be wrong. Aging per se does not account for this breathlessness. Lack of conditioning does. A woman who jogs, swims, or walks regularly—and who does not smoke —has enough respiratory reserve to breathe easy her whole life.

The respiratory system is one of the most resistant to changes over time. Respiration is the process by which oxygen, needed to nourish all the cells of the body, is exchanged with carbon dioxide, the by-product of oxygen metabolism. Oxygen is consumed from the air when we breathe in; by the time we breathe out, the breath is mostly carbon dioxide. This exchange occurs in the alveoli, the tiny air sacs clustered in the lungs with walls no thicker than those of a soap bubble. (The comparison is apt, because the alveoli stay pliable through the action of surfactant, a substance that works much like detergent does to keep the surface of the air sacs slippery and pliable.)

From the alveoli, of which there are some 300 million, oxygen seeps into nearby capillaries and from there enters the bloodstream for a journey through the body. When the blood returns to the lungs, it is full of carbon dioxide, which seeps back into the alveoli and passes out through the lungs to be exhaled—through the tiny bronchioles, or air passages, to the thicker bronchi, and finally through the two main bronchial tubes that carry the carbon dioxide to the windpipe and out the nose or mouth. As an individual continues to breathe, taking in air loaded with nourishing oxygen, the cycle is repeated, again and again, without interruption.

The healthy action of the respiratory system depends, first of all, on pliable bones and muscles around the lungs—the rib cage, which rises and falls with each breath; the diaphragm, a dome-shaped muscle beneath the lungs whose movement changes the pressure in the chest cavity and thus makes the lungs move; and the cilia, the tiny hairlike projections in the nose, windpipe, and bronchial tubes that sweep impurities out of the system. With age, each of these components becomes somewhat less flexible, and so the efficiency of respiration imperceptibly diminishes. The effect is usually a greater tendency toward breathlessness after physical exertion. But in a healthy individual, no matter what her age, this breathlessness can be minimized by slow and steady training through aerobic exercise.

Age Changes in Lung Capacity

One of the most consistent findings among gerontologists is that an individual's forced vital capacity (FVC) decreases with age. In fact, this finding is so universal that some experts have computed a formula through which FVC can determine a person's functional (as opposed to chronological) age, and maybe even his or her remaining life expectancy. The lower a person's FVC, the closer he or she is to death; this relationship is true for both sexes, although it seems to be more clearly the case for women.[1]

Forced vital capacity is the amount of air that can forcibly be expelled after a big inhalation. A woman can measure it by taking a deep breath and exhaling into a metered box; such an instrument is available for under $100 to clinics, doctor's offices, and even individuals. "This pulmonary function measurement," notes Dr. William Kannel, professor of medicine at Boston University, "seems truly a measure of living capacity."[2]

Kannel has been involved in the Framingham Study, a project that since 1948 has followed the health status of more than 5,000 residents of one Massachusetts town. And he found that FVC declines steadily in both sexes. Women in their 30s begin with an average FVC of about 30 deciliters, and this declines by about 3.1 deciliters every ten years. Between the ages of 45 and 74, a woman with a low vital capacity (12 to 35 deciliters) is four times more likely to die than a woman with a high vital capacity (44 to 85 deciliters).[3]

Why the relationship between FVC and mortality? Kannel and his colleagues can offer only theories. FVC seems to be "a measure of vigor," he says, because it is closely related to such performance results as hand-grip strength. And it seems to be "an indicator of biologic aging" as well, reflecting not simply lung compliance but compliance of the entire chest wall.

The close relationship between pulmonary function and other physical measurements, such as the flexibility of the chest wall, makes lung power an especially sensitive measure of an individual's overall well-being. But it also means results must be interpreted with caution. Over the years, for example, scientists have found that lung capacity declines with age. When a cross-section of individuals were examined, the older group traditionally would exhibit lower lung capacity than the younger group. But lung capacity—the maximum amount of air an individual can inhale—is closely linked to height. The taller a woman (or a man), the greater her lung capacity. And that is where the misinterpretations have arisen.

Older people, considered as a group, are almost always shorter than younger people. This is because of both a general increase in height from one generation to the next over the last half-century and an individual's own slight decline in height over the years. If height is removed from consideration, lung capacity seems to stay constant throughout life.[4]

Certain anatomical lung changes also have been shown to occur with age—but, as with so many observed age changes, no one can be sure whether the changes are inevitable with age or are simply the result of the sedentary life-style of most of today's older Americans. One common age-related change has been called ductectasia, a change in the tiny ducts of the alveoli (air sacs) within the lung. It is never seen before age 40, and its incidence increases with age so that it affects about 80 percent of 80-year-olds studied.[5] But tomorrow's generation of 80-year-olds, who might have been exercising vigorously for 60 years, might experience far less ductectasia.

Another lung disorder that becomes more common with age is interstitial fibrosis, a condition in which fibrous material accumulates in the lungs and thickens the walls of the alveoli. The fibrous tissue also obstructs the air passages, or bronchioles, to which the alveoli are attached. In its chronic form, interstitial fibrosis begins in middle age; its symptoms—which include shortness of breath, chest pain, and coughing that may bring up sputum stained with blood—develop slowly. An additional, unexplained symptom of the disease is clubbing of the fingers, in which the fingernails curve around the ends of the fingers and the fingertips become flattened like spatulas.[6]

But in some ways, the respiratory tract grows stronger with age. A lifetime of exposure to the viruses that cause the common cold (called rhinoviruses) builds up a woman's immunity so that, by mid-life, she is catching fewer and less severe colds each year.[7]

Lungs and Life-style

Smoking. There's no question about it, and no delicate way to put it: If you smoke, your lungs will go to hell. A wide range of conditions affects smokers' lungs, including emphysema, frequent respiratory infections, chronic lung disease (which in turn increases the risk of pneumonia and heart failure), chronic bronchitis, and lung cancer.

The increase in lung cancer deaths in recent years is quite alarming, especially for women. It reflects the trend among many Americans—white women in particular—toward heavier cigarette smoking. Between 1950 and 1980, according to the National Cancer Institute, the death rate for lung cancer among white women increased by nearly 200 percent (compared to 188 percent for nonwhite women, 185 percent for nonwhite men, and 116 percent for white men[8]). The most recent figures of the American Cancer Society estimate that lung cancer is a more serious problem for women than ever before. In 1983, these figures show, 17 percent of all cancer deaths in women were from lung cancer, compared to 18 percent for breast cancer.[9]

The Surgeon General of the United States has estimated that, if present trends continue, by the mid-1980s lung cancer will outstrip breast cancer as the leading cause of cancer deaths in women. Smokers are also far more likely than nonsmokers to die of other cancers, including cancers of the throat and mouth, and of cardiovascular disease and other conditions. A woman smoker between the ages of 44 and 54 who has been smoking for 20 years has a death rate 78 percent higher than that of a nonsmoking woman of the same age.[10]

As women enter the work force and engage in stressful life-styles more similar to men's, they find that behaviors such as smoking in public are more widely condoned. So, convinced that they have indeed come a long way, young, ambitious women today are more likely to smoke in numbers resembling the incidence of smoking in men of a generation ago. According to data collected by the National Center for Health Statistics, the woman most likely to smoke today is young, educated, and career-oriented. If she hasn't begun smoking by age 20, she is unlikely to. But there are exceptions, as the table on page 155 shows. Women with high-status *and low-status* jobs are the ones most likely to smoke,

Which Women Smoke?

The Public Health Service Office of Smoking and Health has compiled a profile of the woman most likely to smoke, based on her employment and age. The findings are as follows:

BY EMPLOYMENT*

You have a 50 percent chance of smoking if you are employed as a
> Buyer
> Clerk
> Waitress

You have a 40 to 45 percent chance of smoking if you are employed as a
> Foreman
> Hairdresser
> Manager
> Real Estate Agent

You have a 40 percent chance of smoking if you are employed as a
> Bookkeeper
> Editor
> Nurse

You have a 20 percent chance of smoking if you are employed as a
> Librarian
> Schoolteacher

BY AGE**

You have the highest chance of smoking if you are in your mid 20s.

Age range	Percent of smokers
20–24	36.1
25–34	31.6
35–44	34.9
45–64	30.8
65 or over	16.8

* Source: National Center for Health Statistics.
** Source: National Center for Health Statistics, *Health, United States, 1983* (Washington, D.C.: U.S. Department of Health and Human Services).

probably because employment at either end of the scale makes for a high degree of stress.

There are some signs that this trend might be reversing. Teen-age girls showed a worrisome increase in smoking rates in the late 1970s, but this increase seems to have abated. Women aged 20 to 65 have actually decreased their incidence of smoking, from about 40 percent in 1965 to 33 percent in 1983.[11]

Women smokers do damage not only to their own bodies but to those of their children. A pregnant woman who smokes even half a pack a day is twice as likely as a nonsmoker to have a miscarriage, twice as likely to have a baby who is small for gestational age, and 30 percent more likely to have a baby who dies in the first month after birth.[12] This is because the cigarette smoke decreases the level of hemoglobin in the mother's bloodstream, making it harder for her to carry needed oxygen to her fetus via the placenta. The smoke also indirectly constricts the arteries leading to the placenta, so this essential fetal organ is undernourished and the baby, in turn, is undernourished too.

The damage can continue even after the baby is born. Parents who smoke near their children are likely to affect them through "passive smoking," causing eye and throat irritation and a greater susceptibility to respiratory infections. Children born to smoking mothers tend to grow up shorter than average, and are more likely to lag behind their peers on reading scores.[13] And the presence of at least one smoker in the household has been linked to one of the most terrifying childhood conditions of all, sudden infant death syndrome (SIDS). One study found that 60 percent of women whose babies died of SIDS smoked during pregnancy or after the baby's birth.[14]

How does cigarette smoke do its dirty work? It acts in the lungs very much the way it acts in the air, as an irritant that the body tries to combat. When smoke gets in your eyes, your eyes start to water and turn red; your nose and throat start clogging with mucus in an effort to soothe away the noxious fumes. When a smoker inhales, the same thing happens in the lungs. The lungs are usually kept clean by the sweeping action of the cilia that line the respiratory passages; cigarette smoke, especially from menthol cigarettes, paralyzes the delicate cilia. As the cilia are impaired, the lungs secrete more mucus, which coats the cilia and further inhibits them. The more mucus that is secreted, the more the self-cleaning mechanism is clogged up. So the debris collects inside the lungs, damaging the alveoli and the bronchial passages and setting them up for infections and, eventually, cancer.

Lung damage from smoking, while dramatic, is *not* irreversible. As soon as a person stops smoking, the lungs begin to improve. Within five years of quitting, the chances of death from a smoking-related disease are halved; after 15 years, the ex-smoker runs the same mortality risk as someone who never smoked. This is true no matter how much, or for how long, the person smoked. So it is never too late to stop. For a few hints about some time-honored ways to stop smoking, see page 161.

Exercise. Aerobic exercise—sustained exercise that uses oxygen metabolism as the source of energy for the muscles—builds and helps maintain lung capacity. The best such exercise for increasing lung power is jogging, but for many mid-life women jogging seems too alien, or too risky, to be of much use. Indeed, women with porous bones might experience problems with shin splints, heel spurs, and jogger's knee if they take up running too late in life. Fortunately, other aerobic exercises work well, too, in building up not only the heart but the lungs: walking, swimming, aerobic dancing, square dancing, bicycling, skating, tennis, cross-country skiing. With an ongoing program of sustained, heart-pounding exercise three times a week, a woman of any age is likely to find that her maximal oxygen uptake has increased. Maximal oxygen uptake—or VO_2 max, for short—is the greatest amount of oxygen a body can take in during vigorous exercise. Ordinarily, VO_2 max decreases by about 33 percent between the ages of 20 and 60.[15] But this is not inevitable. A woman who exercises vigorously throughout life could experience a decline in maximal oxygen uptake as slight as 3 percent during those same 40 years. One study found that women between the ages of 52 and 79 were actually able to *increase* their VO_2 max by 21 percent after just three months in training.[16]

What is the effect of a reduction in maximal oxygen uptake? It means that you may lose your breath sooner when engaged in heavy aerobic exercise. It means you may begin breathing hard at the top of a flight of stairs. It means you may slow down some in your day-to-day physical activities. But it does not mean you stop living a generally healthy life.

Where You Live, Where You Work

Studies are now showing that one year of living in the city is the equivalent, in terms of lung damage, to smoking 20 cigarettes a day for a year.[17] After a lifetime of breathing filthy air, city dwellers begin to feel the toll. According to the American Lung Association, "air pollution can make cardiovascular and respiratory illnesses worse, forces the heart and lungs to work harder, reduces the lungs' ability to exhale air, damages cells in the airways of the respiratory system, and may contribute to the development of such diseases as bronchitis, emphysema, and cancer."

But just as middle-aged lungs begin to benefit from a stop-smoking effort *no matter when in life it is begun,* it's also never too late to move to a location where the air is fit to breathe. This is an option unavailable for most Americans, especially those whose roots are dug deep over 30 or 40 years in one spot, but it is an option worth considering for a person

Keeping Aerobically Fit

Aerobic exercise strengthens the heart, lungs, and blood vessels so that the cardiovascular system is better able to consume oxygen and transport it to the muscles and organs of the body. To be aerobic, exercise must be sustained for a minimum of 20 minutes, from three to five times a week, at your target pulse rate. Aside from increasing heart and lung capacity, regular aerobic conditioning builds healthier bones, reduces stress, prevents heart disease, and provides an effective means of weight control. Overall, it makes the body a more productive and efficient performer.

Which activities qualify as aerobic? Running, jogging, brisk walking and hiking, swimming, cycling, cross-country skiing, rowing, rope-jumping, and aerobic dancing, to name some of the most popular ones. The benefits vary according to the intensity and duration of the exercise. Running six miles in 48 minutes yields far better results aerobically than running four miles in the same time period. Of the racquet sports, none of which provides continuous aerobic effects, squash and racquetball rate higher than tennis, according to Dr. Kenneth H. Cooper, founder of the Aerobics Center in Dallas. The important thing to remember in developing your aerobics program is to give yourself plenty of options. Combining different forms of aerobic exercise can make the conditioning process not only more interesting but better for you.

For those who like lively music and exercising with others, aerobic classes are fun and work the heart, lungs, and all the major muscle groups. A good class consists of a thorough warm-up, 20 to 25 minutes of aerobic movement, followed by calisthenics and a brief cool-down. If possible, sign up for a trial class before you commit to a series, and ask yourself the following questions:

- What is the dance surface made of? A suspended wood floor is ideal. If the surface is linoleum or carpet over concrete, make sure your shoes are well-cushioned. Running shoes, aerobic shoes, or thick-soled court shoes are the recommended footwear.

- Does the teacher give instructions and precautions about how to land when you jog in place (the foot rolls from the ball of the foot to the mid-foot to the heel), how to breathe, how to maintain body alignment?

- Are you encouraged to work at your own speed, even walk through segments if necessary?

If these requirements are met, aerobics can be safe and invigorating.

For an aerobics program you can perform at home, see *Esquire Ultimate Fitness* (book and videocassette). Write Esquire Ultimate Fitness, 2 Park Avenue, New York, N.Y. 10016 for further information.

who is having respiratory trouble. The least one can do is not to multiply the risks: If you must live in a polluted area, you can try to stay away from a polluted workplace. And if you smoke, you can stop.

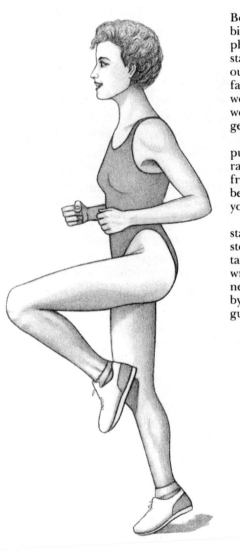

HOW TO FIND YOUR TARGET PULSE RATE

Before you begin a program of aerobics or aerobic sports, get a complete physical exam and stress test. Then start slowly. It's not necessary to work out more than five times per week—in fact, it may be harmful for some women—but you should aim for three weekly sessions performed at your target pulse rate, for at least 20 minutes.

Here's how to determine your target pulse rate: Find your maximum heart rate by subtracting your age in years from 220. Your training range will be between 60 percent and 80 percent of your maximum.

You can check to see that you are staying within your training range by stopping your exercise occasionally to take your pulse. Count the pulse at the wrist or at the carotid artery in your neck for 15 seconds, and then multiply by four. Take note of these further guidelines:

- If you are over 50, or are in poor condition and just beginning an exercise program, take 60 percent of your maximum heart rate to find your target pulse.

- If you are under 50, or are in excellent condition, take 80 percent.

- The average healthy 40-year-old woman has a maximum heart rate of 180 beats per minute (220 minus 40) and a target pulse rate of 144 beats per minute (80 percent of 180). If she is in poor physical condition, her target pulse rate would be 108 (60 percent of 180).

Place of residence has a great deal of influence on one's susceptibility to certain lung conditions as well. Cold, damp weather can lead to repeated bouts of acute bronchitis in persons prone to this condition, and sometimes the only solution is to move to a warmer, dryer climate. The same can be said for allergies, hay fever, and asthma: Warm, dry air seems best for these conditions, and locations where the air is dirty, humid, or full of pollen only makes matters worse. That is why Arizona has the highest percentage of asthmatics and allergy sufferers of any state in the nation; they all move there for the air.

Occupation also has an effect on lung function later in life. Factory workers exposed to aluminum, cotton, synthetic fibers, sugar cane, or talc may, after ten years or so, develop pneumoconiosis (literally, dust in the lungs), in which dust-scarred lungs become less flexible and porous and more susceptible to phlegm-producing coughs and to breathlessness on exertion. Workers substantially increase their risk of developing pneumoconiosis if they also smoke. But even nonsmokers run a risk of developing lung disease, and they should agitate for protective clothing and dust-free environment as the way to minimize the hazards of these potentially dangerous jobs.

Emphysema, a lung condition most commonly caused by smoking, can also be traced to certain occupations. In emphysema, the alveoli at the ends of the bronchioles in the lungs become stretched or ruptured, making the lungs less elastic and interfering with the exchange of oxygen and carbon dioxide that is the goal of respiration. Years of excessive pressure is what damages the alveoli, pressure such as that caused by chronic bronchitis, asthma, or two specialized professions: glass-blowing and playing a wind instrument. Although men are currently at higher risk for emphysema, women may catch up in the future, as they have begun smoking in greater numbers.

Repairing Damaged Lungs

The single most significant thing a woman can do to keep her lungs healthy is to stop smoking. Although smoking does great damage to the lungs, there is one saving grace: The damage can be undone.

Women are likely to resist quitting smoking for one reason: They say it will make them gain weight. In a way, they are right. One study of 57,000 women who quit smoking found that those who had been smoking half a pack a day gained up to five pounds after quitting, and those who had been smoking two packs a day gained up to 30 pounds. But, as some experts have pointed out, it would take a gain of 50 to 75 pounds to create health hazards comparable to the health hazards of smoking just one pack of cigarettes a day.

How to Quit

The bad news about smoking has had a positive effect on smokers. According to the American Lung Association, nine out of ten smokers want to quit. Thirty-three million Americans already have, most of them *not* on their first try. If you have tried to quit unsuccessfully, consider yourself in a stage of quitting and try another method with new courage. Here are recommended programs for those who want help:

- The American Lung Association offers self-help manuals called "Freedom from Smoking in 20 Days," and, for after you've quit, "A Lifetime of Freedom from Smoking." The first manual encourages smokers to learn their smoking patterns and then break them—by switching brands often, by depositing and saving butts in a glass jar, by waiting several minutes before lighting up when the urge to smoke hits—and gradually to eliminate cigarettes altogether. There is a $5 donation for the manuals. For information call your local chapter of the American Lung Association.

- The American Cancer Society sponsors "Quit Clinics" through a national program called Fresh Start. The clinic organizes small groups of smokers who meet once a week for several weeks for support while they learn to cut back gradually. Many of the clinics are free; some require a small donation to the American Cancer Society. If you prefer to quit on your own, the Society will send their pamphlet called "The Quitter's Guide." Call your local Cancer Society for more information.

- The SmokEnders program has helped 300,000 people quit smoking since 1969. Its founder, ex-smoker Jacquelyn Rogers, has devised an eight-week program of weekly meetings. During the first five weeks, participants are allowed, even encouraged, to smoke as much as they wish. After the fifth meeting, they can smoke one last cigarette before bed and, according to one instructor, "The next morning they are free." The final three meetings are to reinforce the new, learned, nonsmoking behavior. Participants sign a form at the outset of the course asking them not to reveal the method. The cost of the course is high, approximately $300, with discounts offered if you join with a friend. For more information call toll-free 1-800-243-5614.

All of these programs encourage companies to establish clinics at the workplace for employees who smoke. The employer's incentive is to improve the health (and thus the rate of absenteeism) of its work force, and protect the rights of nonsmokers. The workplace is an excellent place to quit: Smokers are with their fellow quitters all week for 40 hours of constant support and mutual surveillance. And employers sometimes sweeten the deal by offering extra vacation days or other rewards to smokers who quit successfully.

Most physicians advise against dieting during the first four weeks of a stop-smoking regimen. They say this is the time when withdrawal is most difficult, and any crutch a woman can find to get her through it is acceptable. Find the reason why you smoke—as a prop? as a habit? as a way to keep your mouth and fingers occupied?—and try to replace it with something less hazardous to your health. If food or chewing gum or biting your nails is the replacement, that's okay for a while.

Within two months of going cold turkey, the gnawing hunger for nicotine will have abated, and if you've gained the average five to 15 pounds, you can begin dieting now.

If you need a little financial incentive to get motivated to quit, try this: An economic policy analyst recently reported that women between the ages of 40 and 44 could save from $3,000 to $13,600 in medical costs and lost wages by quitting today. This same economist computed that each pack of cigarettes smoked costs about $3 in "hidden costs" likely to occur over a lifetime as a result of a smoker's increased risk of lung cancer, heart disease, and emphysema.

Another way of keeping the lungs soft and supple for a life-time is through exercise. But the exercise must be done in the right place, and at the right time. Some scientists have suggested recently that vigorous exercise in a polluted environment may actually be doing more harm than good. Air pollution not only makes exercising more difficult— causing a drop in performance and creating symptoms such as head-ache, chest pains, fatigue, and nausea—but it can do at least temporary damage to the lungs. During vigorous exercise, an individual breathes through the mouth, bypassing the scrubbing action of the nose passages and breathing in large volumes of dirty air deep into the lungs. Jogging in an urban area for 30 minutes is said to be the same as smoking a pack of cigarettes.[18]

According to Ronald White of the American Lung Association, city streets are probably the worst place for a person to jog. Because of the stop-and-go traffic pattern, with cars, trucks, and buses belching out pollutants at every red light, the pollution level is even worse than alongside a highway. The ALA recommends that joggers stay away from heavy traffic altogether and exercise in early morning or late eve-ning when the air is cleanest. Just by being aware of the possible risks, a woman can avoid lung damage but continue to walk, jog, or run her way to maintaining well-toned lungs.

Maintenance: The Respiratory System

The respiratory system is resilient: The lungs can repair themselves, as long as the damage done to them is not ongoing. That means if you smoke, stop. Here are just a few of the reasons to quit:

- Smoking is the single largest preventable cause of death in the United States.
- Every year 340,000 Americans die prematurely from diseases caused by cigarette smoking.
- The Surgeon General has estimated that, if the present trends continue, lung cancer will soon outstrip breast cancer as the leading cause of cancer deaths in women.
- A pregnant women who smokes even half a pack a day is twice as likely to miscarry as a nonsmoker. The mother who smokes risks causing eye and throat irritation and a greater susceptibility to respiratory infections in her children.

On the positive side, stopping the habit at any age can dramatically reduce the risk of contracting heart disease, lung cancer, or emphysema.

- Damaged cilia within the lungs will regrow in about six months after all smoking has stopped. Studies have shown improvement in pulmonary function as early as three weeks after the last cigarette has been smoked.
- The physiological benefits are many. No longer will nicotine cause your heart to beat faster and your blood pressure to rise; no longer will it affect your automatic nervous system in other dangerous ways.
- No longer will you have to deal with a fuzzy mouth, lowered taste sensations, and yellow stains on your teeth.
- No longer will you suffer as many coughs and colds, or be as likely to get laryngitis and sinusitis.

Some people are able to stop smoking on their own; others need group support. Some effective methods of quitting are listed on page 161.

Deep breathing can help both ex-smokers and nonsmokers relieve tension and maintain healthy lungs throughout life. The American Lung Association recommends the following method of deep-breathing whenever stress seems to be getting the best of you:

1. Lie flat on your back with your mouth closed, hands folded on your stomach, and your knees flexed. Let your shoulders relax and inhale as deeply as you can—to the count of eight. Push your stomach out as you inhale.
2. Hold your breath to the count of four.
3. Exhale slowly to the count of eight.
4. Repeat this inhale-hold-exhale cycle five times.

And aerobic exercise, which is essential for cardiovascular fitness, is also an excellent way to build and maintain lung capacity. Choose a sport or sports that you enjoy, that are convenient for you to do regularly, and that have the approval of your doctor. See Keeping Aerobically Fit, pages 158–159.

8

You Are What You Eat

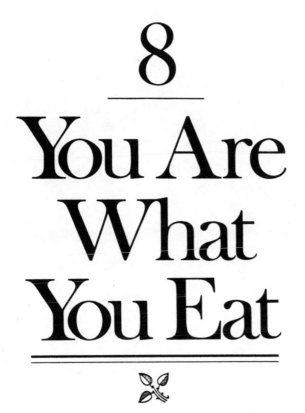

"The nutritional sins of youth and middle age are paid for in old age," says Carlton Fredericks, popular author and radio personality. So it behooves a woman in her 20s or 30s to establish eating patterns today that will carry her healthily into her middle years and beyond. Habits engraved now will be hard to break in another 30 years; why not just start off with the habits that need never be broken?

But the problem is that even the experts disagree on just what is the healthiest way to eat. A consensus is slowly emerging from mainstream nutritionists that certain foods should probably be avoided to increase an individual's chances for a long and healthy life. But few agree on just which foods should be avoided—and which foods should be eaten regularly. Just when the scientists seem to agree, a new study makes it appear not only that they were wrong but that the exact opposite is true.

Nutrition scientists don't mean to be argumentative, and they don't mean to leave the public in such confusion. But nutrition is an inexact science, and for every study that says a particular nutrient is good for you in one way, it seems another study discovers that that same nutrient is bad for you in another way. Polyunsaturated fat (found in margarine, fish, and safflower and corn oil), for instance, is associated with a decrease in risk of heart disease—and an increase in risk of certain cancers. What is a person to do?

The answer: Be moderate. Fad diets and nutrients-of-the-month can prove to be hazardous in surprising ways, but moderation is almost always risk-free. Nutritionists who have followed the eating habits of long-lived groups of people concur that the best way of eating is the most traditional way:

- Eat breakfast every day.
- Eat a variety of foods.
- Eat foods in their most natural, least refined state.
- Maintain your ideal weight.
- Avoid excess fat (especially saturated animal fat) and cholesterol.
- Avoid excess salt and sugar.
- Eat foods with starch (complex carbohydrates) and fiber.
- Drink only moderate amounts of alcohol.
- Drink six to eight glasses of water a day.

The benefits of healthy eating go beyond weight control. A woman whose diet is full of the foods she needs will look and feel better her whole life long. Think of a woman of 40, 50, or 60 who looks terrific—fresh skin, clear eyes, shining hair, a zip to her step. Chances are she eats the kind of diet we all should eat, with lots of fruits and vegetables and very few processed foods, sugar, or salt.

Bookshelves are crammed with testimonials of women who gained new beauty and energy just from eating the right foods. These claims must be viewed with some skepticism, considering the commercial incentive behind them, but they do carry in them a grain of truth. We are what we eat. A woman can indeed become more attractive, and can feel more energetic—no matter what her age—if she turns her diet in the right direction.

The rules of healthy eating become more and more important as a woman ages. Eating a daily breakfast and not eating between meals are two of the seven health habits found in one classic study to characterize a group of long-lived Californians (the other habits are getting seven or eight hours of sleep a night, never smoking cigarettes, moderate or no use of alcohol, maintaining an ideal body weight, and exercising regularly [1]). In mid-life, breakfast is essential to preventing a mid-morning drop in blood sugar that can send a woman into binge eating, mental confusion, or heart palpitations.

Similarly, excess fat is especially dangerous for women approaching mid-life because it is associated with some of the cancers for which women in this age group are at highest risk, particularly breast cancer and uterine cancer. Too much salt can elevate hypertension, which tends to increase with age in this country, and too little water can exacerbate constipation, which also becomes more common with age because of the loss of tone in the digestive system.

Digestive Changes with Age

Digestion is the process of breaking down food—mechanically and chemically—and converting it into forms readily absorbed by the body. Metabolism is the process by which these new, readily absorbed forms of foodstuff are utilized. Both the digestive and the metabolic systems undergo relatively few changes over time, but some changes do indeed occur. These changes, which are examined below, can alter the way a woman utilizes her food over the course of a lifetime.

Reduced motility. Intestinal motility refers to the ability of the digestive

The Human Digestive Plant

The reason man can consume a bewildering array of foods is that our bodies possess complex processing plants that can take everything from soup to nuts and break it down into absorbable products. With age, however, the processing plant slows down and careful attention to diet becomes even more essential.

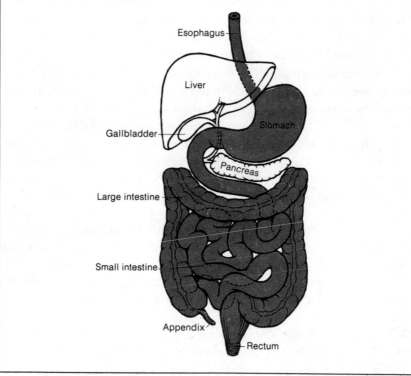

tract to move foodstuffs along through contraction of the intestinal wall. This action, called peristalsis, depends on firm, well-toned intestinal muscles. And as a woman ages, the muscle tone in her gut, like the muscle tone elsewhere in her body, tends to slacken. This increases intestinal "transit time"—the time it takes for a meal to be thoroughly digested and to pass from the body as feces—and makes it more likely for the woman to suffer cramps, bloating, gas, constipation, diverticulosis, and maybe even colon cancer.[2]

But she can make an effort, beginning early in life, to prevent this reduction of motility. The most effective way is by eating a high-fiber diet. This decreases the time it takes for food to pass through the intestine, and gives the intestinal wall an opportunity to expand and contract regularly—the only way to keep those muscles in shape.

Less hydrochloric acid secretion. Because the stomach secretes less acid over the years, some foods that are initially digested by stomach acid, such as red meats and some vegetables, can become increasingly more difficult to digest. In addition, dietary iron from sources like meat is less likely to be converted into a form of iron made "bioavailable"—that is, in a form the body can easily absorb.[3] (Significantly, though, a woman's iron requirements decline after menopause, so it should be a relatively easy matter to balance out.) Decreased hydrochloric acid secretion has a positive aspect, too. It makes heartburn less likely, and reduces the need for over-the-counter antacids as a woman ages. Many of these antacids can leach calcium from the bones, making them especially dangerous for women—who are at high risk of osteoporosis—to use too casually.

Less intrinsic factor secretion. Intrinsic factor is a protein the stomach manufactures to allow vitamin B_{12} to be absorbed. With less intrinsic factor made in late life, it becomes more important for a woman to have a sufficient intake of vitamin B_{12}, since proportionally less of the B_{12} ingested will actually be utilized by the body.[4] Good sources of vitamin B_{12} include meat (especially liver and kidneys), fish, eggs, milk, and oysters. Vitamin B_{12} is involved in the formation of red blood cells and the functioning of the nervous system, and has been offered—with little evidence supporting its effectiveness—as a remedy for excessive fatigue as well.

Fewer digestive enzymes. As a woman ages, many digestive enzymes ordinarily secreted by the pancreas and intestine become less readily available. This means that a mid-life woman might have more trouble utilizing protein, milk products, and fats than she did in youth. It may become difficult for a woman to pack all her nutritional needs into her daily caloric intake—which should be significantly lower than it was a few decades earlier. The decrease in digestive enzymes contributes to the significant malnutrition observed among older women, especially those who live alone. Some nutritionists, attuned to this problem, urge older people to take papaya or pineapple (bromelin) enzymes to assist in the digestion of protein, and pancreatic tissue supplements to provide enzymes that help digest fats, proteins, and carbohydrates.[5]

More trouble with solid foods. An estimated 20 percent of baby food sold in the United States is consumed by the elderly.[6] The less solid food a woman can eat—because of problems with teeth, dentures, swallowing, or heartburn—the less likely she is to consume a nutritionally adequate diet. A woman who can't eat fresh crisp foods is likely to turn to over-processed, overrefined, oversugared foods at mealtime, and she will miss out on the minerals and vitamins contained in "real" food. Blenders and food processors can go a long way in turning this problem around. Recent studies have shown that the fiber content of a fresh fruit or vegetable is virtually the same whether the food is raw or cooked, solid or mashed.[7]

Women's Digestive Complaints

Because of these changes in the digestive system, the older woman is more likely to suffer from one or another of the common digestive complaints. Most of these conditions are relatively innocuous—indeed, many tend to cause no symptoms at all—and they usually can be corrected with improvements in the diet. Still, there are also some serious problems that can create disruption in the digestive system. Any change in bladder or bowel habits, or any unexplained loss of appetite or loss of weight, should therefore be reported to the doctor.

A Healthful Menu Pattern

Author Jane Brody, in her best-seller, *Jane Brody's Nutrition Book,* lists the "menu pattern" developed by the New York City Department of Health and accepted by the U.S. Department of Agriculture in 1980. By adhering to this pattern, a woman would derive about 15 percent of her daily calories from protein, 55 percent from carbohydrates, and 30 percent from fats. With one typical serving from each menu group for each meal, the plan as follows will provide about 2,000 calories a day. The calorie content can be reduced by cutting down portions or cutting out desserts.

Breakfast	*Lunch*	*Dinner*
Fruit	Fruit	Protein food
Egg or substitute	Protein food	Potato or substitute
Cereal or grain	Bread	Two vegetables
Low-fat milk	Salad with dressing	Bread
Coffee or tea	Low-fat dessert	Fruit
	Low-fat beverage	Low-fat milk

Snacks	*Miscellaneous*
Two Fruits	Vegetable oil, 2 Tbsp.
	Margarine, 1 pat
	Refined sugars, jellies, syrups, 1½ Tbsp.

Diverticulosis and diverticulitis. Diverticulosis is an anatomical change in the digestive tract that affects one-third of persons over age 45 and two-thirds of those over age 60. Women are more prone to it than men.[8] But as with so many other problems of the digestive tract, diverticulosis causes no problems in the great majority of people who have it. It is only when the anatomical oddity becomes infected and inflamed that the trouble starts.

Diverticulosis arises when small pouches, or diverticula, form in the lining of the large intestine. They are thought to result from lack of fiber in the diet. If these diverticula remain small, they have no effect on the workings of the colon. When symptoms do occur, they are relatively mild: gas, some stomach cramps, and constipation alternating with occasional diarrhea.

But when the pouches get infected, a painful condition called diverticulitis results. (The suffix "osis" means condition; the suffix "itis" means inflammation.) This occurs in about 15 percent of people with diverticulosis.[9] The pain, which begins in spasms and later becomes chronic, occurs in the lower left of the abdomen, and the painful region is tender to the touch. The pain can become disabling in a matter of hours.

Eating a high-fiber diet (see opposite page) and drinking six to eight glasses of water (in addition to other beverages) daily can soften the stool, which in turn can often prevent diverticulosis. So can avoidance of strong laxatives and enemas, and prevention of chronic constipation. These preventive measures often can keep an established case of diverticulosis from becoming worse. But once diverticulitis develops, a change of life-style is insufficient. Often, an acute flare-up requires immediate hospitalization, so the infection can be combatted with antibiotics, and the stomach can be emptied (often through a nasogastric tube) and given ample time to rest (through intravenous feedings for several days). Rarely, surgery is required to remove the diverticula or the affected region of the colon.

Gallstones. Irreverent medical students still learn that the typical gallbladder patient is characterized by "the four F's"—fat, fecund, forty, and female. While the mnemonic device might be offensive, it *is* accurate. For some unexplained reason, women are twice as prone to gallstones as are men. The highest-risk women are those who are overweight (one-third of whom can expect to develop gallstones), over 40, and the mothers of several children. Autopsy studies have found that 20 percent of all women have gallstones when they die, compared

How to Add Fiber to Your Diet

Nutrition scientists place great stock in fiber. They say that fiber—the undigestable cell wall of plants—can help prevent constipation, diverticulosis, varicose veins, and maybe even colon cancer. Fiber is plentiful in whole grains—whole wheat, whole oats, whole barley—and in all fruits and vegetables, especially in the skin. A woman should aim for 40 grams a day of dietary fiber.

Put bran in your breakfast. Unprocessed bran (preferably coarsely ground) is available in natural food stores and in some supermarkets. Add or subtract bran slowly; if you add too much you can suffer stomach cramps and flatulence, and if you withdraw it too quickly you can become constipated. Begin with one teaspoon of bran sprinkled on your breakfast cereal or yogurt; in a week, add another teaspoon, and so on until your bowel movement is effortless.

Eat carrots. From the point of view of digestive system health, carrots are the only vegetable that provide the benefits of bran, according to Carlton Fredericks. It doesn't matter whether the carrots are raw or cooked. They can easily be added, either shredded or finely chopped, to recipes for muffins, cookies, meat loaf, or hamburger.

to about 8 percent of men. While the cause of gallstones is still unknown, scientists have observed that they tend to occur most frequently in certain ethnic groups, such as American Indian women (70 percent of whom develop gallstones by age 30) and Swedish women (more than half of whom do). This clustering can be traced either to genetic or environmental predisposition. Other women at risk are those who are pregnant, those who are taking estrogen pills for birth control or ERT, and those who are suffering from chronic anemia.[10]

Gallstones are pebble-like accumulations of excess cholesterol from the bile. (Bile is the digestive enzyme manufactured in the liver and stored in the gallbladder that is used to emulsify fat.) The stones can rest unobtrusively in the gallbladder for many years. But the gallbladder is not a stagnant organ. Occasionally it releases bile for fat digestion, transporting the bile through the bile duct into the duodenum (the first 12 inches of the small intestine). If, during one of these journeys, some gallstones travel along with the bile, a stone can get stuck in the narrow bile duct, blocking further flow of bile and causing excruciating pain.

To control gallstones, a woman has one of several choices. She can prevent their development in the first place; she can take steps to reduce the likelihood that they will pass into the bile duct; she can try an experimental medication that seems to dissolve the stones; or she can undergo surgery to have the gallbladder itself removed. (Gallbladder removal has no effect on the functioning of the digestive system.) The best treatment, of course, is prevention.

Gallstones probably are caused by one's diet, but experts are unsure just what about the diet predisposes a person to developing them. Because bile in gallstone patients almost always contains excessive amounts of cholesterol, and the stones themselves are made out of cholesterol, some have theorized that too much cholesterol in the diet causes them. This is one more reason why a woman should reduce her dietary intake of cholesterol, beginning as early in life as possible.

Others have laid the blame for gallstones on a low-fiber diet. Because people on high-fiber diets tend to have lower levels of both fat and cholesterol in their system, some believe that too little fiber in the diet causes gallstones. This is one more reason why a woman should increase her dietary intake of fiber, also beginning early in life.

Once the gallstone condition is established, it seems to be exacerbated by a high intake of fat in the diet. Bile is mobilized to digest fat, and gallstones cause problems only when the bile is in motion. So, once again, we have one more reason to do what the "prudent" nutritionists have all been telling us, this time to reduce the intake of fat in the diet —once more beginning as early in life as possible.

Hiatal hernia and heartburn. According to Maureen Mylander, author of *The Great American Stomach Book,* about half of Americans over age 40 have hiatal hernia, especially if they are overweight or have borne a child.[11] But the great majority of these people never know it. Unless hiatal hernia causes heartburn, it is a benign condition that a woman can live with for half a lifetime.

The diaphragm separates the chest cavity from the stomach cavity, joining the two through a teardrop-shaped opening called the hiatus. The hiatus opens and closes through the action of a tiny valve at the bottom of the esophagus, the "food pipe" through which food descends into the stomach. With age, the muscles of the esophagus weaken, and it is common for the esophageal flap to lose its flexibility altogether. If it remains stuck in the "open" position, the hiatus in the diaphragm remains locked open, too. Through this opening the stomach can gradually push through, resulting in a hernia—that is, the eruption of one organ through an opening into the space of another organ.

Hiatal hernia can cause heartburn when acid from the stomach backs up into the esophagus. This condition, also called indigestion or acid reflux, can cause pain and burning in the chest and, rarely, in the neck and arms. Heartburn can occasionally be mistaken for the pain of a heart attack. Although hiatal hernia, and the heartburn it can cause, is not a dangerous condition, it can be quite annoying. The best treatment is to avoid the accumulation of excess acid in the stomach. Among the best methods for this:

- Avoid foods that cause acid secretion: alcohol, aspirin, chocolate, coffee, garlic, milk, onion, peppermint, and tea.
- Avoid highly spiced and fatty foods, which also can compound the problem.
- Maintain your ideal weight; obesity puts pressure on the stomach, making acid reflux more likely.
- Eat smaller meals.
- After eating, do not lie down, bend over, or exercise for at least two hours.
- Avoid tight clothes.
- Do not smoke; tobacco irritates the stomach.
- Raise the head of the bed about four inches higher than the foot, so that gravity helps to prevent the backup of stomach acid into the esophagus.
- Take antacids, but avoid those that contain aluminum. Aluminum has been associated with neurological conditions such as Alzheimer's disease (see Chapter 11), and tends to put women in neg-

---

Antacids—Which One for You?

Avoid antacids with aluminum	*Look for antacids without aluminum*
Amphojel	Alka-Seltzer
Delcid	Alka-2
Di-Gel	Bisodol
Gaviscon	Citrocarbonate
Gelusil	Eno
Maalox	Marblen
Mylanta	Percy Medicine
Riopan	Titralac
Rolaids	Tums
Simeco	

Source: *Stand Tall! The Informed Woman's Guide to Preventing Osteoporosis* by Morris Notelovitz, M.D., and Marsha Ware, pp. 107–108. Copyright © 1982 by Morris Notelovitz. By permission of Triad Publishing Company, Gainesville, Fla.

ative calcium balance, increasing their risk of osteoporosis (see Chapter 4). Instead, look for over-the-counter antacids that contain added calcium.

Lactose intolerance. The dairy industry likes to tell us that we never outgrow our need for milk, and in many ways that is true. Milk contains a high proportion of protein (in good balance with carbohydrates and fat, especially when taken as skim milk), vitamins A, B, and D, phosphorus, potassium, and, most important for women, calcium. One quart of milk a day will provide all the calcium a postmenopausal woman needs to keep her bones healthy. But while we might never outgrow our *need* for milk, a large percentage of us do outgrow our *stomach* for it.

Lactose intolerance, the inability to digest milk products, is a common condition that often develops in persons over 40; it affects about two-thirds of the adult population worldwide. Women are more susceptible than men, especially women from certain ethnic backgrounds—blacks, Orientals, and Eastern European Jews.[12] In this condition, the enzyme lactase, manufactured in the small intestine to digest lactose (milk sugar), is deficient. The result: Lactose passes undigested from the small to the large intestine, and in the large intestine it is attacked by bacteria never meant to be activated at all. These bacteria can create distressing symptoms, including cramps, diarrhea, and flatulence.

Lactose intolerance exists to varying degrees. Some people experience symptoms only when they ingest excessive amounts of milk, ice cream, or cheese; others have problems when they eat prepared foods that have even a trace of nonfat milk solids or whey in the ingredients. For those with mild lactose intolerance, some "predigested" forms of milk will be easier to stomach, including yogurt, buttermilk, sour cream, and aged cheeses. Sweet acidophilus milk, available in most supermarkets, is milk with lactase added; the lactase is destroyed, however, when the milk is heated. Another alternative is to add the lactase to the milk at home. One popular product for this purpose is called Lact-Aid.

Sometimes lactose intolerance is brought on by a case of the flu. Lactase can be destroyed in the intestine by a viral infection. After the stomach flu or a similar infection, a woman might find that she seems to suffer a relapse when she goes back to her normal diet. If this happens, she should try cutting out milk products for a longer time. Eventually, the lactase will return, although usually not in the same amount as existed previously, especially as the woman ages.

Women who do develop lactose intolerance must be especially attuned to including other sources of calcium in their diets—either as calcium supplements or from nondiary sources such as leafy greens, sardines (with bones), and canned salmon—to avoid the chances of developing osteoporosis.

Spastic colon. Spastic colon, or the "irritable bowel syndrome," has been called "the intestinal equivalent of weeping." [13] It is thought to be related to emotions, erupting most commonly in individuals who are under stress—and who tend to keep their anger, frustration, and resentment to themselves. According to Maureen Mylander, people with spastic colon have been described as "anxious, helpless, and unable to express their feelings" [14]; two-thirds of those with this condition are women. [15]

In irritable bowel syndrome, thought to account for one-half of all gastrointestinal upset, nothing is physically wrong with the digestive system. The symptoms, however, can be quite debilitating, including alternating attacks of diarrhea and constipation, gas pains, cramps, belching, heart palpitations, loss of appetite, and shortness of breath. Doctors told of these symptoms will probably order tests to rule out more serious conditions that could also be the cause, but if they find no abnormalities they can recommend only symptomatic relief:

- Avoid foods likely to irritate the stomach or to exacerbate diarrhea, such as coffee, alcohol, fried foods, or spicy foods.
- Stop smoking.
- Drink plenty of fluids.
- Eat lots of fiber.
- Get enough rest.
- Avoid stressful situations insofar as possible, and work on improving your response to stress.

Most doctors recommend avoiding over-the-counter drugs in treating a spastic colon. Many of these drugs are unnecessarily powerful, especially laxatives for constipation, and because they work directly on the action of the intestine, their overuse can lead to drug dependence.

Metabolic Changes with Age

The older a woman gets, the slower her metabolism becomes. This occurs largely because fat burns calories more slowly than muscle does and, as we have seen, her body contains proportionally more fat over time (see Chapter 2). A woman's caloric needs decline significantly with age, an estimated 2 percent to 8 percent for each decade past the age of 20. This is when exercise becomes especially important as a way to keep off excess pounds. But a woman of 50 who continues to eat as though she were 25—and who exercises even less—is likely to find it surprisingly easy to put on pounds, and surprisingly difficult to take them off.

Overweight. Many women in their 40s and 50s have spent years on the seesaw of weight gain, strict dieting, weight loss, binging, and weight gain again. Swings of 20, 30, even 40 pounds from one season to the next are common, as are closets crammed with two complete wardrobes, one in a woman's "fat size" and one in her "thin size."

According to Dr. Myron Winick, director of the Institute of Human Nutrition at Columbia University, such a woman is engaged in a lifelong struggle against her body's better instincts. She tends toward overweight not because she eats more than other women, but because her body is more efficient at utilizing the calories she does eat. Her body can run on fewer calories than she consumes, and it stores away the excess calories as fat. In times of famine, this is an excellent trick—it means her efficient body can operate on stored energy long after thinner bodies, with "higher metabolisms," have wasted away—but in modern America, where food is plentiful, it does nothing but sabotage a diet.

And eating less is not always the answer. This woman's body is so efficient that when she diets—which the body interprets as a period of food scarcity similar to famine—it simply lowers its metabolic rate, getting by on even *fewer* calories per day and storing the rest, once more, as fat. Despite her best efforts, a woman of this body type will watch in horror as, after a "successful" diet, her weight creeps back up to a level the body considers normal. This weight has been called the body's "set point."

Winick points to studies examining the food intake and activity levels of two groups of people of comparable weight—people who have always been thin and formerly obese people who recently reached their thin goals. "Of two persons who weigh 150 pounds and get the same food, perform the same activities and expend the same energy," he says, "the one who always weighed 150 pounds will remain at that weight while the one who reduced to 150 pounds will begin to gain weight. . . . This ability to gain weight on fewer calories may be the most important reason for obesity in many people."[16] As former President Jimmy Carter said, life is unfair.

One way a woman can beat this unfairness is through exercise. Even early in life, exercise makes the difference. Studies of young girls show that fat children eat the same amount as, or possibly even less than, lean children, but they just don't move around as much. At the pool, for example, chubby girls splash around in the water, and lean girls have swimming races.[17] This sedentary bent can carry over into adulthood, so whatever food a constitutionally heavy woman eats sits heavily on her body—while a constitutionally thin woman burns her food for energy. Exercise can actually lower an individual's set-point "ideal" weight, no matter when it is begun, as long as the exercise is vigorous, prolonged, and engaged in regularly (for at least half an hour at least three times a week).

Diabetes. Other metabolic changes occur with age, too. The body becomes progressively less able to metabolize the glucose (simple sugar) broken down from starches and sweets. This problem, found in the majority of persons after age 60, is exacerbated by obesity. If it progresses, it can turn into a condition known as maturity-onset diabetes.

The incidence of diabetes has long been thought to increase with age. For every 10,000 people in a particular age group, says the American Diabetes Association, there are ten diabetics between the ages of 20 and 40, 100 between the ages of 50 and 60, and 1,000 over the age of 60. Women are at highest risk (60 percent of adult diabetics are women), especially those over 40, those with a family history of diabetes, those who are Jewish or nonwhite, and those who live below the poverty level.[18]

But recently, scientists have reinterpreted the definition of diabetes for mid- and late-life adults. Traditionally, an abnormal result on a glucose tolerance test was the criterion for defining diabetes. (The test measures the body's ability to release insulin, which is needed to metabolize glucose.) These test results are consistently found to be more "abnormal" the older the patient population gets. For patients over 60, at least half have abnormal readings.

When it is shown that more than half of a given population have abnormal scores, experts begin to wonder whether the definition of "normal" is askew. Recently, the scientists studying diabetes reached a consensus: Measures of glucose metabolism must be adjusted to account for age. In one stroke, notes Dr. Reubin Andres, clinical director of the Gerontology Research Center of the National Institute on Aging, "literally millions of individuals have been removed from the diabetes category." With tongue in cheek, Andres calls this a remarkable "public health achievement."[19]

There remains a classification known as "chemical diabetes," applied to an individual who does not have the disease but who does fail the glucose tolerance test. This occurs almost exclusively in persons over age 60. All it means is that an individual should watch his or her intake of sugar, since the body is apparently sluggish about removing glucose from the bloodstream.

Changes in Nutritional Needs with Age

There's a Catch-22 in late-life nutrition that today's generation of young women will have to work hard to avoid: Nutritional needs change with age, but after a certain age it may be harder to eat the right foods. With heartburn, constipation, diarrhea, and gas more common among midlife women, the very foods most important for keeping healthy—raw fruits and vegetables, meats, salads, milk and dairy products—may be the foods that cause the most distress.

Eating right in early life can help make later life healthier. And younger women today are eating right—far more than their mothers did. If they continue their attention to the nutritional recommendations laid out by most experts today, they can expect to reap the benefits of their careful diets for many, many years.

A woman at 50 has different nutritional needs than she did at 30, because her body has changed. But at the same time that she needs lots of vitamins and minerals, she must restrict her overall caloric intake compared to the level she ate 20 years before. Therefore, her food must be "nutritionally dense"—that is, delivering a large proportion of vitamins and minerals per calorie. As a woman ages, she has less and less room in her diet for the "empty calories" of most popular prepared foods, especially sweets.

Some of the most important age-related changes in nutritional requirements are as follows:

- The older a woman gets, the fewer calories she needs.
- A woman past 45 needs less fat in her diet, to reduce her risk of cancer and heart disease and to help her keep her calorie count low.
- A woman past 45 needs more dietary fiber to prevent constipation, diverticulosis, and other gastrointestinal complaints that become more common with age.
- A woman past 45 needs more calcium to prevent osteoporosis. If she has developed lactose intolerance, she should take the calcium in the form of yogurt, nondairy sources, and dietary supplements.

- A woman past 50 needs less iron and folic acid, which had been necessary during the childbearing years to replace the blood components lost with menstruation.
- A woman past 55 needs more chromium (a trace mineral found in grains, meat, beans, and brewer's yeast) to aid in glucose metabolism.
- A woman past 55 needs more vitamin B_{12} (available in meat and dairy products, or in tablets to be dissolved under the tongue) because the reduction of gastric acid makes absorption of this vitamin less efficient.
- A woman taking large quantities of aspirin for the treatment of arthritis needs more iron in her diet.
- A woman taking diuretics for the treatment of hypertension needs more potassium in her diet.

Food and Life-span

For years, scientists have been trying to find a link between food and longevity. The matter is far from settled. Some animal studies imply that the surest way to a long life is to eat as little as possible, beginning in childhood; near-starvation diets in laboratory mice double their average life-spans. But some human studies reach the opposite conclusion: Being too lean, some scientists say, is dangerous to one's health, and persons who are on the portly side as they enter middle and old age might actually live longer than their thinner peers.

Despite the disagreement, though, two notes of concurrence can be found in researchers' recommendations for eating for longer life: reduction of calories and ingestion of plenty of "antioxidants." Antioxidants are food additives that interfere with the action of "free radicals," highly combustible molecule fragments thought to form abnormal, and potentially dangerous, large molecules that interfere with normal functioning. When antioxidants clear out these free radicals, the theory goes, the body can function more smoothly.

Many of the most vocal advocates of the long-life diet practice what they preach. As mentioned earlier, Dr. Roy Walford, a researcher at UCLA, is betting his own future on the value of "undernutrition." Walford himself eats remarkably little. As he describes it in his book *Maximum Life Span*, he eats 2,140 calories a day for five days each week, and then fasts completely (all he takes is water) for two days straight. He believes this regimen will help extend his life-span, as it extends that of laboratory mice, even those whose undernutrition was begun in middle age.[20] (Walford also takes approximately 20 vitamins, minerals, and other additives to act as "radical scavengers and antioxidants [like those] which have extended the life spans of rats, mice, or other animals."[21])

Durk Pearson and Sandy Shaw, authors of the best-selling tome *Life Extension,* are banking almost exclusively on antioxidants and other dietary supplements while they continue to eat "what we like, which includes meats, lots of whole milk and butter, eggs, plenty of fresh fruits and vegetables, daily high-fiber cereal, and even sweets."[22] They outline their daily ration of vitamins and minerals in their book, reaching a daily total of 27 pills, plus three more bedtime-only pills, plus a powder mixture of 19 vitamins, minerals, and additives to be taken four times daily each and every day. The lynchpins of their regimen: vitamins A, B-complex, C, and E; several amino acids (L-arginine, L-cysteine, tryptophan, and L-Dopa); and such antioxidants as dilauryl thiodipropionate, thiodipropionic acid, and BHT.[23]

Carlton Fredericks, the popular radio host and gadfly nutritionist, claims freedom from wrinkles and gray hair in his old age because of *his* recipe of vitamin supplements and antioxidants: vitamin C, vitamin E (taken in the "mixed tocopherols" form), selenium, sulfur-containing amino acids (supplied best in eggs and liver), superoxide dismutase (also recommended as a way to relieve arthritis pain), and lecithin (also recommended as a memory booster).[24]

No one knows whether such single-minded attention to caloric restriction and dietary supplements will pay off in terms of extended life-span —or even in terms of extended youth. Most mainstream scientists recommend only the "prudent diet" of the American Heart Association and National Academy of Sciences, a diet that cuts back on animal fat, sugar, salt, and cholesterol and that includes larger amounts of fruits, vegetables, fish, and grains. They leave the megadoses to the experimentalists.

But one thing is certain: For today's young woman, prudence is likely to pay off. Raised to consider salad, whole-wheat bread, and yogurt a perfectly respectable lunch—or supper—she will grow older with a dietary wisdom her mother never had. She almost certainly will use the nutritional knowledge of the 1980s to stay trim, youthful looking, and energetic far into the next century.

Maintenance: Nutrition

A woman's nutritional needs will vary over the years to accommodate changes in metabolism, digestive capacity, and overall health. Generally, though, eating sensibly and moderately—and starting these habits early— is the surest route to meeting nutritional needs in later life.

- Eat breakfast. In mid-life especially, breakfast is essential to preventing a mid-morning drop in blood sugar that can cause a feeling of weakness and fatigue, lightheadedness, or even heart palpitations.

- Eat a variety of foods. Concentrate on fruits, vegetables, grains and legumes, and calcium-rich foods.

- Avoid excess fat (especially saturated animal fat) and cholesterol-rich foods. Excess fat is especially dangerous for women approaching mid-life because it is associated with some of the cancers for which women in this age group are at highest risk, particularly breast cancer and uterine cancer.

- Limit your salt intake. Too much salt can elevate blood pressure, which tends to increase with age in this country.

- Follow a high-fiber diet. It's essential at any age, but a woman past 45 needs more dietary fiber to prevent constipation, diverticulosis, and other gastrointestinal complaints that become more common with age. See page 173 for ideas on how to add fiber to your diet.

- Drink six to eight glasses of water a day. Your system needs it to aid digestion, guard against constipation. Your skin may benefit also.

- Stay away from sugar. The calories are empty, and, after age 60, when diabetes becomes a substantial threat to women, the body becomes sluggish about metabolizing the simple sugar broken down from starches and sweets.

- In general, as a woman ages her caloric needs decline significantly— an estimated 2 percent to 8 percent for each decade past the age of 20. Eating less is only part of the weight-control answer. The best solution is exercise, preferably that which is vigorous, sustained, and habitual.

9
The
Sensuous
Woman

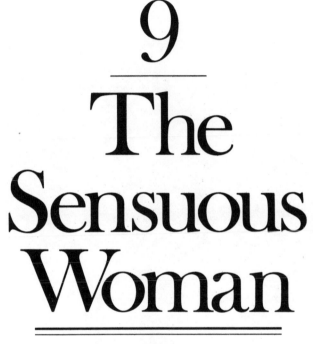

S everal years ago, a group of students at the University of Michigan were engaged in an experiment called "Pre-Experiencing Age." The students, all in their early 20s, wore eyeglasses that distorted their vision, earplugs that muffled their hearing, and special fingertip film that dulled their ability to feel. In short, they adopted the sensory impairments of old age.

Nothing about these students changed except that their senses no longer gave them reliable information about the world they lived in. And a remarkable thing happened. After just a short time of trying to negotiate their daily lives with these impairments, these young people began to act "old." They became crotchety, withdrawn, paranoid. One student grew so depressed that he had to drop out of the experiment.[1]

Old people, of course, cannot drop out. They cannot peel off the gloves and throw away the eyeglasses when sensory deprivation proves too stressful or depressing. They must learn to live in an environment that becomes slightly harder for them to perceive with each passing decade. Although sensory changes are not life-threatening or even truly debilitating, they can have a serious impact on the quality of life in middle and old age.

Like the changes that occur in most other organ systems with age, many of the sensory changes of age may be preventable. But preventing sensory changes often involves changing the environment—sometimes in ways that are nearly impossible. Excess noise, for instance—which has been linked to hearing loss—and excess ultraviolet radiation— which has been linked to cataracts—are virtually ubiquitous. The changes described here, then, will probably occur in most women as they age into the twenty-first century.

But these changes will not affect everyone equally. And here is where mental health comes most evidently into play. If a woman's personality is optimistic and resourceful, the gradual dulling of her senses will present little more than a few new inconveniences. But if she is prone to self-pity and feelings of powerlessness, these same changes can become major handicaps that shut her out of the commerce of the world.

Changed Hearing: Birds Don't Sing

The good news is this: A woman of 65 has only a one-in-four chance of experiencing a hearing loss. While hearing impairment becomes more likely with age, it is *not* inevitable. It can come on in subtle ways, however, and as a woman ages she should be alert to the telltale signs of hearing changes: leaning forward to hear better in a kind of aural "squint"; frequently asking people to repeat themselves; finding social situations, especially those involving large groups of people, more stressful than usual.

The incidence of hearing impairment increases from about 6 percent of the population between 45 and 64 to more than 20 percent of the population over 65.[2] The impairment can begin in a woman as young as age 50. Because it seems to be caused by age itself, this generalized dimming of hearing has been termed "presbycusis" (from the Greek words *presbys*, for elder, and *akousis*, for hearing). But some physicians find presbycusis a meaningless term, as vague and misleading as the term "senility" when applied to mental functioning. Hearing loss, they say, may be *associated* with age, but it is not *caused* by age. The vast majority of cases of hearing loss can be traced to a specific mechanical or neurological cause.

In about half the cases of hearing loss, the individual has a genetic disability that either has been progressing over a lifetime or was programmed to begin causing symptoms only late in life. In the remainder of cases, the problem usually can be traced either to the declining function of the nerves of the inner ear, to hardening of the bones of the middle ear, or to something as simple—and as treatable—as the excessive accumulation of wax.

Hearing begins to decline in a woman's mid-30s, but at first the change is almost imperceptible. By the age of 35, a woman has just slightly more trouble hearing high-frequency sounds, and she needs the sound to be about ten decibels—the level of a barely audible whisper—louder than she needed it to be when she was 25. By the time she is 50, she may have trouble distinguishing among certain consonants—particularly *s, z, t, f,* and *g*—which are high-frequency sounds; this means she might have difficulty in normal conversation.[3]

The location of the hearing problem determines the type of loss that occurs. Wax buildup, for example, leads to a reduction in the sound level that reaches the inner ear. This kind of sound loss, called conduction loss, also occurs in otosclerosis, a genetic condition more common

The Ear: A Built-in Amplification System

Sound waves enter the auricle of the outer ear, travel through the auditory canal to the eardrum and then on to the tiny bones of the middle ear—the hammer, anvil, and stirrup. In the inner ear, the vibrations stimulate minute sensory organs that send electrical impulses along the eighth cranial nerve to the brain. When presbycusis (age-related hearing loss) occurs, it is because these sensory organs, known as hair cells, have degenerated.

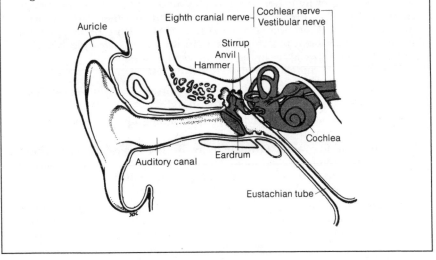

Eighth cranial nerve · Cochlear nerve · Vestibular nerve · Auricle · Stirrup · Anvil · Hammer · Cochlea · Auditory canal · Eardrum · Eustachian tube

in women than men. Both of these conditions are treatable. Wax buildup, which occurs more rapidly the older a woman gets, can be cleared with regular visits to the doctor, who washes the wax out with a warm water bath or, if it is badly impacted, with special tools.

In otosclerosis, the stapes, or "stirrup," becomes embedded in a growth of abnormal spongy bone. The stapes is one of the three bones in the middle ear (nicknamed the hammer, the anvil, and the stirrup because of their respective shapes) that vibrate in response to sound waves that enter from the outer ear and pass into the inner ear. The progress of the disease can only be stopped by an operation called a stapedectomy, which has a 90 percent success rate—and a 2 percent to 5 percent chance of failure and total deafness in the treated ear.[4] In the operation, the stapes is replaced by a tiny metal prosthesis.

If the impairment occurs further inside the ear passage, the sound

Checking Up on Your Ears

A hearing loss can come on quite suddenly as a result of a trauma: an accident, a disease, an explosion. However, most hearing losses, at least those associated with age, develop gradually and so subtly that the afflicted may be unaware of the problem. For that reason, it is important that a woman have her hearing checked regularly by a professional.

Routine checkups can be performed by an *audiologist,* a hearing specialist trained to measure and evaluate hearing abilities and advise on the choice of a hearing aid. Unless you suspect that you are developing hearing loss, a checkup is necessary only every few years. After age 55, however, a hearing examination every year is a good idea. If the audiologist detects a disease or problem that requires treatment other than a hearing aid, he or she will recommend an *otologist,* an M.D. who specializes in the ear, or if the problem involves more than the ear, an *otolaryngologist,* another M.D. who specializes in the ear, nose, and throat.

Here are some guidelines to detect hearing loss:

- Listen to yourself. Are you saying more often "Can you repeat that?" and "Could you please turn up the sound?"

- Are you sometimes startled by people coming up to you because you have not heard them approach?

- Often, the first sounds to fade away are not missed: a clock ticking, the air conditioner humming. The only way to realize the absence of these sounds is to test yourself. Concentrate on the background noises in your home and see if you can hear them clearly.

- Some mistakes that people attribute to forgetfulness may be caused instead by missed auditory cues. If you let the bathtub run over, or a teapot boil until the water is nearly gone, you may simply not have heard the running faucet or the teapot's whistle. If such "accidents" occur more frequently, consider loss of hearing as a cause.

- If you're increasingly puzzled by conversations in which you can't seem to grasp the ideas quickly, don't blame your mind. It could be that you're not hearing every syllable correctly and that your brain is dealing with incomplete messages.

Finally, tinnitus is a symptom of many hearing disorders that is often not subtle and can, in extreme cases, be intolerable. Tinnitus is the medical term for the condition of any ringing, whistling, or buzzing in the ear or head. If it comes about after exposure to a loud noise (like a jet taking off) and disappears quickly, it's not necessary to consult a professional. However, if tinnitus persists, it could be the symptom of a wide variety of disorders—for instance, earwax buildup, an ear infection, or deterioration of the cochlea in the inner ear. Because the cause of tinnitus can involve the nose and throat as well, it's best to see an otolaryngologist.

loss is different. Not only are decibels reduced, as they are in conduction loss, but the sound that does reach the auditory nerve is distorted and difficult to decipher. This hearing loss, called sensorineural loss, is usually caused by damage to the tiny hairlike projections, or cilia, that are found in the snail-shaped cochlea of the inner ear. The hairs, when intact, change the vibrations in the fluid into nerve impulses, ready to be carried along the auditory nerve into the brain.

Cilia can be damaged by medications (especially antibiotics), infections, and, most commonly, noise. Women once were relatively protected from this kind of hearing loss because their work environments were comparatively quiet. But this is less the case today. Modern homemakers are exposed to powerful, noisy equipment (vacuum cleaners, dishwashers, lawn mowers, food processors), and the noise reverberates in our energy-efficient, leakproof homes. Women in factories, especially textile workers, are exposed to noise that often exceeds the government's "possibly unsafe" level of 90 decibels. Women in offices, where the clatter of typewriters, computer printers, and copy machines is common, are also exposed to noise that can become overwhelming when everything is turned on at once. And some of the newest electronic gadgets now available may turn out to damage the delicate cilia of the inner ear, particularly cordless telephones (which can continue to emit a loud ring even after the phone is picked up) and lightweight portable cassette players with earphones.

Experts recommend wearing earplugs around any noisy equipment, and turning the volume down to its lowest setting when wearing stereo headphones. This is especially important because sensorineural hearing loss does not lend itself to improvement either by surgery or by the use of a hearing aid. Once that hearing is gone, it is gone for good.

Hearing aids, while they have improved remarkably in the past 15 years, are not the perfect solution. They are often unattractive (although new, smaller aids worn directly in the ear are being developed), and they increase the decibel level of all sound, even background sound, indiscriminately. A person with a hearing aid has a terrible time at cocktail parties, for instance, because it is difficult to ferret out one voice in a conversation from the amplified voices of everyone else in the room.

Difficulty in hearing does not elicit society's sympathy the way another disability might. Even supposedly sensitive people may forget to include the hard of hearing in ordinary conversation—by something as innocent as turning the other way while speaking. And because social intercourse is often central to a woman's sense of well-being, she may suffer the loss of hearing more acutely than a man. The less well a woman can hear, the more withdrawn, suspicious, and paranoid she is likely to become.

A woman who attempts to cover up a hearing loss may make matters worse. She may misinterpret people's meaning when she fills in for words unheard; she may become a less-than-welcome party guest as her voice rises and her conversation becomes studded with "I beg your pardon's" and "Will you repeat that's." The first step in overcoming a hearing difficulty is admitting that a problem exists and seeking out aids to combat it. And many aids exist—including telephone amplifiers, close-captioned television shows, and lip-reading training—to help a hard-of-hearing woman remain a lively, sociable human being.

Changed Sight: Blues Look Gray

One of the first signs of age a woman experiences is the need for reading glasses. Between the ages of about 35 and 40, she might notice that she is holding her reading matter farther and farther from her nose. A nearsighted woman who already wears glasses might find herself taking them off when she wants to focus on close work. Gradually, she will assume the reading position we remember kidding our mothers about —head tilted back and arms outstretched. The joke used to be that when a person's arms became too short to read comfortably, it was time to see an eye doctor.

When that comfortable focusing distance exceeds the length of one's arms, an individual is said to have presbyopia (from the Greek for "elderly vision"). The condition refers to the gradual inability of the lens to adjust for nearby focusing, and it results from a loss of elasticity in the lens and a loss of power in the muscles that help the lens change shape to focus. Presbyopia is one of the few age-associated changes that probably *is* an inevitable consequence of age; no one has yet suggested that a change in visual hygiene, or a switch to certain foods or exercises, can help prevent the eventual need for reading glasses.

Of all the changes with age that a woman will undergo, presbyopia is one of the most benign and most easily treated. Indeed, even the "stigma" of wearing bifocal spectacles can now be avoided, with new bifocals that have no line between the top distance prescription and the bottom reading prescription, and with bifocal contact lenses. (Bifocal contacts, which are weighted at the bottom to keep them aligned as they float on the cornea, are still uncomfortable for many wearers.) Still,

The Presbyopia Effect

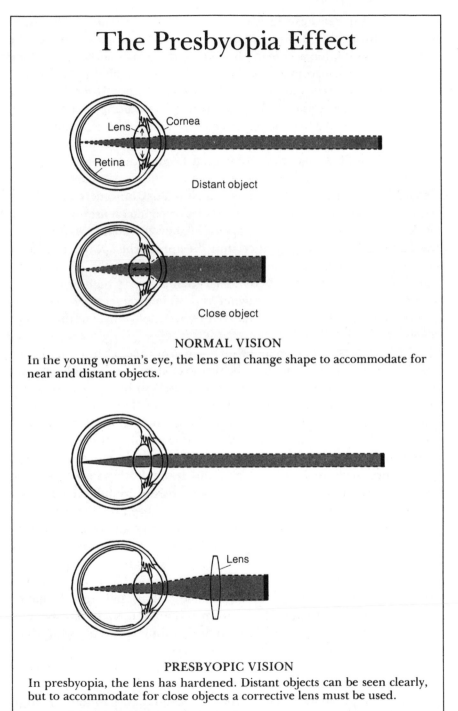

Distant object

Close object

NORMAL VISION

In the young woman's eye, the lens can change shape to accommodate for near and distant objects.

PRESBYOPIC VISION

In presbyopia, the lens has hardened. Distant objects can be seen clearly, but to accommodate for close objects a corrective lens must be used.

when a woman reaches the point where she needs reading glasses, in whatever form, she may panic. Because it usually comes at about the age of 45, this is often a woman's first portent of true middle age. "When this happens, most women don't rush out immediately to get glasses," observes Dr. Barbara Edelstein in *The Woman Doctor's Medical Guide for Women.* "They pretend it will go away, sometimes waiting until they have to stand up to read while the paper lies flat on the table. Sometimes they stop reading altogether. It's probably such a shock to people because it's the first physical change that's completely beyond their control."[5]

On very rare occasions, presbyopia can be temporarily corrected with visual exercises. Dr. Richard Kavner, a New York optometrist, had one patient who didn't want to wear spectacles or contact lenses because she worked on television. But by the age of 50, her 20/300 near-point vision was hampering her performance, and she approached Kavner for a set of exercises to help her see better. Within three months, he says, her acuity was 20/30. "She needs remedial therapy every eighteen months or so, for eight to ten weeks," Kavner says. "Therapy seems to arrest the deteriorating condition for a while, but then the old wheel of time keeps revolving."[6]

Other harmless visual changes with age also occur, beginning in the 50s. At about this time, the pupil begins to change size more slowly, and in darkness it is never quite as large as it used to be. This means that light has a harder time reaching the retina, so that one needs more outside light to see clearly. By the age of 80, a person needs three times more light than at age 20 to achieve the same visual clarity.

As people age, they may notice that their eyes are more sensitive to glare, more likely to produce tears, and less able to adapt to sudden changes in illumination. And their ability to differentiate colors may diminish as well, as the eye's cones—the specialized cells that regulate color vision—gradually deteriorate. They may first notice a disconcerting tendency for anything blue, no matter what shade of blue, to look gray. Gradually, other "cool colors"—particularly greens and purples—will also begin to blur (although the "warm colors"—yellow, red, and orange—generally remain distinguishable).[7] This perceptual change seems to occur less dramatically in women than in men, in part because women usually have a better grasp on the vocabulary of hues with which to express the differences they observe.

Other eye problems that are common with age are less benign. All of them endanger vision, yet they generally can be treated successfully and perhaps even prevented. With earlier detection, new methods of surgical and laser therapy, and better treatment of certain underlying disease processes, tomorrow's older woman will have a better than four-to-one chance of keeping her vision intact for as long as she lives.

Cataracts. Cataracts are so common that they have long been thought to be an inevitable part of aging. But now some experts believe that exposure to ultraviolet radiation is a major cause of cataracts in late life. The conscientious use of protective sunglasses could minimize the chance of developing cataracts. But only certain sunglasses are effective in filtering out ultraviolet light. The Corning Glass Company has devised a special light-filtering sunglass that is recommended for cataract patients, and there is a chance that the use of this type of glass might help prevent the development of cataracts in the first place.[8]

In a cataract, the normally clear lens compresses and becomes more and more opaque. This blocks or distorts the light entering the eye and eventually blurs vision. As the cataract worsens, the now-whitish lens might actually be visible through the pupil of the eye.

Traditionally, ophthalmologists have urged their patients to wait until a cataract was quite severe before recommending surgery. But many eye surgeons will now do the operation as soon as visual impairment becomes a problem. In cataract surgery, the clouded lens is removed. It is then substituted for either with a new, plastic lens inserted in its place or with special eyeglasses or contact lenses that can compensate for the lens-less eye's extreme farsightedness. Such operations, of which more than 500,000 are performed each year, have a success rate of better than 95 percent.

Senile macular degeneration. The most common cause of low vision in persons over 50, affecting about 10 million Americans, senile macular degeneration is responsible for 20 percent of the cases of legal blindness in the United States.[9] It is a progressive disease that affects the macula, the central part of the retina responsible for perception of fine detail. Without a functioning macula, an individual loses central vision, making it difficult to read, sew, count change, or see anything in a close range. While peripheral vision remains intact, which usually allows the person to navigate street crossings alone, the ability to do close work is all but lost.

Senile macular degeneration is usually caused by arteriosclerosis in the tiny blood vessels that supply the retina. This creates little pockets of avascularity (no blood vessels) near the macula, and the region eventually degenerates from lack of nutrients. It is most common in fair people with blue eyes, and least common in blacks, and can be aggravated by the presence of hypertension, diabetes, or disorders of the circulatory or central nervous systems.[10] About the only prevention currently available is the avoidance, or at least treatment, of these predisposing conditions.

For years, macular degeneration was considered untreatable. But recently, some doctors have been able to halt its progression with laser beam therapy directed at the decaying blood vessels. The trick is to begin this treatment within *days* of the onset of the degenerative process. Because the condition usually starts gradually and painlessly, however, this is not always so easy to do.

Some ophthalmologists suggest that all women, and men, past the age of 50 conduct the following quick self-test *every day* to make sure their maculas are intact: Look at a straight vertical line, such as a door frame or light pole, first with your left eye and then with your right. If the straight line appears at all wavy, or if a blank spot appears, call your eye doctor immediately.[11]

Diabetic retinopathy. A common complication of insulin-dependent diabetes, especially in persons whose blood glucose levels are poorly controlled, is destruction of the blood vessels of the retina, or retinopathy. In this condition, which causes about 50 percent of the cases of blindness seen in elderly Americans, blood from these constricted vessels, or from new vessels that grow on the retina to take their place, can leak into the vitreous humor, a jelly-like substance inside the eyeball. When the blood leaves scar tissue on the retina, partial loss of vision results.

Ophthalmologists have successfully treated diabetic retinopathy by plugging leaks with laser beams and, if necessary, replacing the vitreous humor with an artificial substance. The best treatment, of course, is prevention, which includes good regulation of blood glucose and frequent visits to the eye doctor.

Glaucoma. Another eye condition that grows more common with age, and that can lead to blindness if left untreated, is glaucoma. This disorder refers to the excessive buildup of pressure in the eyeball, usually caused by a blockage between the iris and cornea from which the eyeball's aqueous humor ordinarily drains. When the humor cannot drain, internal pressure builds further. Chronic glaucoma develops gradually, resulting in an almost imperceptible loss of peripheral vision after many years. Acute glaucoma, which is more rare, is a medical emergency that may require surgery to relieve the pressure. It occurs in about one in 1,000 persons between the ages of 40 and 65, and about two in 1,000 over 65. It is most common in persons who are farsighted.[12]

Focus on Eye Care

The good news is that most eye disorders and failing vision can be corrected with eyeglasses or surgery, provided the problem is detected in time. Therefore, in order to enjoy a lifetime of good vision, it is critical to get your eyes examined every two years after the age of 40 (or every year if you have a family history of glaucoma) and every year after the age of 55. Below is a glossary of eye care specialists. The general rule of thumb: the longer the title, the more professional training that has gone into earning it.

Ophthalmologists are M.D.'s who, after medical school and a general medical internship, completed at least three years of hospital residency while specializing in eye-related disorders. All ophthalmologists can prescribe glasses, contact lenses, and drugs for eye conditions; some go on to practice surgery.

Optometrists have completed four years of graduate work at a school of optometry for their O.D. degree (doctor of optometry). Optometrists can prescribe eyeglasses and contact lenses for such disorders as nearsightedness, farsightedness, and astigmatism. They cannot, in most states, prescribe drugs.

Opticians have been certified after one or two years of training in lens technology and must continue to meet licensing requirements as established by the Opticians Association of America.

The symptoms of failing vision are sometimes subtle—or at least subtle enough to ignore. Don't ignore them. Get advice from a professional if there is a change in your vision. Below are symptoms that call for a visit to the eye doctor:

- If you notice that you can't read as well as you used to, or that you're holding the newspaper at arm's length, chances are you need glasses.
- An aggravating condition that affects some women over 40 is dry eyes. The symptoms are chronically red, irritated eyes and the feeling that something is in them but that tears can't be mustered to wash it out. An over-the-counter artificial tears solution can be used to clean and lubricate the eyes, but it's important to also consult an ophthalmologist (dry eyes can by a symptom of rheumatoid arthritis).
- If you are diabetic, you should be aware of the symptoms of diabetic retinopathy. In advanced stages of the disease, the woman will see cobweb-like strands caused by the formation of abnormal blood vessels across the retina and/or her vision will be severely clouded.
- Glaucoma is often called the "sneak thief of sight." Its symptoms, if they exist at all, can include occasional blurred vision, the inability to adjust the eyes to a darkened room, seeing rings around light, and reduced peripheral vision.

Glaucoma tends to run in families, and becomes more common after the age of 40, when it affects 1 to 2 percent of the population. It can be detected by a simple, painless test of eye pressure that is part of any regular eye checkup. Because it can develop without warning, those over 40 are urged to see an opthalmologist or optometrist every two or three years.

Changed Taste: Food Seems Blander

The tongue is a remarkably strong and active organ. As the first step in food's passage through the digestive tract, it is outfitted with powerful muscles (for chewing and molding the food into a ball), taste buds, and a profusion of tiny hairlike projections called papillae.

Every tongue is covered with papillae. Around each papilla is a cluster of taste buds, the microscopic organs responsible for our ability to distinguish salty from sour, bitter from sweet. Taste buds that are especially responsive to particular flavors are located in particular regions of the tongue. Near the tip of the tongue are the taste buds that can best distinguish sweet and salty tastes. Toward the back are the buds for bitter tastes. And along the sides are the buds that detect tastes that are sour.

Without taste buds, eating would be bland and monotonous. It might even be somewhat dangerous, since a sharp sense of taste (in combination with the sense of smell) is what alerts us when food has gone bad. But no one's taste buds stay intact forever; indeed, taste buds may be among the first things to go.

Along the circumvallate papillae, a V-shaped row of papillae at the base of the tongue, a 75-year-old has an average of only 88 taste buds—compared to an average of 248 taste buds in childhood. In addition, about half of the taste buds that do remain are atrophied.[13]

Experts are unsure whether this loss of taste buds is an inevitable result of age or the result of a lifetime of bad habits. Poor oral hygiene might well be at least partly responsible. Smoking cigarettes, for example, is known to destroy the taste buds. Other possible causes for loss of taste include iron deficiency, riboflavin deficiency, and other nutritional problems. But little research has been done to find ways to maintain the sense of taste. The gustatory joys that are eliminated when taste declines apparently are thought too minor to mourn for long.

But loss of taste is not always a benign problem. A woman with little taste for food might have a hard time motivating herself to eat sensibly. And if loss of taste translates into a loss of appetite, an older woman runs the risk of becoming malnourished and setting herself up for a host of other problems. One important side effect of a poor diet, as we

Taste and the Tongue

The tastebuds are not the tiny elevations that are visible on the top of the tongue that give it its rough, bumpy texture. Those elevations are called the papillae, and come in a variety of shapes. The tastebuds are embedded in the papillae beneath the surface of the tongue. The deterioration and atrophy of the tastebuds is a normal and inevitable consequence of aging. However, it is thought that good oral hygiene can help prevent some of the deterioration, and thus preserve some of an older person's ability to taste.

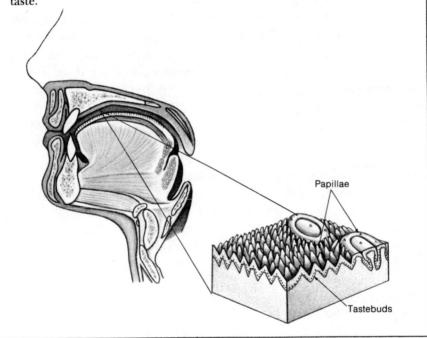

Papillae

Tastebuds

shall see in Chapter 11, is a decline in mental sharpness and the development of "pseudosenility."

Researchers have long thought that a reduction in saliva production contributed, along with the loss of taste buds, to the general diminishing of the sense of taste. And they have long thought that a loss of saliva is inevitable with age. But new research on very healthy older people reveals that loss of saliva is not an age-related change at all; it is almost always a side effect of medication. When persons over 65 who are receiving no medication whatsoever are examined, they are shown to produce as much saliva as they did in their youth.[14] With further research, it might be revealed that the loss of taste buds is similarly an associated condition of some of the other ravages of age, not a result of age itself.

Changed Smell: Perfume Gets Stronger

The sense of smell also has been shown to decline with age. This explains in part why the perfume you remember on your aged Aunt Sally was more pungent than it should have been. For Aunt Sally to smell her own perfume, she really needed to pour it on.

That's the biggest hazard of a declining sense of smell—its potential social impact. A woman who cannot smell well is less likely to notice when she needs to bathe, use deodorant, or brush her teeth, and people might begin to avoid her if she smells unpleasant. Even if she manages to maintain her own hygiene, she might find that social contacts are less appealing from her perspective, too. Smell, for instance, has recently been shown to play a major role in sexual attraction, and she may have a harder time getting turned on by a man who is attracted to her if she cannot smell the scent signals his body sends out.

The sense of smell is also closely related to the sense of taste—and to the enjoyment of food. If you cannot smell the difference, an apple, however sweet, just tastes like a raw potato, and a beautiful cheese soufflé just tastes like air. Loss of smell, like loss of taste, can make malnutrition more likely as a woman ages, and she must pay particular attention to maintaining a well-balanced diet even if it is not that appealing.

Some decline in the sense of smell is thought to occur in almost everyone. But total loss of smell, or anosmia, is a rare condition that usually is caused by an underlying condition such as a head cold, allergy, or nasal polyps. When these causes of anosmia have been eliminated, a neurologist might be needed to evaluate the condition of the olfactory nerves, which are located at the top of the nose and convert smells into nerve impulses that travel to the brain. Damage to these nerves is extremely rare, and referral to a specialist is warranted only if the anosmia is complete and distressing.

Changed Touch: Pain Is Duller

Skin sensitivity changes can be paradoxical. For some older women, the skin loses its sensitivity to external stimuli, such as extremes of heat and cold. But for others, the skin becomes exquisitely sensitive to internal stimuli—such as the mechanism responsible for the sensation of itchiness. Dr. Albert Kligman, a dermatologist at the University of Pennsylvania, says older women frequently are bothered by maddening itchiness all over their bodies, especially in hard-to-scratch places like the back or the vulva. Extreme itchiness may respond to such old-fashioned remedies as a baking soda bath (one teaspoon of baking soda in a bath of lukewarm water). Occasionally, a prescription medication, such as an antihistamine, may provide some relief.

An important way in which skin sensitivity has been shown to change is in perception of temperature changes. A young woman can detect a temperature drop of just 1° F; after age 65, the air temperature may need to drop by as much as 9° F before she is aware of it.[15] This, combined with older persons' failing mechanisms for internal body heat regulation—such as failure to shiver—puts an older woman at special risk of accidental hypothermia, a dangerous drop in body temperature (to lower than 94.6° F) caused by extremely cold surroundings.

While a relatively mild loss of skin sensitivity is to be expected with age, a sudden or total numbness of a particular region is not. When this occurs, it usually can be traced to an underlying problem with the nerves or blood vessels supplying the region. The following syndromes, while they are not caused by age, do tend to become more common as a person ages.

Carpal tunnel syndrome. The carpal tunnel is formed by the bones of the wrist, and nerves linking the brain with the hand travel through it. As a woman approaches menopause, a change in her hormonal balance may lead to accumulation of fluid in her wrist. As her wrist swells, the carpal tunnel presses on the nerve passing through it, leading to tingling and intermittent numbness in the thumb and first two fingers. Shooting pain up the arm often occurs as well, especially at night, and is frequently severe enough to rouse the woman from sleep. Eventually, the affected fingers may become permanently weak or numb.

Doctors treat carpal tunnel syndrome with diuretics to minimize fluid accumulation, a splint worn at night to immobilize the affected wrist, or, in severe cases, an operation in which the tunnel membrane is cut to provide more space for the pinched nerve.

Circulatory problems. A woman with damaged blood vessels will notice the deficiency first in the regions at the periphery of the circulatory system—the fingers and toes. Arteriosclerosis and diabetes are the two most common causes of loss of blood flow to these extremities. When blood flow is impaired, a woman experiences loss of touch sensitivity, weakness, and eventually actual numbness in these regions. Thus women with diabetes or arteriosclerosis must be especially alert to the conditions of their fingers and toes to prevent the development of gangrene.

Staying Sensuous

The sensory changes of old age present a comforting paradox. At the same time that physiological changes may be making a woman less "in touch" with the world around her, psychological changes may actually be heightening her sensuous experiences. As a woman ages, she is likely to become more sharply aware of the telescoping of her remaining time. Many women react to this foreshortening of life by engaging in small tricks to allow them to savor experiences to the fullest. Fully functioning senses are of little use to a woman too busy to use them, and that is what tends to happen to women in their frantic 20s and 30s. But a woman in mid-life who takes the time to stop to smell the roses will not notice that her sense of smell has declined. She will simply sniff a little harder, and whatever scent she catches will be a scent she deeply enjoys.

Maintenance: The Senses

Your five senses can serve you well year after year—as long as you exercise common sense in caring for them, and learn to adjust to sensory changes if they do occur.

EARS

- Remember the telltale signs of hearing loss (see page 190). When you notice a change in your hearing, have your ears examined and your hearing tested.
- Protect yourself from loud noises—one overexposure can cause irreparable damage. At your workplace, check to see if the noisy equipment around you meets government safety standards. Wear earplugs or earmuffs for frequent or prolonged exposure to loud equipment at home like the vacuum cleaner or the lawn mower.
- On noisy subways, it's not a bad idea to insert earplugs for the ride. Both your ears and your nerves deserve to be protected from the screeching and clattering.
- When on a plane, chew gum, suck on mints, or try yawning repeatedly to prevent your Eustachian tubes from plugging up. Because alcohol causes mucous membranes in the Eustachian tubes to swell, avoid alcoholic beverages before or during the flight. If you're traveling with a cold or sinus trouble, the mucous membranes are probably already swollen. Use a nasal decongestant as the plane begins its descent.
- Protect your ears from the elements. The outer ear itself and the skin that covers it are delicate, and must be protected from sunburn and frostbite.
- Older women with hearing difficulties can help themselves in social situations by standing close to and squarely in front of their partners in conversation, in order to receive the sound well and watch lips and facial expression.
- If you have a hearing difficulty, speak clearly and slowly. People will often unconsciously match the pace and volume of their speech to yours.
- When your doctor recommends a hearing aid, get one. You may be surprised how unobtrusive and easy to use the latest models are.

EYES

- Alert your doctor to any of the symptoms of the major eye diseases associated with age described in this chapter, so you can perhaps correct a problem in its early stages.
- Wear good sunglasses. The sun can damage your eyes, especially when reflected by sand, water, and snow. Choose brown and green-tinted lenses instead of pink, yellow, or blue ones. The darker lenses block out the more damaging rays and cause less color distortion. When buying sunglasses, hold them at half an arm's length and focus on a strong vertical line. Move the glasses slowly up, down, and across

continued

the line. If the line appears wavy, there is some distortion in the lenses.

- If you find you can't see as well in dim light, it may be because of a normal eye condition of aging that allows less light to reach the retina. Light up your life: Equip your workplace with a table top lamp for soft (to avoid glare), direct light.

TASTE AND SMELL

- The sense of taste is closely associated with the sense of smell. Tastebuds naturally degenerate over the years, and food may taste blander because of a decline in the sense of smell, too. In any case, it's important for older women to eat regularly and maintain a nutritious diet, even if they're not as enticed by food. Regular exercise helps to stimulate the appetite, especially when the sense of taste has diminished.
- Maintain oral hygiene, so that gum disease and tooth decay do not interfere with taste and smell.
- If you smoke, one more good reason for quitting is that smoking can damage both tastebuds and nasal passages.
- Older women who notice they have lost some of their sense of smell should be careful to maintain all aspects of personal hygiene. Perfume should be applied sparingly, since others may be overwhelmed by a scent the woman no longer can perceive herself.

TOUCH

- It's more difficult for older skin to detect and respond to temperature changes. Older women should not rely solely on their perception of heat or cold, but take care to listen to weather reports and dress appropriately.
- Exercise is an excellent way to keep the blood pumping all the way out to the extremities. Move briskly and vigorously in cold weather, and you'll feel healthier and warmer for it.
- Although the sense of touch diminishes with age, any repeated numbness in the fingers and toes should be brought to the attention of a doctor.

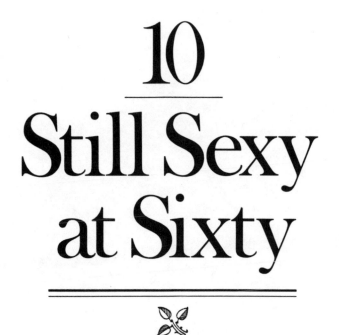

10
Still Sexy
at Sixty

Let us imagine a woman in bed, and let us call her Linda. Linda is 36 years old; she and Frank have been married for 11 years. She has two sons, aged eight and five, and since her last pregnancy she has felt wonderful. She feels especially wonderful about sex.

Now that the children are older, Linda and Frank have more time to themselves. They meet occasionally for a lunchtime rendezvous in a downtown hotel; they have moved their bedroom to the first floor, and they enjoy more privacy than they did when the boys slept fitfully right next door; they escape every now and then to a romantic country inn for a weekend. For Linda, lovemaking has become at once familiar and fascinating. Frank's vasectomy, which he had two years ago, has relieved Linda of the hassles of a diaphragm. Now that Linda has returned to her prepregnancy weight and is up to five miles on her after-work jog, she feels proud of her body and is thrilled to have her husband admire it. Her breasts and belly might be a little less taut than when she first met Frank, but he doesn't seem to mind. And Linda feels more sexually responsive than ever. In fact, these days it is usually Linda who initiates lovemaking—to Frank's delight—and there are times she wishes they could go on all night.

Tonight, though, as she lies in bed next to Frank, Linda worries that this lovemaking idyll will soon end. She has noticed that Frank takes a longer time to become aroused. Even though she knows that is normal for his age (he is 39), she can't help feeling that maybe she just isn't sexy enough. And what will happen as she approaches menopause? Will she become less responsive, less interested in sex, less able to turn Frank on?

Linda need not worry. As long as she and Frank stay compatible and communicative, their sex life will likely stay as good as it is—and might even get better. There is indeed sex after 60, and the sex can be every bit as good as it was at 30, 40, and 50.

Now consider Emma, who is 60 years old. Emma is a respondent to the Starr-Weiner report, a major study of sexual attitudes and behavior published in 1981 by Drs. Bernard Starr and Marcella Bakur Weiner of the City University of New York. "Has sex changed since the menopause?" the Starr-Weiner questionnaire asked. Emma's reply: "Why should it? One fear has certainly been discarded—pregnancy. If I continue to feel good about myself, I see no reason for menopause to make any difference . . . unless to enhance sex." [1]

Emma's views are echoed by older women everywhere. Women in their 30s might worry about the loss of sexuality, but women in their 60s know better. A woman can stay sexually responsive, and sexually active, for a lifetime.

Starr and Weiner interviewed 800 persons over the age of 60—518 women, 282 men—with an open-ended questionnaire. The results showed that sex life does indeed continue in the "twilight years." More than 40 percent of the women interviewed—compared to 27 percent of the men—said sex feels better now than when they were younger. Another 40 percent of the women—and 37 percent of the men—said sex feels as good. Their answers were backed up with enthusiastic comments. "It took me until I was 34 to know what satisfactory sex was," said one woman, age 66. "It's nice," said another, age 65 and happily retired, "not to have to calculate how getting amorous might upset the morning [getting-to-work] routine."

The respondents had surprisingly liberal sexual attitudes, too. More than 95 percent of them said they "like sex"; 90 percent approve of sex without marriage; 85 percent of the women and 76 percent of the men condone masturbation; and when asked, "What about sex embarrasses you the most?" 57 percent of the men and women answered, "Nothing."

The Psychology of Mid- and Late-life Sex

One reason that sex improves with age is that mature women often are better able to tell their partners—directly and without any shame—what will please them sexually. "Once I decided the rest of my life is for me," one 49-year-old woman told Rosetta Reitz, author of *Menopause: A Positive Approach,* "I was shocked how easy it became to get what I want. There's hardly a thing I can think of sexually that I want to experience that I can't. I'm amazed, and wonder why it took me so long not to be afraid to ask."[2]

Still, even though sex improves for so many, the fact that sexiness is equated with youthfulness makes many women past 40 fear they have lost their allure. The specter of declining sexuality can make these women shy: They avoid their husbands, hesitate to embark on love affairs, won't even look in the mirror or stroke their own bodies for fear that the changes they see and feel will humiliate them. Sadly, these anxious women create their own vicious cycle. Yes, age does bring with it some changes in sexual anatomy and physiology, but the changes are

The Sexual Plateau

While changes in sexual anatomy and function occur in mid-life, a young woman can take heart from the fact that her sexual responsiveness will reach a peak in her late 30s and remain on a high plateau into her 60s. In contrast, men begin a slow decline in responsiveness beginning in their late teens.

Many factors influence a woman's mid-life enthusiasm for sex:

- Hormones work in her favor. The libido is determined by androgen, the male hormone, which is manufactured throughout a woman's life. During her reproductive years, estrogen and progesterone are also manufactured, and they can mask the effects of androgen. After menopause, however, androgen circulates in the body unopposed, and for that reason, a woman's sex drive can actually increase with age.
- Women, as opposed to men, retain indefinitely the potential for reaching multiple orgasm during intercourse and masturbation.
- Middle-aged couples often have more time and privacy to enjoy sex. Once the children have left home, and careers and housekeeping are less time-consuming, many couples experience an "empty nest honeymoon."
- Women interviewed during mid-life reported a heightened receptivity to all things sensual and a better understanding of what makes sex satisfying for them. Postmenopausal women also felt that sex was more enjoyable without the fear of unwanted pregnancy, and the bother and interruptions caused by contraceptives and menstruation.

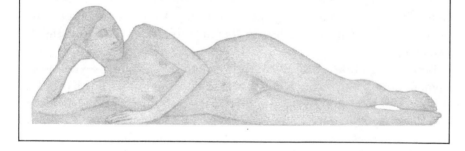

worst for women who allow them to interfere with sexual behavior. As we will see later in this chapter, recent research has shown that women with active sex lives—orgasm, however it is accomplished, one or two times a week—rarely experience the "senile vagina syndrome," nor do they suffer functional changes from age-related changes in the clitoris, uterus, or cervix. This may be a chicken-and-egg conclusion, but one thing is clear: In sex, you really must use it or lose it.

Sexual expression has always been related, in women perhaps more than men, to the need for intimacy, for caressing, for body contact. Young women interviewed by sex researchers tend to rate the hugging aspect of lovemaking as highly as they rate the sexual stimulation itself. With age, the psychological desire for body contact can become almost a physical demand—and one that becomes at times more urgent than the physical need for orgasm.

"Lovemaking," says Dr. Ruth Weg, professor of biology and gerontology at the University of Southern California, "gradually becomes more caring, gentle, and prolonged in the important search for person-oriented intimacy. . . . The older woman has learned the sensitivity and giving, the caressing and gentle play, the whispers and the humor, the holding, the sensuous joys of body warmth that make up the second language [of sex]. The sex act may or may not be part of the conversation at any one time."[3]

Ever since Alfred Kinsey's ground-breaking report, *Sexual Behavior in the Human Female,* appeared in 1953, scientists have known that women remain at a sexual plateau for many years more than men. Kinsey found that, for women, the frequency of masturbation and other "sexual activities which are not dependent upon the male's initiation of socio-sexual contacts" remain constant from the late teens into the 50s and 60s. Women's rate of sexual *intercourse* does decline somewhat in the 50s and early 60s, Kinsey found, probably for lack of available partners or because the partners stop initiating lovemaking. Men, on the other hand, begin a slow and steady decline in sexual responsiveness as early as the late teens.

Best-selling author Gail Sheehy called the out-of-synch sexual development between men and women "the sexual diamond." The basic idea, put forth in her book *Passages,* is that men reach their sexual peak early, at around age 18, and thereafter begin a slow lifelong decline, while women don't peak sexually until the late 30s, after which they stay on a high plateau of sexual functioning until far into the 60s or 70s.

The fact that age-matched couples are sexually out of synch for most of their lives together can put a strain on the best of marriages. A woman may begin to feel more erotic, more potent, and more needful of sex at about the same time her husband is feeling less sexy and is, if anything, worrying about his ability to perform. Couples who are aware of these differences, and who express their feelings easily to each other, usually can surmount the strain. One survival tactic is for a woman to take more of the initiative. As one 68-year-old woman told researchers for the Starr-Weiner report, "Now I wake him up when I'm in the mood, and afterward I even roll over and sometimes fall back asleep. He's been doing that for years!"[4]

Recently, Consumers Union (CU) conducted a nationwide mail survey of more than 2,000 readers of its publication, *Consumer Reports,* to determine the sexual habits, attitudes, and practices of persons over age 50.[5] One of the topics probed was menopause—particularly its effect on sex. The CU researchers concluded that menopause rarely creates distressing symptoms, and even more rarely interferes with sexual expression. Of the respondents to the CU survey, for instance, only 35 percent said they had experienced vaginal dryness since menopause. In fact, menopause often heightens sexual pleasure for a woman by removing the fear of pregnancy, the bother of contraceptives, and the interruption of a monthly period.

The authors did conclude, however, that postmenopausal women are slightly more likely to remain more sexually active when they are on estrogen replacement therapy (ERT), a controversial medical treatment discussed in Chapter 5. Some women even report that sexual comfort is the most compelling reason for staying on ERT. For example, one respondent, a 54-year-old widow from New England who expects to remarry soon, experienced vaginal atrophy and dryness when she went through menopause at age 46. She started taking estrogen the following year, then stopped briefly and resumed once more. "Onset of menopause caused dryness and thinning of vaginal membranes, and pain and bleeding with intercourse," she explains. "Interest and desire were not decreased but pleasure was." She says her problems were "completely eliminated" by ERT.[6]

Of the 1,764 postmenopausal respondents to the CU survey, 408 take estrogen and 1,356 do not. The estrogen-takers are a more sexually active group: 93 percent of them are sexually active, compared to 80 percent of the nontakers. But there is no proven cause-and-effect relationship between ERT and sexual activity. It might be that added interest in sex *to begin with* led those 408 women to take estrogen in the first place.

Even when postmenopausal changes in sexual anatomy do occur, and are *not* treated with ERT, they need not interfere with a healthy and rewarding sex life. A 54-year-old divorced woman from the midwest is one dramatic example of this. She indicates in the CU survey that since menopause she has experienced vaginal atrophy, as well as insufficient vaginal lubrication on arousal. She says these conditions interfere with her sex life—but her behavior gives evidence to the contrary. This 54-year-old woman is engaged in a very active sexual relationship with a 35-year-old man—a man she has known since he was 15—with whom she has sex once a day or more, and she masturbates about once a week in addition. When asked to rate her life enjoyment, her satisfaction with her relationship, and her enjoyment of sex with her partner, she gives each the highest possible rating—and on the sex satisfaction scale, she pens her rating with three exuberant check marks.

During mid-life, many women are for the first time free to make love whenever they want to, without the presence of children or the pressures that come with juggling career, housekeeping, and motherhood. The CU researchers call this period the "empty nest honeymoon." "Now that the children are grown and gone," writes a 56-year-old woman from Oklahoma who has been married for 34 years, "we are delighted to be a 'single couple' once again and have been on a honeymoon ever since we have been alone. We find that our shared experiences have made us closer, wiser, and funnier. Our little understandings—communicated by a lifted eyebrow during some cocktail party, the little words that are a private joke within the family, and the ability to sit down and talk about feelings—have all come with age. We like being able to make love in the afternoon, if we wish, or to wait a few days longer than usual if one or another of us is not in the mood. It is a *lovely* time of life."[7]

Changes in Sexual Anatomy

Still, aging does bring with it some alterations in a woman's genitalia, and this can—though it usually does not—have an effect on sexual functioning. As her estrogen and progesterone levels diminish, a woman experiences changes in the size and shape of her genitalia. Beginning about eight years after menopause, a woman's vulva will decrease in size. Her mons, labia majora, and labia minora will also lose fatty tissue, and will shrink and flatten. A woman's clitoris gets slightly smaller, too, although this is not thought to have any effect on sexual sensation. Her cervix, ovaries, and uterus will also shrink. During orgasm, the uterus may contract spasmodically rather than in the rhythmic pattern of her younger years, but most women cannot feel—or do not care about—the difference.

Perhaps the most significant anatomical change in later years is the change in vaginal tissue. In many women, the vagina gets thinner, decreases in length, and loses elasticity. Fewer glands are available to lubricate the vagina, causing many women to complain that they can never get wet enough for comfortable penetration. (Vaseline, K-Y Jelly, natural oils, or, if necessary, prescription estrogen creams can often solve the problem of lack of lubrication.) All these changes are called the "senile vagina syndrome."

But the senile vagina syndrome is not inevitable. The best rejuvenator of the vagina is continuous use—that is, orgasm and sexual intercourse as often as possible. Even women without partners can retain the moistness and resiliency of their youth by masturbating at least once a week. In addition, Kegel exercises (see Chapter 5) performed regularly, about 50 times a day, can help keep the vagina well-toned and elastic.

According to Ruth Weg of the University of Southern California, the phases of sexual response in women change over time. The excitation phase is longer: It takes five minutes, rather than 15 to 40 seconds, for an older woman to achieve vaginal lubrication, and it takes longer for

Still Sexy After All These Years

The Consumers Union report, which studied the sexuality of 1,844 women over the age of 50 (as well as 2,402 men), found a gradual decline in sexual activity from decade to decade, as follows:

PROPORTION OF SEXUALLY ACTIVE WOMEN

Married	
In their 50s	95 percent
In their 60s	89 percent
In their 70s and beyond	81 percent
Unmarried	
In their 50s	88 percent
In their 60s	63 percent
In their 70s and beyond	50 percent

The only measure of sexuality that did not decline with age, the CU report notes, is the frequency of masturbation among women who masturbate: It holds steady at about .7 times per week, on the average, through the 50s, 60s, 70s, and later. The proportion of women who masturbate, however, does decline, from 47 percent of women in their 50s, to 37 percent of women in their 60s, to 33 percent of women in their 70s or older.

Based on *Love, Sex and Aging: A Consumers Union Report* by Edward M. Brecker and the editors of Consumers Report Books. Copyright © 1984 by Consumers Union of the United States, Inc. Reprinted by permission of Little, Brown & Company.

the clitoris to elevate in response to stimulation. The orgasmic phase is shorter, with the decrease usually beginning around the age of 50. Uterine contractions are reduced in number from two or three per orgasm to one or two. And, as in men, the resolution phase (the period of time required for the body to return to its pre-aroused state) is shorter, too.[8]

Physiologically, a woman's sexual desire stays the same her whole life; if anything, it might increase after menopause. Libido is determined by the male hormone androgen, which is produced by the adrenal glands. During a woman's reproductive years, the androgen competes with relatively high levels of the female hormones estrogen and progesterone, which mask its effects. But after menopause, when the female hormones abate, androgen continues to be manufactured—and it circulates in the system unopposed. So a woman's hormones are actually working to bring her a heightened sex drive in her later years.

Sexuality and Illness

Over the years, women (and men) are more and more likely to encounter chronic disabilities. Sometimes these conditions have a direct effect on sexual behavior; lifelong diabetes, for instance, can lead to physiological impotence in the middle years. Sometimes these conditions have a less direct effect; impotence or decreased libido can be side effects of certain medications (such as those prescribed for hypertension), and discomfort during conventional lovemaking can accompany some chronic conditions (such as severe osteoporosis or severe arthritis). In all these situations, though, love and imagination can triumph.

Consider this 72-year-old Missouri woman married to an 80-year-old man who has not had a full erection in eight years, and whose joints are so painful that intercourse even with an erection is out of the question. "He is such a delightful, delicious caresser," she wrote in response to the CU survey, "that he can give me an orgasm without [intercourse]. He does not crave this activity as often as I do, but the quality is worth waiting for."[9]

There is no question that health affects sexual activity. The CU researchers found that the proportion of women who are sexually active (who masturbate or have sex with a partner or both at least once a week) is highest among those in excellent or very good health—69 percent—and drops to 63 percent among those in good health and 54 percent among those in fair or poor health. But even among those in fair or poor health, nearly three-quarters report *some* continued sexual activity.

Diseases and conditions most likely to inhibit sexual functioning include diabetes, multiple sclerosis, thyroid deficiency, depression, arthritis of the hip, and musculoskeletal disorders of the pelvis and lower back. In women, says Dr. Helen Singer Kaplan, director of the Human Sexuality Teaching Program at New York Hospital, pain during intercourse can come from prolapse of the uterus, post-hysterectomy scarring, or genital infection.

Certain medications, particularly antihypertension medication, are also known to have a possible effect on an individual's sex drive and, in men, ability to achieve erection, The effect of the drug varies from one individual to the next, and depends on the dosage, type of drug, and other variables. Physicians are unlikely to consider impairment of sexual function a significant side effect in a woman over 50 or so, because many doctors still blindly accept the stereotype that a mid-life woman is past her sexual prime. It is up to the patient herself to complain and ask for a change in dosage or brand if she thinks her medication is interfering with her sex life.

The CU researchers found that women on antihypertension medica-

Drugs and Sex

As a woman ages, she is more and more likely to be taking medications that are known to interfere with sexual functioning. Her doctor might not consider this a significant side effect in a woman over 50, but chances are the woman does. Often, the sexual impairment resulting from one drug can be corrected under a physician's guidance by reducing the dosage or switching to another brand.

EFFECT ON SEXUAL BEHAVIOR OF HYPERTENSIVE DRUGS

	Women on antihypertensive medication	*Healthy comparison group*
Sexually active	78 percent	86 percent
High or moderate sexual frequency	59 percent	71 percent
High enjoyment of sex	59 percent	70 percent

tion did indeed experience a slight decline in the frequency and intensity of sexual activity. They compared their 336 respondents taking such drugs with a group of 819 "extremely healthy" women who rated their own health as "good" or "excellent" and who had none of the diseases that most frequently impair sexual function. Their results are summarized in the box on page 215.

After a heart attack, men and women are often afraid to engage in sexual intercourse. They still remember stories about heart attack survivors who recovered only to return to their mistress's arms and die *in flagrante delicto.* (They forget the punch line, though: Seven out of ten of the people who die during sexual intercourse are having extramarital affairs.[10] The moral is not that a weakened heart cannot handle any sex at all, but that it cannot take on sexual liaisons that carry with them the intensity or anxiety that extramarital affairs usually do.) Sex, many still believe, is too exciting, too vigorous, too great a strain on the heart—so, despite their doctors' advice, they refrain.

Recently, physicians have discovered that the *best* route to post-heart-attack vigor is through exercise, which is why they urge their patients to begin walking, jogging, bike-riding—and making love—within 12 to 16 weeks. Sexual intercourse places no more strain on a heart than climbing two flights of stairs. Most patients are advised to resume sex at the same time they're advised to resume other comparable physical activities. And even for those who have pain on climbing two flights of stairs, lovemaking is still possible. Dr. Richard A. Stein, director of the Cardiac Exercise Laboratory and Medical Service, SUNY-Downstate, tells these patients to take their nitroglycerin dose 15 to 30 minutes before having sex.[11]

Hysterectomy is another condition that the CU researchers found could have an adverse impact on sexual expression. Physiologically, there is no reason why a hysterectomy should have anything to do with libido, sexual intercourse, or orgasm. To some women, though, the loss of the uterus does seem to have an actual physical effect during intercourse.

"I felt no diminution in my femaleness and femininity after the operation," a 62-year-old widow, who had a hysterectomy when she was 41, told the CU researchers. "But I noticed a pronounced difference in my interior at once. Only males have averred to me that the operation itself has no effect on sexual response. As a woman, I go on record as saying the uterus plays a secondary or accompanying role in coitus—

acts or functions as a sounding board does in a piano. It reflects the orgasmic contractions, intensifying the sensations."[12]

Of 1,844 woman respondents in the CU survey, 635 (34 percent) have had hysterectomies: 31 percent of those in their 50s, 34 percent of those in their 60s, 43 percent of those in their 70s or older. Although the CU researchers expected to hear many complaints of declining sexuality and lost femininity—especially among women aged 35 to 45 who might not have completed their families—the overall impact of the surgery on sexual activity was "quite modest, with small to negligible differences." Of women with hysterectomies, 82 percent are still sexually active, versus 86 percent of healthy controls, and 68 percent (versus 70 percent of controls) still have a high enjoyment of sex.

New Combinations

The most important factor limiting older women in their sexual expression is lack of opportunity. The older a woman gets, the less likely she is to find an available man her age. For every 100 women in a particular age range, there are 97 men between ages 25 and 44, 91 men between ages 45 and 64, 68 men over age 65,[13] and only 45 men over age 85. A significant proportion of mid- to late-life women are widowed. The average of widowhood is 56; by the age of 65, 52 percent of women are widowed, as are 68 percent of women over 75. The loneliness of the mid- to late-life widow is heightened by the fact that a significant proportion of men of her age—about 78 percent—are still married,[14] or are divorced and on the prowl for women in their 30s.

Why are so many more women alone in their middle years? Because women live longer than men. The life expectancy of a woman born in the 1950s is about 8 years longer than the life expectancy of a man born at the same time. (For more on this "gender gap" in life expectancy, see the box in Chapter 1, page 5.) Female longevity has been attributed to several causes. For one thing, women tend to have healthier life-styles. At least until recently, women smoked less, ate less fat, and worked in less dangerous jobs than men, so they were less likely to die of smoking-related, diet-related, or toxin-related diseases such as cancer, heart disease, and atherosclerosis. Women are also less likely to take physical risks, making them less vulnerable to death from accidents, suicide, or homicide.[15] These life-style differences have narrowed in recent years —the proportion of young women smokers has increased in the last ten years, and with it the death among women from lung cancer—so the life-span differences might change by the year 2000.

In addition, women seem to have a biological advantage over men. Females of most species, especially species most closely related to us, are generally longer-lived than males. At any given age, from conception right through the 70s and 80s, a female has a lower chance of dying than a male. A man in his late 60s is twice as likely to die as is a woman of the same age. A 65-year-old woman can expect to live another 18 years, a 75-year-old woman another 12; a man, on the other hand, can expect to live another 14 years when he reaches 65, and another 9 years when he reaches 75.[16]

The result, often, is that there simply are not enough men over the age of 65 to go around. Because of this imbalance, many women are now seeking new kinds of relationships in their search for intimacy. With so many women living, and sleeping, alone, the need for a caring and responsive partner is widely felt. Not every woman can find the traditional ideal of a mate: a man who is two or three years older, two or three inches taller, a little more assertive, and a good deal better-paid than she. Instead, more and more women in their middle years are beginning to look for love with younger, sometimes considerably younger, men.

Widespread acceptance of such liaisons, however, may be a long time coming. While "May-December" relationships have long been tolerated when the "May" half was female, the response is quite different when the relationship is reversed, and the middle-aged woman is the *older* half. One 48-year-old woman had to give up her affair of two years with a 28-year-old man because of the stares and titters of the world in which they moved. "The strain was too great," she is quoted as saying in Jane Porcino's book, *Growing Older, Getting Better*. "Everywhere we went together, people asked me if he was my son (they would never dare do that to a male who came in with a young woman on his arms) . . . And so, despite a very compatible intellectual and sexual relationship, we decided to separate."[17]

Some women, of course, seem to get away with it easily. When the television actress Mary Tyler Moore, aged 46, married a 29-year-old urologist in 1983, few people made fun of her. For women who are celebrities—Dinah Shore, Elizabeth Taylor, Joan Collins—relationships with younger men are considered acceptable. Part of the reason is that standards are different for stars; part of the reason is that these women look so good (that is, so young) that no one thinks they're making fools of themselves. But for ordinary people, the world still has trouble accepting a May-December romance when the "wrong" half is the younger one.

"People are people, and making love (and revolution) is good," says Maggie Kuhn, a political activist who never married and has had sexual relationships with people of various ages. "Age is irrelevant."

Kuhn, who is known for her feisty speeches—all the more startling because of her fragile, white-haired-granny appearance—has also suggested that older women should consider seeking sexual intimacy from other women. The scarcity of available men might well be enough to send heterosexual women into homosexual liaisons in their later years. But many women find lesbianism an undesirable alternative. Whenever Kuhn makes this suggestion during a speaking engagement, she is met by an uncomfortable silence.

In the CU survey, only 11 percent of the women polled said they had felt sexually attracted to another woman; 5 percent said they felt this attraction after the age of 50. And of *this* tiny minority, only 23 percent have acted on their impulses. In contrast, 56 percent of the men who have been turned on by other men since age 50 report that they've had homosexual liaisons.

Keeping Sensually Alive

"Love continues to soar and soar and sexual relationships become intensified," one 67-year-old woman says. "There should be no concern over possible loss of sex feelings; they do not deteriorate."[18] Indeed sex can and usually does get better and better as a woman ages. Not only is a woman in mid-life more sexually responsive than ever before, in spite of some sensory changes, but in old age she often has a heightened receptivity to all things sensuous—to the things in the world that she can see, smell, hear, and, perhaps most dramatically, touch.

"Elementality—the enjoyment of the elemental things of life—may develop in late life precisely because older people are more keenly aware that life is short," write Dr. Robert Butler and Myrna Lewis in *Sex After Sixty*. "Responsiveness to nature, human contact, children, music, to beauty in any form, may be heightened. Healthy late life is frequently a time for greater enjoyment of all the senses—colors, sights, sounds, smells, touch."[19] A woman in this state of continual arousal is truly a sensuous woman.

The way to stay alive sensuously is to use the senses continually. A woman who holds herself aloof, or who has allowed herself to fall into ritualistic habits of lovemaking, is not expanding her sensual potential. But a woman who feeds her tactile experiences—who exposes her skin to baths, massages, oils and creams, and the sensations of the fresh air —will keep up her appetite for more. Skin-to-skin contact is the best source of heightened sensuality, and this does not only mean contact with a potential lover. A woman who literally stays in touch with others —including close friends, children, even pets—will maintain her awareness of her own sensuality her whole life long.

Maintenance: Sexuality

Maintaining sexuality is a difficult concept at any age: It means dealing with complicated emotions and relationships, and knowing what's normal and right for you.

When thinking about your sexuality as you grow older, keep in mind the positive results of studies on aging and sexuality. For example, of the 518 women who responded to the Starr-Weiner study, 37 percent said that sex feels just as good after 60 and another 40 percent said that it actually feels better. There are many reasons why a woman can expect to stay sexually responsive and active throughout her life.

However, there is no denying that certain changes associated with growing older can have a less positive effect on a woman's sexuality, and may require her to make some adjustments in her sexual behavior.

- In many women the vagina gets thinner and loses its elasticity, especially after menopause. With fewer glands to lubricate the vagina, it can be more difficult for her to achieve the wetness for comfortable penetration. Use Vaseline, K-Y Jelly, or other natural oils for lubrication. Remember that the best rejuvenator of the vagina is frequent use, through orgasm and the Kegel exercises described on page 109.

- The phases of sexual response may also change over time: It may take longer for the older woman to get excited and achieve vaginal lubrication; the orgasmic phase is shorter and the uterine contractions are reduced in number; and the resolution phase—the period of time the body needs to return to its pre-aroused state—is shorter. Men experience similar changes. The best advice for older couples is to be communicative about the changes and adapt their lovemaking to their new rhythms.

- Some diseases associated with aging, and the medications taken for them, can alter sexual function, particularly medications for hypertension (see page 215). Inform your doctor of the problem—it could be corrected by changing the dosage, or switching brands of medication.

- From what the sex experts tell us, it is health-promoting for women to stay sexually active as long as they have the desire to do so. As a woman grows older, she can protect her potential for a satisfying sex life by maintaining her overall fitness and by staying actively involved with other people, with her work, and with her community.

11
The Myth of Senility

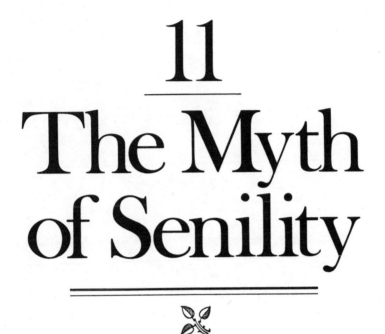

$\mathbf{F}$or a typical bright, active woman in her 30s, the most terrifying prospect of growing older is losing her brainpower. A few new wrinkles or a less taut abdomen are superficial changes, really, but a loss of mental abilities would threaten her basic self-concept. But there is nothing to fear. The odds are overwhelmingly in favor of this bright, active woman retaining her intellectual power far into the so-called twilight years.

Of course, age all by itself does not impart wisdom. Intellect doesn't suddenly appear in a woman who has spent her entire adult life worrying about ring-around-the-collar and reading Harlequin romances. For a woman for whom the life of the mind is important, however, there is good news: Most old people are as smart at 70 as they were at 30. And in tests of accumulated knowledge, such as vocabulary or the popular board game Trivial Pursuit, they actually may be smarter.

The healthy life-style of the baby-boom generation will pay dividends in old age in terms not only of physical health, but of mental health as well. With better educations, more stimulating careers, and more enriching opportunities than their mothers and grandmothers, women of the baby boom are spending their adult lives exercising their minds as vigorously as they exercise their bodies. So they probably can look forward to retaining their mental sharpness for as long as they live.

"Senility," that catch-all diagnosis that has come to mean confusion, forgetfulness, and disorientation in old age, is by no means inevitable. In fact, only about 5 to 10 percent of persons over the age of 65 have Alzheimer's disease, one of the few conditions accurately labeled "senile dementia." (Alzheimer's disease accounts for about 60 percent of the cases of senile dementia in the United States; another 20 percent can be traced to circulatory problems in the brain, and the rest to a combination of the two or to other, rare neurological diseases.[1]) But Alzheimer's disease, tragic as it is, is the exception, not the rule. It is a neurological disease probably caused by some combination of genetics, environmental toxins, and viral exposure. It is not the result of simple aging. For the vast majority of men and women, old age brings with it only a few intellectual changes—slowness, forgetfulness, and absentmindedness—that are, by and large, quite easily compensated for.

"The problem in old age is not so much how to have ideas," says Dr. B. F. Skinner, the Harvard psychologist, "as how to have them when you can use them."[2] In his recent book, *Enjoy Old Age,* Skinner advises keeping a pad and pen on the night table for middle-of-the-night inspirations that otherwise would be forgotten; taking action at the time it occurs to you to do so, such as putting an umbrella by the door as soon as you hear the forecast of rain; and using social ruses to hide such embarrassing lapses as forgetting an acquaintance's name. Memory almost always declines somewhat with age, but forgetfulness need not be debilitating. As Skinner puts it, "In place of memories, memoranda."[3]

It is important to differentiate the normal mental changes of age from the abnormal ones. *Some* forgetfulness is normal; forgetfulness to the degree seen in Alzheimer's disease is pathology. In Alzheimer's disease, memory loss and disorientation become progressively worse. At first, an individual might exhibit such apparently harmless traits as forgetfulness, slovenliness, and withdrawal. Eventually, this progresses to more profound changes such as inability to reason, loss of judgment, loss of memory, loss of orientation, inability to calculate, and, finally, inability to care for oneself or even to remember one's own name.

Neurologists like to make clear the distinction between normal aging and pathology by using two vivid terms: benign forgetfulness and malignant forgetfulness. Benign forgetfulness is when you misplace your glasses. Malignant forgetfulness is when you forget you ever wore glasses.

The Brain at Forty

In the spring of 1982, some Japanese scientists caused a minor flurry by reporting their findings that women's brains atrophy more rapidly than men's. Dr. Jun Hatazawa and colleagues at Tohoku University performed brain scans of 154 men and 147 women, aged 20 to 79, and concluded that men's brains begin shrinking in their 40s, but women's brains begin shrinking in their 30s.[4]

The Japanese findings were replicated by a group of pathologists at the Dundee (Scotland) General Hospital. According to the Scottish pathologists B. M. Hubbard and J. M. Anderson, "This may partly explain the very high incidence of senile dementia amongst aged women."[5] (They failed, however, to take into account the fact that old women are more likely to live to the advanced old age—80 years plus—when senile dementia reaches its highest prevalence rate of about 20 percent.)

Despite these findings, most neuroscientists say that the signs of aging in a 40-year-old brain—a woman's or a man's—generally have little

Brain Changes

The brain at 40 is smaller, lighter, and wetter, and it gradually pulls away from its sheath, the cortical mantle (see detail below). The valleys, or gyri, that separate the ridges of the brain matter become wider and deeper. And throughout her life, at an accelerated rate after the age of 20, a woman loses brain cells. Brain cell loss occurs in various regions of the brain including the cortex, the locus ceruleus (the region that controls sleep and perhaps intelligence), and the hippocampus (the seat of learning, memory, and perhaps pleasure). However, the physical changes that occur in the healthy, aging brain seem to have little effect on cognitive function.

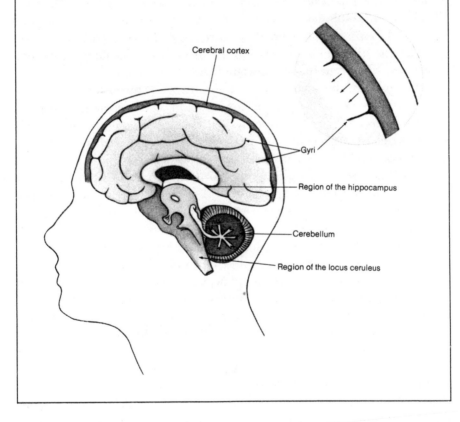

impact on the way the brain functions. Still, the physical changes are there. In the same way one's body loses tone with advanced age, so too does one's brain. The valleys, or gyri, that separate the ridges of brain matter become wider and deeper, and the entire brain pulls in from its encasement, the cortical mantle, like a sagging skin.

The brain at 40 is smaller, lighter, and wetter than it was at brain maturity (which is at about the age of two). Between the ages of 20 and 80, the brain loses about 7 percent of its overall weight. Brain cells, or neurons, are the only cells in the body that do not divide; once a neuron atrophies it is lost forever.[6]

Conventional wisdom has it that about 100,000 brain cells are lost daily beginning at about age 20 (out of some 10 to 100 *billion* brain cells altogether). But many scientists now protest that it is impossible to quantify this loss with any precision.

Cell loss occurs at different rates in different regions of the brain. Some parts of the brain don't seem ever to lose neurons. The number of cells in the vestibular nucleus, a small group of neurons in the brainstem that helps maintain head posture, does not diminish with age. Neither does the number of cells in the inferior olive, a larger group of cells in the hindbrain that is associated with motor control.

Other parts of the brain lose a lot of neurons. The cortex is the most dramatic example. In the cortex, the seat of higher intellectual functioning, the most rapid cell loss occurs between birth and the age of 30. Cortical cell loss then continues more slowly until, by the age of 90, the cortex has roughly one-half the brain cells it had in youth. Other brain regions that lose a significant number of neurons include the locus ceruleus, which affects sleep stages and perhaps intelligence, and the hippocampus, generally considered to be the seat of learning, memory, and perhaps even pleasure.[7]

Over time, the brain also begins accumulating some troublesome lesions, known as neuritic plaques and neurofibrillary tangles, that tend to interfere with the transmission of nerve impulses from one brain cell to another (see box, page 235). Plaques and tangles seem to form in all individuals, although they are so numerous in cases of Alzheimer's disease that they are considered a hallmark finding for postmortem diagnosis of the condition.

Changes have been measured, too, in the levels of neurotransmitters in the brain over time.[8] Neurotransmitters are the chemical substances that ferry nervous impulses from one neuron to another; without them, messages cannot get across the space between brain cells. The most significant age-associated loss in neurotransmitters has been found in the chemicals in the cholinergic system (which includes an enzyme precursor and an inhibitor as well as the transmitter itself, acetylcholine). The precursor, and probably acetylcholine as well, has been shown to decline by as much as 70 percent in healthy aged brains. Significantly, the cholinergic system is known to be involved in the retrieval of memories.

Of the 25 known or suspected neurotransmitters, most remain at relatively constant levels in healthy older persons. A few, in addition to acetylcholine, seem to decline as part of normal aging, including dopamine, epinephrine, and norepinephrine. One neurotransmitter, monoamine oxidase, may increase with age, but its presence in high levels has been linked to depression. And some researchers suspect that beta-endorphin, the brain's morphine-like painkiller, might also increase with age. Some studies of pain sensitivity have shown that old people have a better ability to mobilize beta-endorphin and use its pain-killing effect to best advantage.[9]

Is Senility a Myth?

"I can't seem to remember anything anymore," the woman might complain. "I go to the store, and I can't remember what I wanted to buy. I go out, and I can't remember whether I locked the door. I sit down to read, and I can't remember where I left my glasses. Sometimes I even forget what I had for breakfast that very morning."

How serious is this woman's problem? Should she worry about her forgetfulness? Is she exaggerating? Does her memory loss signal some underlying condition? Is she just terribly absentminded, or is she "going senile?"

The answer to these questions might depend on the woman's age. If she were 45, we might suspect that she is under stress—or we might think she is exaggerating a simple case of absentmindedness. If she were 55, we might say she is beginning to experience some serious age-related forgetfulness. And if she were 65 or older, we might say she is indeed "going senile."

The plain fact is that, no matter what her age, this woman's memory problems are in all likelihood perfectly normal. If she is quite young, however, she is unlikely to complain about them. Only when a person passes 40 or so is she likely to fear that she is "going senile" every time her glasses are mislaid.

Contrary to our expectations, senility is not inevitable with old age. Most older women—and older men—retain their mental abilities right to the end of life. There are two exceptions to this optimistic rule. Almost everyone will, with time, become slower in terms of ability to learn, to think, and to retrieve information; and almost everyone will, with time, become more forgetful.

The Normal Mental Changes of Old Age

When Olympic runner Mary Decker turns 65, she will no longer be able to run the mile in 4.5 minutes. But that doesn't mean she won't be able to run, and probably faster and longer than others her age. Similarly, when author Ann Beattie turns 65, she will probably not be able to churn out stories and novels as fast as she once did. But that doesn't mean she won't be able to write, and even to write as well as ever.

It is important to remember that a person's cognitive skills (which include thinking, perceiving, understanding, and reasoning) will undergo some change as a natural part of normal aging. There is nothing shameful in this, and the changes need not be particularly burdensome for a man or woman who expects them and accepts them. But because so many persons believe that "senility" is inevitable with age, the small foibles that are part of normal aging can take on a paralyzing significance. Every time an older woman forgets a phone number or mislays her eyeglasses, she may wonder whether she has already taken

---

Counting Sheep

As a woman ages, she sleeps less, and she spends a declining proportion of her sleep in restorative REM sleep. The changes are gradual, though, and for women they tend to occur most perceptibly after menopause—some 20 years after men start noticing changes in *their* sleeping patterns. These changes are normal, but the unusual woman who does not experience these normal changes is likely to fare better than her more typical peer. According to Dianne Hales, author of *The Complete Book of Sleep*, women who spend as much time in REM sleep as they always did tend to exhibit fewer changes in mental functioning.

SLEEP CHANGES OVER TIME

Typical sleep pattern in an 80-year-old	*Typical sleep pattern in a 20-year-old*
18 minutes to fall asleep	8 minutes to fall asleep
80 percent of night spent asleep	95 percent of night spent asleep
6 hours' total sleep time	7.5 to 8 hours' total sleep time
1 hour in REM sleep	2 hours in REM sleep

Source: Dianne Hales, *The Complete Book of Sleep*. Copyright © 1981. Addison-Wesley Publishing Company, Inc. Reprinted with permission.

the first step in the dreaded slide toward mental emptiness. Tragically, her fear can magnify the problem, turning a normal failing into an incapacitating handicap.

The myth about memory loss and intellectual decline with age is as powerful—and as destructive—as it is because the aged themselves have spent a lifetime believing it. We grow up expecting our grandparents, and then our parents, gradually to lose mental functioning, and as a result we treat them in ways that ensure that the myths will come true. When the time comes that we ourselves defined as "old," we look for those same symptoms in ourselves.

"Society's prejudices indoctrinate us before they hit us," says Alex Comfort, the noted British geriatrician. "How many 20-year-olds realize that sexual capacity and normal intelligence are lifelong in healthy humans? On this basis we obligingly drown ourselves as persons when the clock points to the appropriate age."[10]

Psychologists call it a self-fulfilling prophecy when a condition comes about because of one's *expectation* that it will come about. In this way, "senility" can be a self-fulfilling prophecy, and a tragic waste of human resources and individual lives. But socially induced senility may soon come to an end. Old people who remain active and alert have become plentiful enough these days to convince young people that mental health is the rule, not the exception. Women and men in their 30s today, the first generation to grow up believing that senility is not inevitable, will make plans that take for granted their own continuing intellectual growth. And, one can hope, their optimistic expectations will become the self-fulfilling prophecy of the next generation, when the "twilight years" are seen as years of expanding opportunities, continued learning, and, with luck, some growing wisdom.

Another reason to expect attitudes about aging and intelligence to change can be found in psychological circles. Traditionally, psychologists have derived their impressions about normal aging from intelligence test scores, which almost universally are lower in older test subjects than in younger test subjects. But these studies have been misleading, for two reasons. First, they compared old and young persons taking the same test at the same time, a study design called cross-sectional. But the old and young subjects had quite different backgrounds; the older the subject, the lower his or her educational attainment and the less skilled he or she was in the tricks of test-taking. When intelligence studies were redesigned to look for changes in test scores of the same individual over many years—that is, when the results were interpreted longitudinally rather than cross-sectionally—almost no decline could be found.[11]

The second hazard of traditional intelligence tests is that they depend on a rapid *speed of response* for an individual to perform well. A slight slowness of response is one of the most common, and least troublesome, intellectual changes of age, and timed tests fail to handicap older subjects for this slowness. But on self-paced tests, in which speed of response is not taken into account, the scores of the older subjects are almost as high as those of the younger ones.

The relationship between speed of response and intellectual "decline" was shown dramatically in a classic study at Wayne State University. Dr. Robert Kastenbaum assigned a series of decision-making tasks to his college-aged subjects, and gradually, without their knowledge, he accelerated the pace of the task. At first the students had five minutes in which to make their decisions. But Kastenbaum gradually shortened it to four minutes, then three, then two. As the tempo quickened, these young students began to "act old."

"Some narrowed their focus," Kastenbaum reports. "Some became almost stultified, some jittery and agitated. Even though many of them were aware that we were speeding things along, they still took it out on themselves when they couldn't perform fast enough. They were angry at themselves, angry that what had started out as a manageable task had become so complicated." [12]

Beginning in middle age, individuals slow down when they have an intellectual task to perform. "The index file doesn't age," Alex Comfort has said, "but the secretary is older and takes longer to put new cards in or to bring cards you want." [13] In other words, the memory is still tucked away somewhere, but older people just take longer finding it.

This delay in memory retrieval can start as early as the mid-30s. In one study of memory retrieval, three groups of people—young (19 to 21), middle-aged (33 to 43), and old (58 to 85)—were asked to memorize lists of numbers of varying lengths, and then to respond yes or no to flash cards of digits presented one at a time (yes if the number on the card had appeared on the memorized list, no if it hadn't). As the length of the list grew, from one number to three to five to seven, all age groups took longer to say yes or no when confronted with a flash card. But the additional digits slowed down the middle-aged and old groups more than they slowed down the young. The conclusion: Beginning in middle age, the rate of search diminishes, and this slowing down becomes progressively more detrimental as one must search an ever-larger memory store.[14]

Some forms of mental functioning need never change. One example of this is general intelligence—at least as measured by standardized tests like the Wechsler Adult Intelligence Scale. Psychologists who use the longitudinal study design have found that on the intelligence test measure most closely associated with "true" intelligence, their subjects exhibited a systematic increase over time. The improvement of this measure, called "crystallized intelligence"—which reflects such abilities as verbal comprehension, numerical skills, and inductive reasoning—continued "right into old age," the psychologists noted. "Even people over 70 improved from the first testing to the second."[15]

The Abnormal Mental Changes of Old Age

It is important to differentiate the normal from the abnormal in mental functioning of the middle-aged and elderly. If a woman gradually becomes more forgetful, but her lapses are harmless and easily compensated for, she can assume that she is experiencing a normal change. But if her memory loss is quite sudden, occurring over the course of a few short months, and if it interferes with her day-to-day functioning, she needs a physician's attention. In this situation, the woman may be suffering from a condition known as pseudosenility.

Pseudosenility is a reversible mental state caused by one of 100 or so *treatable* physical conditions. It can affect individuals at any age, but it is most dangerous in persons past the age of 50. Because so many people assume that mental decline is inevitable in the middle-aged and elderly, any sudden forgetfulness or disorientation in an older man or woman might seem quite unremarkable. But pseudosenility is in fact a medical emergency. If the underlying condition remains undiagnosed, the mental decline, which began as something treatable, might never be improved.

The most common cause of pseudosenility is depression, especially in women. Depression is a chameleon, likely to disguise itself as any of a wide range of physical or mental illnesses. And it is thought to affect twice as many women as men.

A depressed woman of any age has a weak self-image that is usually fed by stereotypes. When a teen-ager is depressed, she is acutely conscious of the conventional notion of adolescence as a time of turmoil and rebelliousness, and she may take her behavioral cues from that stereotype. In old age, the most widely held stereotype available to a depressed woman is that of a forgetful old lady in "second childhood." When asked to describe their day-to-day functioning, depressed old people are likely to sigh and say, "It's not so good; I forget a lot." The emphasis in such a statement, though, is not on the forgetfulness; it's on the sadness.

Treatment of depression in the aged should be as vigorous as it is for younger patients. "Contrary to popular professional opinion," notes Dr. Robert Butler, a psychiatrist and chairman of the geriatrics department at Mt. Sinai Medical Center in New York, "older persons can make effective use of the whole gamut of mental-health services, including psychotherapy, psychoanalysis, group psychotherapy, drug therapy, oc-cupational, physical and recreational therapies, behavioral modification therapies, family and marital counseling, and last, but by no means least, sex counseling and therapy. . . . Old people are eminently capable of [psychological] change [because] they stand so near to death. They have things to accomplish before it is too late. [16]

Another frequent cause of pseudosenility is drug intoxication. Older people are likely to be taking at least one or two prescription medica-tions for chronic medical conditions, plus one or two over-the-counter drugs for their aches and pains. This is especially true for women; surveys show that a physician is most likely to prescribe medications, particularly psychoactive or pain-killing drugs, when the patient is a woman. Any one of these drugs is likely to create adverse side effects in the elderly, since all drugs take longer to be metabolized as a person ages. When these drugs are taken in combination, they can be especially damaging.

Adverse drug reactions can take many forms in younger patients—drowsiness, hives, nausea, hyperactivity. In older patients, they tend to take one form above all others: a change in mental function. Certain common drugs—such as digitalis, diuretics, oral antidiabetes drugs, an-algesics, steroids, and sedatives—actually can induce brain disorder, which, if not corrected in time, can lead to irreparable damage. Other drugs may simply throw off the physiological balance of the aged brain just enough to create confusion and memory loss. Finally, some drugs may create physical side effects (usually an increased slowing of re-sponse, which exaggerates the normal slowing down of age) that are distressing enough to disorient an elderly person who hasn't been suf-ficiently warned to expect these reactions.

Other causes of pseudosenility include hormone dysfunction (particularly disorders of the thyroid, pancreas, and adrenal gland), kidney infection, heart attack, malnutrition, anemia, gallstones, fecal impaction, and even a bad cold. Because so many illnesses show up first in the elderly as confusion, any sudden bout of "senility" must be considered treatable until proven otherwise. The prospects are good; for every 100 confused old people who show up in the doctor's office, as many as 20 or 30 of them can be treated and cured.

Alzheimer's Disease

About 10 percent of the aged do suffer from senile dementia, a brain disease that affects an estimated 1 million to 2 million Americans over 65, men and women equally. The majority of these people have Alzheimer's disease, a disease of the brain cells that leads to profound memory loss, disorientation, personality changes, and eventually death. About 120,000 deaths in the United States have been attributed to Alzheimer's disease each year.

Alzheimer's disease is devastating—but it is no more inevitable than heart disease or cancer. It is not even a disease of old age only, occasionally affecting individuals as young as 40. (Indeed, the disease was first

Clogging Up the Brain

Neuritic plaques and neurofibrillary tangles are the troublesome brain lesions found in great numbers in persons with Alzheimer's disease. But most people develop at least some plaques and tangles if they live long enough. In the general population, a sharp rise in the prevalence of plaques and tangles has been detected after the age of 40.

Age	Percent of persons with neuritic plaques in the neocortex	Percent of persons with neurofibrillary tangles in the hippocampus
30–40	13	0
40–50	18	5
50–60	40	20
60–70	48	52
70–80	70	90

Source: Robin Marantz Henig, *The Myth of Senility: Misconceptions About the Brain and Aging* (New York: Anchor Press/Doubleday, 1981), p. 45.

described in 1906 in a 55-year-old woman who died of what was then called "pre-senile dementia.")

In the past five years, an extraordinary amount of public and professional attention has been directed toward Alzheimer's disease. Scientists are pursuing several theories about what might cause it. Among the most promising:

- the theory that it is passed on genetically (Alzheimer's disease does seem to run in families, and tends to occur in families with higher-than-normal rates of other genetic diseases such as Down's syndrome);
- the theory that it results from excess accumulation of aluminum in the brain (high levels of aluminum have been found in Alzheimer's brains, and in the brains of persons with other forms of dementia as well); and
- the theory that it is caused by a slow-acting virus that lodges in brain cells, remains dormant for 20 or more years, and is reactivated by some stress to the body—a scenario known to account for at least two rare neurological diseases that also create dementia.

Diagnosis of Alzheimer's disease can only be made conclusively on autopsy—in other words, you cannot know a person has Alzheimer's disease until after death. But some tests have proved helpful in ruling out other possible causes of dementia and in pointing toward a probable diagnosis of Alzheimer's disease. Among these are psychological tests of memory and orientation, a CAT scan (a brain X-ray to detect anatomical changes in the brain), and a PETT scan (which records brain activity by visualizing the metabolism of radioactive glucose in the brain).

On autopsy, a diseased brain shows characteristic changes: a proliferation of neurofibrillary tangles and neuritic plaques, especially in the brain regions concerned with thought and memory, and a severe decline in the level of brain chemicals in the cholinergic family of neurotransmitters—the transmitters involved in memory retrieval.

Because the body of an Alzheimer's victim often stays relentlessly healthy, the mental deterioration can continue for ten or 15 years, or even more. One woman with Alzheimer's disease is described by her son, nine years after her condition was diagnosed, as "passing away cell by cell, wasting with excrutiating slowness, withering—I hardly know how to describe . . . this awful erosion, this endless leaking away."[17]

For now, Alzheimer's disease has no cure. Researchers have experienced limited success with some drugs, but only in terms of improving a patient's mood, not in reversing or even slowing the cognitive decline. Currently, a diagnosis of Alzheimer's disease is a diagnosis of inexorably progressive memory loss, finally leaving the victim unable to think, speak, or even use the bathroom. The only good thing that can be said about Alzheimer's disease is that most people will not experience it.

Staying Bright in the Twilight Years

Take a tip from the old age masters: If you want to maintain intellectual vigor throughout a lifetime, use your brain. This means setting up mental challenges again and again to keep the mind agile and flexible. Exercise is as crucial to maintaining intellectual functioning as it is to maintaining physical functioning.

A woman whose job demands creative thinking has a built-in advantage; she uses her mind every day. But for women who are retired, or who have never had careers, the challenges must be sought after. Reading is one way to keep involved and alert. Learning a new skill—a new language, perhaps, or a new musical instrument—is useful at any age. Getting involved in a community improvement project or a political campaign is a good way to focus one's planning ability and organizational skills—skills that generally improve with age.

Finding younger friends, beginning in one's 30s and 40s, is also excellent insurance against emotional and intellectual isolation in old age. Margaret Mead, the noted anthropologist, advocated this technique of surrounding oneself with youth in one's old age. "Change all your doctors, opticians, and dentists when you reach fifty," she advised in a 1977 interview, when she was 76. "You start out when you are young with everybody who looks after you older than you are. When you get to be fifty, most of these people are sixty-five or older. Change them all and get young ones. Then, as you grow older, you'll have people who are still alive and active taking care of you. You won't be desolate because every one of your doctors is dead." [18] The same advice can be made about one's friends—not necessarily to toss out the old, but vigorously to pursue the new, and to do so when you are young enough to have the energy for making new friends.

We tend to live and function in age-segregated ghettoes, but this can only create loneliness and withdrawal in old age. If all your friends are from your generation, and you are lucky enough to live a long time, your old age is likely to be clouded with feelings of abandonment as your dear friends die. But if you cultivate friendships with younger people during your middle age, you will continue to have a new store of friends still alive when *you* are old, friends who can help you stay involved in the world outside yourself. And there's nothing like involvement for staying "young," interested, and alive.

Maintenance: The Brain

The woman who otherwise approaches old age with confidence may yet be terrified at the thought of losing her mental abilities. She should know that normal aging does not mean the loss of brainpower. Studies show that most people are as smart at age 70 as they were at age 30.

However, because there are age-related diseases that do impair mental functioning, it's important to be able to distinguish between the normal and abnormal effects of aging on the brain.

- Memory loss is a symptom of both normal and abnormal aging of the brain. A woman should not be alarmed if she misplaces her glasses. But if memory loss is severe enough to interfere with her day-to-day functioning, she should see her doctor. Memory loss, disorientation, and mental deterioration can be caused by many factors, including Alzheimer's disease.

- Severe depression is a condition that should not be chalked up to age. A woman who is chronically depressed needs help. She shouldn't blame herself, or try to suffer through it alone.

- A dependency on certain drugs, or the combination of certain drugs in the body, can have a wide range of effects, such as a slowing of physical response, confusion, memory loss, and eventually pseudosenility and brain damage. Your doctor should know if you drink alcoholic beverages or take drugs, including aspirin and other pain killers.

To keep her mind functioning well, a woman needs to keep her brain active. For women who have exercised their minds vigorously throughout life, this is a welcome and easy task. Seek out ways to challenge your brain: Learn a new skill, get involved in a community project, continue to be creative, and indulge your appetite for reading whenever you have the chance.

Getting enough sleep is also important for good mental health, and is a problem for some older women. Here are tips to combat occasional bouts of insomnia:

- Maintain a regular schedule during your waking hours: Eat balanced meals; exercise, or simply take a brisk walk daily; get to bed at the same time in the evening. Your body functions better if you follow its regular, natural rhythms.

- Relax before you turn off the lights and try to sleep. Listen to music, read in bed, do gentle stretching exercises.

- Try not to use your bedroom to study your financial situation, or to attend to office work. If you associate your bedroom with relaxing pastimes, sleep, and sex—and not with the kinds of anxieties that can keep you up at night—you will sleep better.

12
Future Stock

The ancient Greeks told the story of Eos, the goddess of the dawn, who fell in love with the handsome young Tithonus. She asked Zeus to grant Tithonus eternal life, and her wish was granted. But the wish was incomplete; Eos had forgotten to ask for eternal youth. So Tithonus was condemned to grow old forever. "Helpless at last, unable to move hand or foot, he prayed for death, but there was no release for him," writes Edith Hamilton in *Mythology*. "He must live on forever, with old age forever pressing upon him more and more. At last in pity the goddess laid him in a room and left him, shutting the door. There he babbled endlessly, words with no meaning." [1]

The horrible spectre of Tithonus's eternal senility haunts us when we think of "living forever." That is why eternal *youth*, not eternal *life*, has been pursued so vigorously through the centuries. Myths about the fountain of youth abound in Hindu, Hebrew, Greek, and Roman legend; youth potions have been hawked since Egyptian times; the quest for "springs of youth" accounts for some of the adventures of King Arthur's knights, Ponce de Leon's explorers, and scores of wealthy European ladies at the spas of Bath and Vichy. And recently, the phenomenal success of books such as *The No-Aging Diet* is proof of the public's insatiable hunger for advice on how to stay young forever.

Unfortunately, there is no magical, or easy, path to eternal youth. The secrets of staying young are the rules we have been reiterating throughout this book. They are not easy rules to follow, because they require tough changes in life-style today for uncertain benefits tomorrow. If you cut back on red meat now, will you really have a "younger" cardiovascular system in 20 years? And will it be worth all those juicy steaks you had to forego?

Staying young, by the way, is not the same thing as living longer. According to Dr. Jordan Tobin of the National Institute on Aging, there is little proof that any of the manipulations commonly pursued in the name of long life—even the old standbys like lowfat diets and aerobic exercise—will in any way extend one's life-span. "If you want to live longer," he says, "there is only one thing we can say that, based on the data, probably contributes to a longer life: Wear your seat belt."

Aging in the Twenty-First Century

In the year 2015, a woman of 65 will have a lot going for her. Because of her improved life-style, embarked on back in 1985 (when she was 35 years old), this woman may look and feel like a 45-year-old woman does today. If she has maintained healthy eating habits and exercised regularly, she will have the body shape and muscle tone of a woman in her 40s. If she has kept her heart and lungs strong, she can continue the rugged physical activities she engaged in 20 years before—and embark on new activities as well. If she stopped smoking, or never started, she may be spared the cancer and heart disease that plagued her mother's generation in *their* 60s. And if, in addition, she has consumed enough calcium, maintained her teeth properly, done her Kegel exercises, and protected herself from the sun, she may avoid the small pitfalls of the aging body that tend to occur in a 65-year-old woman today.

The steps to healthier aging require some modification in the life-style to which our mothers aspired. In a previous generation, women and men believed the luckiest individual was the one for whom no pleasure was denied. The American dream life-style was a hedonistic one. While there is indeed a certain appeal to a pampered existence in which physical exertion is unnecessary and sensuous appetites are easily appeased, most people today engage in such habits for no more than two-week vacations. Now that they know the health costs of overeating and underexercising, more and more Americans are following the experts' advice. For the sake of their bodies and in some cases their souls, today's 30-year-olds have begun to redefine the ideal life-style as a kind of healthy asceticism. And as they age, they will continue to benefit from this new definition.

For a healthy old age, a woman must have a healthy youth, a youth in which good eating and exercising habits are as natural as breathing. The rules for healthy aging therefore apply to women at every age. We have stated these rules over and over again as we investigated the aging of each organ system of a woman's body. Here they are once again.

THE TEN COMMANDMENTS OF HEALTHY AGING

1. Do not smoke.
2. Do not sunbathe, and wear a protective sunscreen when you must expose yourself to the sun.
3. Change your diet to include more fruits, vegetables, dairy

products, and grains. Eat less fat, animal protein, salt, sugar, and cholesterol, and eat a variety of foods.

4. Get enough calcium.

5. Exercise vigorously on a regular basis, at least one-half hour three times a week.

6. Maintain a normal weight, within 10 percent in either direction of the "ideal weight" on insurance tables.

7. Drink six to eight glasses of water a day.

8. Do Kegel (pelvic floor) exercises 50 times a day, and achieve orgasm through intercourse or masturbation at least once a week.

9. Floss your teeth daily, and have them cleaned professionally two or three times a year.

10. Keep up a wide range of interests, an optimistic attitude, and a sense of community with family, friends, neighbors, even pets.

A woman who is 65 in the year 2015 will have more going for her than her personal life-style. She will be aging in a cultural milieu in which the whole world seems to be getting older. Men and women of the postwar baby boom—those born between 1947 and 1965—have, on the strength of sheer numbers, virtually defined the "best" age to be throughout their collective lifetime. In 2015, when an estimated 25 percent of the American population is over 65,[2] old age will carry quite a different connotation than it does today, when the elderly are just 11 percent of the population.

Baby-boomers have always changed the cultural context of their own experiences. In the 1950s, when they were young, elementary schools erupted on the landscape, and advertisers tried to get to the money earners by appealing to their kids. In the 1960s, the center of action was on high school and college campuses, and the choices of these young people, from the miniskirt to the sexual revolution, were fashions of the day. In the 1970s, those of the baby-boom generation declared that no one over 30 was to be trusted; later, when they passed 30, that attitude quietly disappeared. And when this generation got busy in the 1980s creating a baby boomlet of their own, scores of books and articles suddenly appeared about pregnancy, childbearing, parenting, and how to choose the best fold-up stroller.

When the baby-boomers have all gone gray, there is every reason to believe that their self-preoccupation will continue to set trends. Suddenly, it will be good to be old. We are already seeing signs of this, as they push the date of their "mid-life crisis" at least a decade past when their parents encountered it. A generation ago, a woman began to feel "over the hill" when she passed her thirtieth birthday. These days, a woman usually doesn't face the fact of her own aging process until at least the age of 40.

With this new cultural definition of an acceptable age, one can hope as well for a reorientation of society's attention, so that persons over 65 can at last demand and receive the resources and services they require.

A Changing Life-span?

All the good health habits in the world have not yet extended the human life-span. While life expectancy, the age by which one-half of the population will die, has changed significantly since Roman times—from about 22 in 100 B.C. to 40 in the mid-1800s, 50 near the turn of the century, and about 75 today—life-span has remained frustratingly constant. The upper limit of the human life-span is and has always been about 110 years; the only news here is that today more people than ever before are attaining this advanced age. Researchers in the field of longevity want to push that limit. They want to expand the human life-span to 120 years, 130 years, 140 years or beyond. Some critics wonder whether this is really a good idea; after all, they point out, society cannot bear the cost of maintaining a race of Tithonuses. Longevity researchers counter that their goal is to extend *productive* life; if they are successful, they say, the added years of life will be years equivalent to the years of middle age.

To figure out what would make us live longest, longevity researchers first must discover what makes us age and die. For the past 20 years, they have been devising and testing theories that might explain aging at the cellular and organism levels. No one theory has yet been accepted as accounting for all aspects of aging. No one scientist has yet proposed that his favorite aging mechanism is the single determinant of the rate at which an individual ages. But a few theories have stood the test of time, and today are considered the leading theories to begin explaining how a person ages.

Free-radical theory.[3] This popular theory was first proposed by Dr. Denham Harman, a chemist at the University of Nebraska, in 1966. Free radicals are highly unstable pieces of molecules that are on the prowl for other molecules to link up with. When a free radical attaches

Toward the Bionic Woman

In the twenty-first century, if you need a spare body part, chances are you'll be able to get it. Already, dramatic improvements in technology and in methods of suppressing the body's immune system have made possible these tissue transplants and artificial prostheses.

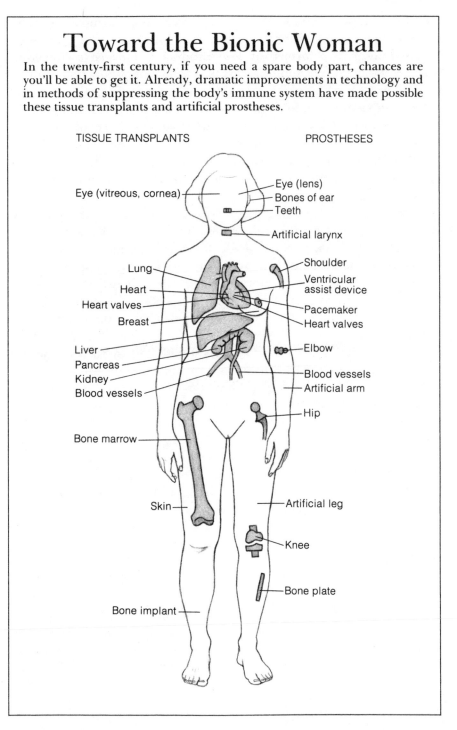

TISSUE TRANSPLANTS   PROSTHESES

Eye (vitreous, cornea)
Eye (lens)
Bones of ear
Teeth
Artificial larynx
Lung
Shoulder
Ventricular assist device
Heart
Heart valves
Pacemaker
Breast
Heart valves
Liver
Elbow
Pancreas
Kidney
Blood vessels
Blood vessels
Artificial arm
Hip
Bone marrow
Skin
Artificial leg
Knee
Bone plate
Bone implant

itself to a healthy molecule, the resulting "cross-linked" molecule is too large, and too contorted, to perform its work properly.

Free radicals are formed as a by-product of oxygen metabolism, which is the basic function of all living cells. Their production is inevitable, then, unless it is inhibited by the introduction of certain chemicals called antioxidants. Antioxidants now are being marketed as a possible key to longevity. Among the most popular: vitamin C, vitamin E, BHT (bis-hydroxytoluene), SOD (superoxide dismutase), and selenium. Antioxidant therapy forms the basis for the "life extension" diets promoted by Roy Walford in *Maximum Life Span* and by Durk Pearson and Sandy Shaw in *Life Extension*.

Endocrine theories and the "death hormone."[4] Removing the pituitary gland—the "master gland" of the endocrine system, which gives orders for all other hormonal secretions—is a rather extreme step to take in pursuit of a longer life. But Dr. W. Donner Denckla did just that—with astonishing results. In laboratory rats at Harvard University, Denckla removed the pituitary gland and kept the rats alive with daily injections of some of the pituitary hormones they needed. According to Denckla, the rats without pituitaries aged far more slowly than intact rats. Their coats turned brown again, their kidneys stopped aging, their cardiovascular and immune system functions returned to youthful levels. The reason: When the pituitary gland was removed, so was the source of a hormone that Denckla calls DECO (for decreasing oxygen consumption hormone) and that his popularizers call the "death hormone."

Denckla thinks that DECO may be the orchestrator for all the aging in the body. He doesn't know *why* or *how,* only that it seems responsible for aging in the lungs, heart, and brain. He is now trying to isolate DECO in the hopes of producing an antagonist that would deliver the promise of extending the lives of human beings.

The thymus is another endocrine gland thought to play a central role in the aging of the organism. For years, scientists have known that the thymus gland, which is located in the chest just behind the breastbone, has an unusual life cycle: It is quite large during childhood, and gradually shrinks until by late adolescence it has disappeared altogether. The isolation of its principal hormone, thymosin, made clear the gland's function in maintaining the health of the immune system. And it set scientists to wondering whether the disappearance of the thymus gland is somehow central to the aging of the immune system, and of the organism itself.

In his book *Prolongevity*, Albert Rosenfeld, a prominent science writer, predicted in 1976 that thymosin "may be one of the first important anti-aging drugs to reach the marketplace."[5] Although it has been outpaced by the antioxidants, which already claim title to being anti-aging drugs, the value of thymosin in retarding aging may yet prove to be significant.

The aging clock. A preset cellular clock was first demonstrated in the 1960s by Dr. Leonard Hayflick of the Wistar Institute in Philadelphia.[6] Hayflick took bits of lung tissue from human embryos and kept them alive in as supportive an environment as a laboratory dish could muster. The lung cells divided regularly and the cell colony doubled over and over again. But the colony did not live forever. After the cells had doubled approximately 50 times, the colony gradually died out. Hayflick theorized that the body cells of an embryo are engineered to divide only a finite number of times, and then to die.

Subsequent manipulations with his embryonic lung cells confirmed Hayflick's suspicions. Lung cells taken from an older organism divided fewer than 50 times, usually in proportion to the age of the individual from which they were derived. In other words, lung cells from an individual midway through the expected life-span divided only 25 times. Embryonic cells that were frozen after approximately 30 doublings and then thawed out seemed to "remember" where they had left off, doubling only another 20 times or so before they died. And when the nucleus of an embryonic cell was inserted into the cytoplasm (cell body) of an older cell, the old cell took its orders from the young nucleus and went through another 50 doublings before it died. (Conversely, when an older nucleus that had already gone through 30 doublings was inserted into a younger cell body, the cell colony doubled only 20 more times.)

As the cells approached what has come to be known as the "Hayflick limit," they began to look old. They became larger, and were riddled with increasing amounts of lipofuscin, the pigment accumulation responsible for, among other things, "age spots" of the skin.

Hayflick's research has been widely accepted as evidence that cells carry a sort of biological clock, embedded in the nucleus, that is set to wind down at a particular age. If this is so, there is little that scientists can do to prolong the life-span; all they can do is to prolong life expectancy so that a greater proportion of persons live out their fully allotted time.

Women: The Long-Lived Sex

One observation regarding life-span has remained remarkably consistent through the ages, and indeed across the species: Females live longer than males. A white 65-year-old woman is likely to live to 83, four years longer than her male counterpart. And a woman of 32 can expect to live to be nearly 80 if she's white, nearly 77 if she's black—seven to eight years longer than a man of the same race and age.

The gap between men and women has actually widened in the past 30 years. In 1950, life expectancy for a baby girl was 71, and for a baby boy it was 65½—a difference of five and one-half years. But for a baby girl born in 1978, the life expectancy is 77—nearly eight years more than for a boy born the same year.[7]

What accounts for this difference? Are women biologically hardier, or are they just more adept at avoiding the major killers? Researchers believe it's a little of both. Because females are longer-lived in almost every animal species, there does seem to be some inherent biological advantage in being female. Some think there is some protection in the redundancy of having two "X" chromosomes. (The chromosomal configuration known as "XX" is what makes someone female, and the configuration known as "XY" is what makes someone male.) That way, if there is an error on one X chromosome, a female has a second, probably error-free, X chromosome to compensate for it.

But biology is not everything. A consensus seems to be growing that women's longer life expectancy is more a result of behavioral advantages than biological ones. Dr. Ingrid Waldron of the University of Pennsylvania has been a leading proponent of this view. She attributes the great majority of the "excess mortality" in males to life-style differences.

According to Waldron, 40 percent of excess male mortality can be traced to arteriosclerotic heart disease, which in turn can be traced to greater cigarette smoking among men and "probably a greater prevalence of the competitive, aggressive Coronary Prone Behavior Pattern." Another 33 percent of excess male mortality, Waldron says, can be accounted for by "accidents, suicide, and cirrhosis of the liver. Each of these is related to behaviors which are encouraged or accepted more in men than in women in our society—for example, using guns, being adventurous and acting unafraid, working at hazardous jobs and drinking alcohol."[8]

Women also may deal with the stress they do encounter in a healthier, more life-enhancing way than men do. As a group, women are more likely than men to express their emotions and seek out psychological support from professionals, friends, and family. Because of the contribution that stress makes to many degenerative diseases, some observers think that a woman's tendency to work through her problems—compared to a man's tendency to bottle them up inside—might help contribute to her greater life expectancy.

If women's life-styles really do help lead to longer lives, then women in the next century might not be as protected as they like to think they are. Social observers have seen a decided "masculinization" of life-style in recent years, with women behaving more and more like men. Some of this has come about with the rising numbers of women in the workplace. With women now negotiating the terrain of the outside world, they are encountering many of the health and safety hazards traditionally reserved for men, including exposure to dangerous workplaces and the increased likelihood of car or plane accidents as they clock more miles traveled each year. And jobs, no matter what their inherent risk, tend to place women under more stress than men, because the vast majority of working women still have all the cooking, cleaning, and child-rearing responsibilities after they get home.

Women still tend to cope with stress more healthily than men, turning to each other or to professionals for counseling and support. But some women are turning instead to the crutches men have always used, such as cigarettes or alcohol, or are finding new substances of their own to abuse, such as prescription tranquilizers or caffeine- and saccharin-laden diet sodas.

We cannot predict the impact on a woman's health and longevity of being employed outside the home throughout her adult life. There are indeed some hazards associated with women's new work status—stress, workplace accidents, failure to recover from childbirth after a brief maternity leave—and we have yet to see how these risks will affect the health of women in their 50s, 60s, and beyond. But just as likely is the possibility that women's work will bring with it some wonderful *improvements* in an older woman's health, most probably because of the changes it portends for a woman's relationship to the world around her.

Outside employment helps a woman establish an identity and a community beyond her husband and children. In late life, when her nest has emptied, this woman will still stay connected to her surroundings through her work and her friendships. A woman who has been engaged for much of her life in rewarding work is most likely to perceive herself, and be perceived by others, as a committed individual whose existence in this world makes a difference. As this woman ages, she will stay "young" in a way that no amount of exercise, creams, or antioxidant pills can accomplish. With the health and vigor that come about from social involvement, this woman—the older woman of the twenty-first century—will truly be able to live until she dies.

NOTES AND SOURCES

CHAPTER 1: HOW A WOMAN AGES

1. Gloria Steinem, "50 Is What 40 Used to Be—And Other Thoughts on Growing Up," *Ms.*, vol. 12, no. 2, June 1984, pp. 109–110.

2. Linda Campanelli, "Women and Aging." A lecture presented at the National Institutes of Health, Bethesda, Md., September 1983.

3. Roy L. Walford, *Maximum Life Span* (New York: W. W. Norton, 1983); Albert Rosenfeld, *Prolongevity* (New York: Alfred A. Knopf, 1976); Kenneth R. Pelletier, *Longevity* (New York: Delacorte Press, 1981).

4. Stanton H. Cohn et al., "Compartmental Body Composition Based on Total-Body Nitrogen, Potassium, and Calcium," *American Journal of Physiology*, vol. 239, 1980, pp. E524–E530.

5. Jennifer Robinson, "Body Image in Women over Forty," *Melpomene Institute for Women's Health*, October 1983, p. 12.

6. Steinem, *op. cit.*, p. 109.

7. Albert Kligman, "The Skin and Aging." Presented at a conference on "Mental Health Aspects of Physical Disease in Late Life," National Institutes of Health, Bethesda, Md., March 31, 1984.

8. Barbara A. Gilchrest, "Age-Associated Changes in the Skin," *Journal of the American Geriatrics Society*, vol. 30, no. 2, February 1982, pp. 139–142.

9. Charles W. Finley et al., "Periodontal Therapy: A Summary Status Report—1983," American Academy of Periodontology, 1983.

10. Morris Notelovitz and Marsha Ware, *Stand Tall! The Informed Woman's Guide to Osteoporosis* (Gainesville, Fla.: Triad Publishing Co., 1982), p. 38.

11. Sally Squires, "Menopause: Beyond the Myths," *The Washington Post*, Oct. 24, 1984, p. D7.

12. Stephen Kiesling, "Breath Test for Life Span?" *American Health*, March/April 1983, p. 25.

13. Jane Porcino, *Growing Older, Getting Better* (Reading, Mass.: Addison-Wesley, 1983), p. 294.

14. *Ibid.*, p. 300.

15. Ruth Weg, "More Than Wrinkles," in L. E. Troll, J. Israel, K. Israel, eds. *Looking Ahead: A Woman's Guide to the Problems and Joys of Growing Older* (Englewood Cliffs, N.J.: Prentice Hall, 1977), pp. 32-35; also, Helen Singer Kaplan, "Sex and Aging." Presented at a conference on "Mental Health Aspects of Physical Disease in Late Life," National Institutes of Health, Bethesda, Md., March 30, 1984.

16. "Sex and the 'Senile Vagina,' " *Science News*, vol. 123, May 21, 1983, p. 328.

17. U.S. Bureau of the Census, *Statistical Abstract of the United States, 1981* (Washington, D.C.: U.S. Department of Commerce, 1981), p. 25.

18. Bernard D. Starr and Marcella B. Weiner, *The Starr-Weiner Report on Sex and Sexuality in the Mature Years* (New York: McGraw-Hill, 1982), p. 285.

19. Robin Marantz Henig, *The Myth of Senility: Misconceptions About the Brain and Aging* (New York: Anchor Press/Doubleday, 1981), p. 119.

20. A. R. Omran, "A Century of Epidemiologic Transition in the United States," *Preventive Medicine*, vol. 6, no. 1, March 1977, pp. 30–51, cited in Pelletier, *Longevity, op. cit.*

21. Toni L. Goldfarb, "For Robust Life, Try Wedded Bliss," *American Health*, November/December 1982, pp. 98–99.

CHAPTER 2: THE SHAPE OF THINGS TO COME

1. Bureau of the Census, *Current Populations Report: Population Estimates and Projections*, series P-25, no. 952 (Washington, D.C.: U.S. Department of Commerce, 1984), p. 77.
2. Gail Sheehy, *Passages* (New York: E. P. Dutton, 1976).
3. Sandra Rosenzweig, *Sportsfitness for Women* (New York: Harper & Row, 1982), p. 96.
4. Stanton H. Cohn et al., "Compartmental Body Composition Based on Total-Body Nitrogen, Potassium, and Calcium," *American Journal of Physiology*, vol. 239, 1980, pp. E524–E530.
5. *Ibid.*, p. E527.
6. Doreen Glucken with Michael Eberhart, *The Body at Thirty* (New York: M. Evans & Co., 1982), pp. 33–34.
7. Elizabeth Martin, *The Over-30 6-Week All-Natural Health and Beauty Plan* (New York: Clarkson N. Potter, 1982).
8. Isadore Rossman, "Anatomic and Body Composition Changes with Aging," in Caleb E. Finch and Leonard Hayflick, eds., *Handbook of the Biology of Aging* (New York: Van Nostrand Reinhold, 1977), p. 199.
9. E. Gutmann, "Muscle," in Finch and Hayflick, *op. cit.*, p. 461.
10. *Ibid.*
11. Laurence E. Morehouse and Augustus T. Miller, Jr., *The Physiology of Exercise*, 7th Edition (St. Louis: C V. Mosby, 1976), p. 327.
12. Elissa Melamed, *Mirror Mirror: The Terror of Not Being Young* (New York: Linden Press, 1983), p. 143.
13. *Ibid.*, p. 144.
14. Ralph Leslie Dicker and Victor Royce Syracuse, *Consultation with a Plastic Surgeon* (New York: Warner Books, 1975).
15. Curtis Bill Pepper, *We the Victors* (New York: Doubleday, 1984), p. 62.
16. *Ibid.*, p. 60.
17. Jane Brody, *Jane Brody's The New York Times Guide to Personal Health* (New York: Avon Books, 1983), p. 646.
18. Ernest Aegerter, *Save Your Heart* (New York: Van Nostrand Reinhold, 1981), p. 120.
19. *Ibid.*, p. 97.
20. Roy L. Walford, *Maximum Life Span* (New York: W. W. Norton, 1983), p. 153.
21. Jane Brody, *Jane Brody's Nutrition Book* (W. W. Norton, 1981), p. 409.

CHAPTER 3: A WRINKLE IN TIME

1. Elissa Melamed, *Mirror Mirror: The Terror of Not Being Young* (New York: Linden Press, 1983), p. 72.
2. Joan Israel, "Confessions of a 45-Year-Old Feminist," in Lillian E. Troll, Joan Israel, and Kenneth Israel, eds., *Looking Ahead: A Woman's Guide to the Problems and Joys of Growing Older* (Englewood Cliffs, N.J.: Prentice-Hall, 1977), p. 66.
3. Carol A. Nowak, "Does Youthfulness Equal Attractiveness?" in Troll, Israel, and Israel, *op. cit.*, p. 61.
4. *Ibid.*
5. "Wrinkle Riddles," *Science Digest*, September 1983, p. 84.
6. Kathleen Jonah, "Ageless Skin," *Self*, January 1984, p. 94.
7. Victor J. Selmanowitz, Ronald L. Rizer, and Norman Orentreich, "Aging of the Skin and Its Appendages," in Caleb E. Finch and Leonard Hayflick, eds., *Handbook of the Biology of Aging* (New York: Van Nostrand Reinhold, 1977), p. 497.
8. Barbara A. Gilchrest, "Age-Associated Changes in the Skin," *Journal of the American Geriatric Society*, vol. 30, no. 2, February 1982, p. 140.
9. Elizabeth Martin, *The Over-30 6-Week All-Natural Health and Beauty Plan* (New York: Clarkson N. Potter, 1982), pp. 106–107.

10. "The Unveiling of a New Ford," *Time,* October 23, 1978, p. 97.

11. Melamed, *op. cit.,* p. 142.

12. Susan S. Lichtendorf, *Eve's Journey: The Physical Experience of Being Female* (New York, Berkley Books, 1983), page 144.

13. *Physician Characteristics and Distribution in the United States, 1982 Edition* (Chicago: American Medical Association, 1983), p. 41.

14. *Ibid.,* p. 153.

15. Gilchrest, *op. cit.,* pp. 139–140.

16. Linda Allen Schoen, ed., *The AMA Book of Skin and Hair Care* (New York: Avon Books, 1976), p. 134.

17. *Ibid.,* p. 103.

CHAPTER 4: TEETH, BONES, AND JOINTS

1. D. L. Anderson, "Periodontal Disease and Aging," *Gerontology,* vol. 1, no. 1, 1982, pp. 19–23.

2. Morris Notelovitz and Marsha Ware, *Stand Tall! The Informed Woman's Guide to Preventing Osteoporosis* (Gainesville, Fla.: Triad Publishing Company, 1982).

3. Jane Porcino, *Growing Older, Getting Better: A Handbook for Women in the Second Half of Life* (Reading, Mass.: Addison-Wesley, 1983), pp. 248–249.

4. Figures provided by the National Institute for Dental Research (NIDR), National Institutes of Health, Bethesda, Md.

5. Figures provided by NIDR.

6. Judith E. Randal, "To Avoid $2,000 Gum Surgery, Acid Breath and Loose Teeth," *American Health,* vol. 1, no. 1, March/April 1982, pp. 82–85.

7. Harry W. Daniell, "Postmenopausal Tooth Loss: Contributions to Edentulism by Osteoporosis and Cigarette Smoking," *Archives of Internal Medicine,* vol. 143, September 1983, pp. 1678–1682.

8. Bruce J. Baum, "Research on Aging and Oral Health: An Assessment of Current Status and Future Needs," *Special Care in Dentistry,* vol. 1, no. 4, July/August 1981, pp. 156–165.

9. Notelovitz and Ware, *op. cit.,* p. 17.

10. *Ibid.,* pp. 88–112.

11. Myron Winick, *For Mothers and Daughters* (New York: William Morrow, 1983), pp. 20–21.

12. Notelovitz and Ware, *op. cit.,* p. 51.

13. Stanton H. Cohn et al., "Effect of Aging on Bone Mass in Adult Women," *American Journal of Physiology,* vol. 230, no. 1, January 1976, pp. 143–148.

14. *Ibid.,* p. 147.

15. Notelovitz and Ware, *op. cit.,* p. 26.

16. Porcino, *op. cit.,* p. 229.

17. Notelovitz and Ware, *op. cit.,* pp. 42–43.

18. *Ibid.,* p. 37.

19. *Ibid.,* p. 51.

20. *Ibid.,* p. 63.

21. *Ibid.,* p. 64.

22. *Ibid.,* p. 65.

23. *Ibid.*

24. *Ibid.,* pp. 67, 70.

25. *Ibid.,* p. 102.

26. *Ibid.,* p. 60.

27. *Ibid.*

28. James F. Fries, *Arthritis: A Comprehensive Guide* (Reading, Mass.: Addison-Wesley, 1979), p. 156.

29. *Ibid.,* p. 58.

30. Barbara Edelstein, *The Woman Doctor's Medical Guide for Women* (New York: Bantam Books, 1983), p. 183.

31. Fries, *op. cit.*
32. Edelstein, *op. cit.*, p. 71.
33. Fries, *op. cit.*, p. 78.
34. *Ibid.*

CHAPTER 5: BABIES AND BEYOND

1. Cynthia Cooke and Susan Dworkin, *The Ms. Guide to a Woman's Health* (New York: Doubleday, 1979), p. 323.
2. Katharina Dalton, *Once a Month* (Pomona, Calif.: Hunter House, 1979).
3. Paula Weideger, *Menstruation & Menopause* (New York: Dell Publishing Company, 1977), pp. 22–26.
4. Penny W. Budoff, *No More Menstrual Cramps and Other Good News* (New York: Putnam, 1980), pp. 25–26.
5. J. Irwin, E. Morse, D. Riddick, "Dysmenorrhea Induced by Autologous Transfusion," *Obstetrics & Gynecology*, vol. 58, 1981, pp. 286–290.
6. *The Tampax Report.* Conducted by Research and Forecasts, Inc., New York, N.Y., June 1981.
7. Dalton, *op. cit.*
8. Christine Moore, "Bye-Bye, Ms. American Pie," *Washington Post Magazine*, Nov. 27, 1983, p. 16.
9. Susan West, "Fertility Fizzle," *Science 82*, May 1982, p. 12.
10. "WD Asks the Experts: How Much Does Age Affect Fertility?" *Woman's Day*, August 10, 1982, pp. 61ff.
11. Susan S. Lichtendorf, *Eve's Journey: The Physical Experience of Being Female* (New York: Berkley Books, 1983), p. 144.
12. Jeffrey R. M. Kunz, editor-in-chief, *The American Medical Association Family Medical Guide* (New York: Random House, 1982), p. 593.
13. Jane Porcino, *Growing Older, Getting Better: A Handbook for Women in the Second Half of Life* (Reading, Mass.: Addison-Wesley, 1983), p. 66.
14. Victor Berman and Salee Berman, "Who Runs a Higher Risk? A Consultation About Childbearing After 30," in Gail Sforza Brewer, ed., *The Pregnancy After 30 Workbook* (Emmaus, Pa.: Rodale Press, 1978), p. 5.
15. Jane Brody, *Jane Brody's Nutrition Book* (New York: W. W. Norton, 1981), p. 335.
16. Susan Morse, " 'Clearly on the Upswing,' " *The Washington Post,* January 16, 1984, p. B5.
17. U.S. Department of Health, Education, and Welfare, *Antenatal Diagnosis: Report of a Consensus Development Conference* (Washington, D.C.: National Institutes of Health, 1980), p. 48.
18. "First Birth After 30," *The New York Times,* July 31, 1984, p. 61.
19. Carole Spearin McCauley, *Pregnancy After 35* (New York: E. P Dutton, 1976), p. 15.
20. Cited in McCauley, *op. cit.*, p. 15.
21. Porcino, *op. cit.*, p. 65.
22. U.S. Public Health Service, *The Health Consequences of Smoking for Women* (Washington, D.C.: Department of Health and Human Services, 1983).
23. Myron Winick, *For Mothers and Daughters* (New York: William Morrow, 1983), p. 110.
24. Data from the March of Dimes national office.
25. Winick, *op. cit.*, p. 114.
26. Thomas H. Green, Jr., *Gynecology: Essentials of Clinical Practice* (Boston: Little, Brown, 1977), p. 566; Lillian E. Troll, "Poor, Dumb, and Ugly," in *Looking Ahead: A Woman's Guide to the Problems and Joys of Growing Older*, Lillian E. Troll, Joan Israel, and Kenneth Israel, eds. (Englewood Cliffs, N.J.: Prentice Hall, 1977), p. 5.
27. Green, *op. cit.*, p. 566.
28. John S. Rinehart and Isaac Schiff, "Hormonal Imbalance, Hormonal Treatment," *Menopause Update*, vol. 1, no. 2, 1983, pp. 13–16.

29. The Diagram Group, *Woman's Body: An Owner's Manual* (New York: Paddington Press, 1977), p. F-03.

30. Lichtendorf, *op. cit.*, p. 174.

31. The Diagram Group, *op. cit.*, p. F-03.

32. Cooke and Dworkin, *op. cit.*, p. 287.

33. Lichtendorf, *op. cit.*, p. 178.

34. *Ibid.*, p. 171.

35. "Sex and the 'Senile Vagina,'" *Science News,* vol. 123, May 21, 1983, p. 328.

36. Green, *op. cit.*, p. 566.

37. Porcino, *op. cit.*, p. 172.

38. *Ibid.*, p. 172.

39. Trudy L. Bush, Linda D. Cowan, et al., "Estrogen Use and All-Cause Mortality," *JAMA,* vol. 249, no. 7, February 18, 1983, pp. 903–906.

40. Andrea Rowand, "The (Anti-Cancer?) Pill," *Science News,* vol. 125, June 30, 1984, p. 404.

41. Green, *op. cit.*, pp. 401, 402, 421, 457, 503.

42. Porcino, *op. cit.*, p. 179.

43. *Ibid.*, p. 179.

44. *Ibid., p. 181.*

CHAPTER 6: THE HEART OF THE MATTER

1. U.S. Bureau of the Census, *Statistical Abstract of the United States 1981* (Washington, D.C.: Department of Commerce, 1981), p. 76.

2. T. Gordon, W. B. Kannel, M. C. Hjortland, et al., "Menopause and Coronary Heart Disease," *Annals of Internal Medicine,* vol. 89, 1978, pp. 157–161.

3. Trudy L. Bush, Linda D. Cowan, Elizabeth Barrett-Connor, et al., "Estrogen Use and All-Cause Mortality," *Journal of the American Medical Association,* vol. 249, no. 7, February 18, 1983, pp. 903–906; also, P. K. Ross, A. Paganini-Hill, T. M. Mack, et al., "Menopausal Estrogen Therapy and Protection from Death from Ischaemic Heart Disease," *Lancet,* vol. 1, 1981, pp. 858–860.

4. Gina Kolata, "New Puzzles over Estrogen and Heart Disease," *Science,* vol. 220, June 10, 1983, pp. 1137–1138.

5. William B. Kannel, personal interview.

6. Thomas J. Thom and William B. Kannel, *Annual Review of Medicine 1981,* vol. 32, p. 431.

7. U.S. Bureau of the Census, *op. cit.*, p. 121.

8. *Ibid.*

9. Bonnie Liebman, "The Sodium-Hypertension Connection," *Nutrition Action,* December 1982, p. 7.

10. John H. Laragh, "Giving Salt a Fair Shake, *Health,* February 1983, p. 32.

11. Veterans Administration Cooperative Study Group on Antihypertensive Agents, "Effect of Treatment on Morbidity in Hypertension—II. Results in Patients with Diastolic Blood Pressure Averaging 90 Through 114 mm Hg," *Journal of the American Medical Association,* vol. 213, 1970, pp. 1143–1152.

12. Gina Kolata, "New Cholesterol Clues: Diet vs. Stress," *American Health,* March/April 1984, pp. 43–47.

13. Jane Brody, *Jane Brody's Nutrition Book* (New York: W. W. Norton, 1981), p. 62.

14. W. F. Enos, R. H. Holmes, J. Beyer, "Coronary Disease Among United States Soldiers Killed in Action in Korea: Preliminary Report," *Journal of the American Medical Association,* vol. 152, 1953, pp. 1090–1093.

15. Jeffrey R. M. Kunz, *The American Medical Association Family Medical Guide* (New York, Random House, 1982), p. 372.

16. Information provided by the National Heart, Lung, and Blood Institute, Bethesda, Md.

17. Dag S. Thelle, Egil Arnesen, and Olav H. Forde, "The Tromso Heart Study: Does

Coffee Raise Serum Cholesterol?" *The New England Journal of Medicine,* vol. 308, no. 24, June 16, 1983, pp. 1454–1457.

18. Jane Porcino, *Growing Older, Getting Better: A Handbook for Women in the Second Half of Life* (Reading, Mass.: Addison-Wesley, 1983), p. 239.

19. Kunz, *op. cit.,* p. 405.

20. Carleton Fredericks, *Carlton Fredericks' Nutrition Guide for the Prevention & Cure of Common Ailments & Diseases* (New York: Simon and Schuster, 1982), p. 167.

CHAPTER 7: BREATHING EASY

1. Stephen Kiesling, "Breath Test for Life Span?" *American Health,* March/April 1983, p. 25.

2. William B. Kannel, Edward A. Lew, et al., "The Value of Measuring Vital Capacity for Prognostic Purposes," *Transactions of the Association of Life Insurance Medical Directors of America,* vol. 64, 1980, p. 67.

3. *Ibid.,* p. 69.

4. Robert A. Klocke, "Influence of Aging on the Lung," in Caleb E. Finch and Leonard Hayflick, eds., *Handbook of the Biology of Aging* (New York: Van Nostrand Reinhold, 1977), p. 435.

5. *Ibid.,* p. 433.

6. Jeffrey R. M. Kunz, ed., *The American Medical Association Family Medical Guide* (New York: Random House, 1982), p. 368.

7. *Ibid.,* p. 342.

8. "Lung Cancer Is Linked to Rise in Death Rates," *The New York Times,* February 24, 1984.

9. Paul D. Stolley, "Lung Cancer in Women—Five Years Later, Situation Worse," *The New England Journal of Medicine,* vol. 309, no. 7, August 18, 1983, pp. 428–429.

10. Jean Reese and Louise Kruse, "Women and Smoking," in Gail Hongladarom, Ruth McCorkle, and Nancy Fugate Woods, eds., *The Complete Book of Women's Health* (Englewood Cliffs, N.J.: Prentice-Hall, 1982), p. 115.

11. U.S. Public Health Service, *The Health Consequences of Smoking for Women* (Washington, D.C.: Department of Health and Human Services), p. 34.

12. Jane Brody, *Jane Brody's The New York Times Guide to Personal Health* (New York: Avon Books, 1983), p. 363.

13. *Ibid.*

14. U.S. Public Health Service, *op. cit.,* p. 226.

15. Klocke, *op. cit.,* p. 440.

16. *Ibid.*

17. Information from Ronald White, American Lung Association, New York, N.Y.

18. Dr. John Nicholson, Cornell Medical Center, New York City, quoted in "Air Pollution Alert," *Running Times,* November 1983.

CHAPTER 8: YOU ARE WHAT YOU EAT

1. Lester Breslow and James E. Enstrom, "Persistence of Health Habits and Their Relationship to Mortality," *Preventive Medicine,* vol. 9, 1980, pp. 469–483.

2. Myron Winick, *For Mothers & Daughters* (New York: William Morrow, 1983), pp. 212–213.

3. *Ibid.,* p. 215.

4. *Ibid.*

5. Carlton Fredericks, *Carlton Fredericks' Nutrition Guide for the Prevention & Cure of Common Ailments & Diseases* (New York: Simon and Schuster, 1982), p. 129.

6. Winick, *op. cit.,* p. 214.

7. Jane Brody, *Jane Brody's Nutrition Book* (New York: W. W. Norton, 1981), pp. 146–147.

8. Maureen Mylander, *The Great American Stomach Book* (New Haven, Conn.: Ticknor & Fields, 1982), p. 158.

9. *Ibid.,* p. 160.

10. *Ibid.*, p. 132.

11. *Ibid.*, p. 108.

12. Brody, *op. cit.*, p. 252.

13. Mylander, *op. cit.*, p. 151.

14. *Ibid.*, p. 153.

15. Jeffrey R. M. Kunz, ed., *The American Medical Association Family Medical Guide* (New York: Random House, 1982), p. 478.

16. Winick, *op. cit.*, p. 171.

17. Jane Brody, *Jane Brody's The New York Times Guide to Personal Health* (New York: Avon Books, 1983), p. 117.

18. Jane Porcino, *Growing Older, Getting Better: A Handbook for Women in the Second Half of Life* (Reading, Mass.: Addison-Wesley, 1983), p. 273.

19. Reubin Andres, "Aging, Diabetes, and Obesity: Standards of Normality," *The Mt. Sinai Journal of Medicine,* vol. 48, no. 6, November/December 1981, p. 489.

20. Roy L. Walford, *Maximum Life Span* (New York: W. W. Norton, 1983), p. 157.

21. *Ibid.*, p. 140.

22. Durk Pearson and Sandy Shaw, *Life Extension: A Practical Scientific Approach* (New York: Warner Books, 1982), p. 371.

23. *Ibid.*, p. 465.

24. Fredericks, *op. cit.*

CHAPTER 9: THE SENSUOUS WOMAN

1. Robin Marantz Henig, *The Myth of Senility: Misconceptions About the Brain and Aging* (New York: Anchor Press/Doubleday, 1981), p. 242.

2. Robert Ruben, "Hearing Impairment in the Elderly." Presentation at the conference "Mental Health Aspects of Physical Disease in Late Life," National Institutes of Health, March 29, 1984.

3. Jane Porcino, *Growing Older, Getting Better* (Reading, Mass.: Addison-Wesley, 1983), p. 295.

4. Jeffrey R. M. Kunz, *The American Medical Association Family Medical Guide* (New York: Random House, 1982), p. 332.

5. Barbara Edelstein, *The Woman Doctor's Medical Guide for Women* (New York: Bantam Books, 1983), p. 8.

6. Richard Kavner and Lorraine Dusky, *Total Vision* (New York: A&W Visual Library, 1978), p. 59.

7. Porcino, *op. cit.*, p. 303.

8. Information provided by the National Eye Institute, National Institutes of Health, Bethesda, Md.

9. Porcino, *op. cit.*, p. 303.

10. *Ibid.*

11. *Ibid.*, pp. 303–304.

12. Kunz, *op. cit.*, p. 321.

13. Edgar A. Tonna, "Aging of Skeletal-Dental Systems and Supporting Tissues," in Caleb E. Finch and Leonard Hayflick, eds., *Handbook of the Biology of Aging* (New York: Van Nostrand Reinhold, 1977), p. 485.

14. Bruce Baum, "Research in Aging and Oral Health: An Assessment of Current Status and Future Needs," *Special Care in Dentistry,* vol. 1, no. 4, July/August 1981, pp. 156–165.

15. Kunz, *op. cit.*, p. 721.

CHAPTER 10: STILL SEXY AT SIXTY

1. Bernard Starr and Marcella Bakur Weiner, *The Starr-Weiner Report on Sex and Sexuality in the Mature Years* (New York: Stein and Day, 1981), p. 187.

2. Quoted in Susan S. Lichtendorf, *Eve's Journey: The Physical Experience of Being Female* (New York: Berkley Books, 1983), p. 162.

3. Ruth B. Weg, "Beyond Babies and Orgasm," *Educational Horizons,* vol. 60, no. 1, 1982, p. 167.

4. Starr and Weiner, *op. cit.*

5. Edward Brecher and the editors of Consumer Reports Books, *Love, Sex and Aging: A Consumers Union Report* (Boston: Little, Brown, 1984).

6. *Ibid.,* p. 291.

7. *Ibid.,* p. 58.

8. Ruth B. Weg, "More Than Wrinkles," in Lillian E. Troll, Joan Israel, and Kenneth Israel, eds., *Looking Ahead: A Woman's Guide to the Problems and Joys of Growing Older* (Englewood Cliffs, N.J.: Prentice-Hall, 1977), pp. 34–35.

9. Brecher, *op. cit.,* p. 354.

10. Robert N. Butler and Myrna L. Lewis, *Sex After Sixty* (New York: Harper & Row, 1976), p. 29.

11. Brecher, *op. cit.,* p. 275.

12. *Ibid.,* p. 278.

13. Bureau of the Census, *Statistical Abstract of the United States 1981* (Washington, D.C.: U.S. Department of Commerce, 1981), p. 25.

14. Jane Porcino, *Growing Older, Getting Better* (Reading, Mass.: Addison-Wesley, 1983), pp. 42–43.

15. Ingrid Waldron, "Why Do Women Live Longer Than Men?" *Journal of Human Stress,* vol. 2, March 1976, pp. 2–13.

16. Lois M. Verbrugge, "Women and Men: Mortality and Health of Older People," in M. W. Riley, B. B. Hess, and K. Bond, eds., *Aging in Society: Selected Reviews of Recent Research* (Hillsdale, N.J.: Lawrence Erlbaum Associates, 1983), p. 145.

17. Porcino, *op. cit.,* p. 191.

18. Edward Brecher and the editors of Consumer Reports Books, *Love, Sex and Aging: A Consumers Union Report* (Boston: Little, Brown, 1984), p. 74.

19. Butler and Lewis, *op. cit.,* pp. 143–144.

CHAPTER 11: THE MYTH OF SENILITY

1. Robin Marantz Henig, *The Myth of Senility: Misconceptions About the Brain and Aging* (New York: Anchor Press/Doubleday, 1981), p. 257.

2. B. F. Skinner, *"The Experience of Old Age."* Presentation to the American Psychological Association convention, August 1982.

3. *Ibid.*

4. J. Hatazawa, M. Ito, et al., "Sex Differences in Brain Atrophy During Aging," *Journal of the American Geriatrics Society,* vol. 30, no. 4, April 1982, pp. 235–239.

5. B. M. Hubbard, J. M. Anderson, "Sex Differences in Age-Related Brain Atrophy" (Letter), *Lancet,* June 25, 1983, p. 1447.

6. Henig, *op. cit.,* p. 26.

7. *Ibid.,* pp. 30–31.

8. *Ibid.,* pp. 40–43.

9. L. Lasagna, F. Mosteller, et al., "A Study of Placebo Response," *American Journal of Medicine,* vol. 16, 1954, pp. 770–779.

10. Alex Comfort, *A Good Age* (New York: Simon & Schuster, 1976), pp. 10–11.

11. Paul Baltes and K. Warner Schaie, "Aging and IQ: The Myth of the Twilight Years," *Psychology Today,* vol. 7, March 1974, pp. 35–40.

12. Robin Marantz Henig, "Exposing the Myth of Senility," *The New York Times Magazine,* December 3, 1978.

13. Comfort, *op. cit.,* p. 135.

14. T. R. Anders, J. L. Fozard, and T. D. Lillyquist, "The Effects of Age upon Retrieval from Short-Term Memory," *Developmental Psychology,* vol. 6, 1972, pp. 214–217.

15. Baltes and Schaie, *op. cit.*

16. Robert N. Butler, *Why Survive? Being Old in America* (New York: Harper & Row, 1975), pp. 228–230.

17. Anthony Brandt, "A Woman of Character," *Esquire,* August 1984, p. 17.

18. Grace Hechinger, "Growing Old in America: An Introduction with Margaret Mead," *Family Circle*, July 26, 1977, p. 27.

CHAPTER 12: FUTURE STOCK
1. Edith Hamilton, *Mythology* (New York: New American Library, 1969), p. 290.
2. Robert N. Butler, *Why Survive? Being Old in America* (New York: Harper & Row, 1975), p. 16.
3. Albert Rosenfeld, *Prolongevity* (New York: Alfred A. Knopf, 1976), pp. 43–49.
4. *Ibid.*, pp. 66–74, 82–87.
5. *Ibid.*, p. 84.
6. *Ibid.*, pp. 50–65.
7. Lois M. Verbrugge, "Women and Men: Mortality and Health of Older People," in M. W. Riley, B. B. Hess, and K. Bond, eds., *Aging and Society: Selected Reviews of Recent Research* (Hillsdale, N.J.: Lawrence Erlbaum Associates, 1983), p. 145.
8. Ingrid Waldron and Susan Johnston, "Why Do Women Live Longer Than Men?" (Part II), *Journal of Human Stress*, June 1976, p. 19.

BIBLIOGRAPHY

Berland, Theodore and Gordon L. Snider. *Living with Your Bronchitis and Emphysema.* New York: St. Martin's Press, 1972.

Birren, James E. and K. Warner Schaie. *Handbook of the Psychology of Aging.* New York: Van Nostrand Reinhold, 1977.

Botwinick, Jack. *Aging and Behavior.* New York: Springer Publishing, 1978.

Brecher, Edward and the Editors of Consumers Report Books. *Love, Sex and Aging: A Consumers Union Report.* Boston: Little, Brown, 1984.

Brewer, Gail Sforza, ed. *The Pregnancy After 30 Workbook.* Emmaus, Pa.: Rodale Press, 1978.

Brody, Jane. *Jane Brody's The New York Times Guide to Personal Health.* New York: Avon Books, 1983.

Brody, Jane. *Jane Brody's Nutrition Book.* New York: W. W. Norton, 1981.

Budoff, Penny W. *No More Menstrual Cramps and Other Good News.* New York: G. P. Putnam's Sons, 1980.

Butler, Robert N. and Myrna L. Lewis. *Sex After Sixty.* New York: Harper & Row, 1976.

Cherry, Sheldon H. *For Women of All Ages.* New York: Macmillan, 1979.

Chovanian, Aram V. and Lorraine Loviglio with Patrick O'Reilly. *Boston University Medical Center's Heart Risk Book.* New York: Bantam Books, 1982.

Comfort, Alex. *A Good Age.* New York: Simon and Schuster, 1976.

Cooke, Cynthia W. and Susan Dworkin. *The Ms. Guide to a Woman's Health.* New York: Doubleday, 1979.

Danon, D., N. W. Shock, and M. Marois, eds. *Aging: A Challenge to Science and Society, Vol. 1, Biology.* New York: Oxford University Press, 1981.

Diagram Group, The. *Woman's Body: An Owner's Manual.* New York: Paddington Press, 1977.

Dicker, Ralph Leslie and Victor Royce Syracuse. *Consultation with a Plastic Surgeon.* New York: Warner Books, 1975.

Edelstein, Barbara. *The Woman Doctor's Medical Guide for Women.* New York: Bantam Books, 1983.

Finch, Caleb and Leonard Hayflick, eds. *Handbook of the Biology of Aging.* New York; Van Nostrand Reinhold, 1977.

Fredericks, Carlton. *Carlton Fredericks' Nutrition Guide for the Prevention & Cure of Common Ailments & Diseases.* New York: Simon and Schuster, 1982.

Fries, James F. *Arthritis: A Comprehensive Guide.* Reading, Mass.: Addison-Wesley, 1979.

Galton, Lawrence. *"How Long Will I Live?"* New York: Macmillan, 1976.

Glucken, Doreen with Michael Edelhart. *The Body at Thirty.* New York: M. Evans & Co., 1982.

Hales, Dianne. *The Complete Book of Sleep: How Your Nights Affect Your Days.* Reading, Mass.: Addison-Wesley, 1981.

Haynes, Suzanne G. and Manning Feinleib, eds. *Second Conference on the Epidemiology of Aging.* Bethesda, Md.: National Institutes of Health, 1980.

Henig, Robin Marantz. *The Myth of Senility: Misconceptions About the Brain and Aging.* New York: Anchor Press, 1981.

Holt, Linda Hughey and Melva Weber. *The American Medical Association Guide to WomanCare.* New York: Random House, 1984.

Hongladarom, Gail Chapman, Ruth McCorkle, Nancy Fugate Woods, eds. *The Complete Book of Women's Health.* Englewood Cliffs, N.J.: Prentice-Hall Inc., 1982.

Kunz, Jeffrey R. M., ed. *The American Medical Association Family Medical Guide.* New York: Random House, 1982.

Lichtendorf, Susan S. *Eve's Journey: The Physical Experience of Being Female.* New York: Berkley Books, 1983.

Lynch, James J. *The Broken Heart: The Medical Consequences of Loneliness.* New York: Basic Books, 1977.

Marshall, John L. with Heather Barbash. *The Sports Doctor's Fitness Book for Women.* New York: Delacorte Press, 1981.

Martin, Elizabeth. *The Over-30 6-Week All-Natural Health and Beauty Plan.* New York: Clarkson N. Potter, Inc., 1982.

McCauley, Carole Spearin. *Pregnancy After 35.* New York: E. P. Dutton & Co., 1976.

Melamed, Elissa. *Mirror, Mirror: The Terror of Not Being Young.* New York: Linden Press, 1983.

Morehouse, Laurence E. and Augustus T. Miller, Jr. *Physiology of Exercise.* St. Louis: C. V. Mosby, 1976.

Mylander, Maureen. *The Great American Stomach Book.* New York: Ticknor & Fields, 1982.

Notelovitz, Morris and Marsha Ware. *Stand Tall: The Informed Woman's Guide to Preventing Osteoporosis.* Gainesville, Fla.: Triad Publishing, 1982.

Nudel, Adele. *For the Woman over 50.* New York: Avon Books, 1978.

Obley, Fred A. *Emphysema.* Boston: Beacon Press, 1970.

Orbach, Susie. *Fat Is a Feminist Issue.* New York: Berkley Books, 1979.

Ornish, Dean. *Stress, Diet & Your Heart.* New York: Holt, Rinehart and Winston, 1982.

Pearson, Durk and Sandy Shaw. *Life Extension: A Practical Scientific Approach.* New York: Warner Books, 1982.

Pelletier, Kenneth R. *Longevity: Fulfilling Our Biological Potential.* New York: Delacorte Press, 1981.

Porcino, Jane. *Growing Older, Getting Better: A Handbook for Women in the Second Half of Life.* Reading, Mass.: Addison/Wesley, 1983.

Rose, Louisa, ed. *The Menopause Book.* New York: Hawthorn Books, 1977.

Reichman, Stanley. *Breathe Easy: An Asthmatic's Guide to Clear Air.* New York: Thomas Y. Crowell Company, 1977.

Rosenfeld, Albert. *Prolongevity.* New York: Alfred A. Knopf, 1976.

Rosenzweig, Sandra. *Sportsfitness for Women.* New York: Harper & Row, 1982.

Schoen, Linda Allen, ed. *The AMA Book of Skin and Hair Care.* New York: Avon Books, 1976.

Sheehy, Gail. *Passages.* New York: E. P. Dutton & Co., 1976.

Starr, Bernard D. and Marcella Bakur Weiner. *The Starr-Weiner Report on Sex and Sexuality in the Mature Years.* New York: Stein and Day, 1981.

Stoppard, Miriam. *Being a Well Woman*. New York: Holt, Rinehart and Winston, 1982.

Troll, Lillian E., Joan Israel, and Kenneth Israel, eds. *Looking Ahead: A Woman's Guide to the Problems and Joys of Growing Older*. Englewood Cliffs, N.J.: Prentice-Hall, 1977.

Waldo, Myra. *The Prime of Life and How to Make It Last*. New York: Macmillan, 1980.

Walford, Roy L. *Maximum Life Span*. New York: W. W. Norton, 1983.

Weideger, Paula. *Menstruation & Menopause*. New York: Delta Books, 1977.

Winick, Myron. *For Mothers & Daughters: A Guide to Good Nutrition for Women*. New York: William Morrow & Co., 1983.

INDEX

About the Author

Robin Marantz Henig is a health and medical writer whose work has appeared in *The New York Times Magazine, Woman's Day, American Health, Redbook, Human Behavior,* and other publications. She is the author of *The Myth of Senility,* which won the National Media Award of the American Psychological Association, and of *Your Premature Baby.* Henig, who will be 65 in the year 2018, lives near Washington, D.C., with her husband, Jeff, and their two young daughters.